Knowledge Systems Design

PRENTICE HALL
ADVANCES IN COMPUTER SCIENCE SERIES
Editor: Richard P. Brent

Knowledge Systems Design

John K. Debenham

School of Computing Sciences
University of Technology, Sydney

PRENTICE HALL

New York London Toronto Sydney Tokyo

Printed and bound in Australia by
Impact Printing, Brunswick, Victoria

1 2 3 4 5 92 91 90 89

ISBN 0-13-516428-1

National Library of Australia
Cataloguing-in-Publication Data

Debenham, J. K. (John K.).
  Knowledge systems design.

  Includes index.
  ISBN 0-13-516428-1.
  1. Expert systems (Computer science). 2. Data base design. I. Title.
006.3'3

Library of Congress
Cataloguing-in-Publication Data

Debenham, J. K.
  Knowledge systems design.

  (Prentice Hall advances in computer science series)
  Bibliography: p.
  Includes index.
  1. Expert systems (Computer science) 2. Data base design.
  I. Title. II. Series.
QA76.76.E95D43 1989   006.3'3   88-30655
ISBN 0-13-516428-1

Prentice Hall, Inc., Englewood Cliffs, New Jersey
Prentice Hall of Australia Pty Ltd, Sydney
Prentice Hall Canada, Inc., Toronto
Prentice Hall Hispanoamericana, SA, Mexico
Prentice Hall of India Private Ltd, New Delhi
Prentice Hall International, Inc., London
Prentice Hall of Japan, Inc., Tokyo
Prentice Hall of Southeast Asia Pty Ltd, Singapore
Editora Prentice Hall do Brasil Ltda, Rio de Janeiro

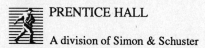 PRENTICE HALL

A division of Simon & Schuster

Contents

Preface

This is a book about design - the design of knowledge-based systems. It is written for those who have an interest in building expert systems and deductive database systems. It is written in particular for those who have an interest in building *maintainable* expert systems and *maintainable* deductive database systems. The text, therefore, will appeal to computer professionals, postgraduate students and senior undergraduate students.

The text contains a detailed description of a method for designing expert knowledge-based systems and deductive database systems. This method is complete and extends from initial knowledge acquisition to knowledge base implementation and knowledge base maintenance. It is claimed that the method presented is suitable for team work. This method represents and analyzes the knowledge in a way that is quite rigorous and yet is independent of any particular expert system shell or computer language.

The majority of expert systems constructed in large corporations during the mid- to late 1980s have not been fully integrated with the central computing resources, in particular with the corporate databases. There are two main reasons for this; first, the lack of suitable, reliable, integrated knowledge base management system software, and second, the lack of design methodologies which permit "knowledge" to be gathered, modeled, analyzed, normalized and implemented with the same degree of precision as is typically applied to "information". This book addresses the second issue and its text should be of prime interest to those large corporations with a commitment to building up a large, integrated, corporate knowledge base.

The work reported here began in 1982 with a joint research project with Mike McGrath of Telecom Australia. At that time we rebuilt the substantial Telecom Telephone Accounting System for the Sydney region as a deductive database using logic programming. This was a large database of some 250 mega-bytes of "information" and a substantial and complex set of rules or "knowledge". It is believed to be the first large, commercial database actually implemented in logic. This design exercise involved a very large number of design decisions made at the time on a more or less *ad hoc* basis. However, this experiment clearly defined the major problems which this text now attempts to solve. Since that time, research has concentrated on assembling a set of systematic techniques for solving the major problems encountered in that early experiment. This set of techniques is now complete and is reported herein.

A key feature of our method is the construction of a "normalized model" of the application. The normalized model consists of a formal part and an informal part. The formal part of the normalized model is called the "system model"; it contains all the information required by a programmer to implement the system. The informal part of the normalized model is called the "application model"; it consists of a description of the application in stylized natural language. Thus, the application model acts as both the

1

documentation for the system model and as the specification of the application with which a nontechnical domain expert can easily interact. The normalized model is in normal form in a fairly elaborate sense which is a direct extension of the well established normal forms for information. Our normal forms include, in particular, a set of technical normal forms for knowledge. The idea behind the normal forms is that each real "thing" in the application should be represented in one place, and in one place only, in the normalized model. This should greatly assist the knowledge base maintenance process.

The text is illustrated with examples expressed in logic programming. Logic programming was chosen because it is both very simple and widely understood when compared with other knowledge languages. We would like to stress that we are *not* necessarily promoting logic programming as an ideal language for implementing expert, knowledge-based systems or deductive databases. We would also like to stress that the ideas presented in this text are quite independent of logic programming; the general principles discussed and the examples given may easily be re-expressed in any other suitable formalism or general purpose expert system shell.

It is important to appreciate that the work reported here is not intended to be a complete account of expert systems or deductive databases. In fact no attempt is made to present material on expert systems or deductive database systems that is generally available in the current literature. For example, the reader whose principal interest is the design of expert systems is assumed to be familiar with (Waterman, 1986); the reader whose principal interest is the design of deductive database systems is assumed to be familiar with (Kerschberg, 1986). The reader is also assumed to be familiar with the design of databases, the managerial difficulties in maintaining databases, the elements of knowledge processing, and, preferably, the use of at least one expert system shell. For example, "machine learning", which is a powerful technique that may be applied to the generation of knowledge from hard data, is not discussed at all; see, for example, the work of Quinlan. Also, for example, "plausible inference", which lies at the heart of many expert systems shells, only receives a mention in passing (Horvitz, Bresse and Henrion, 1988). This is not then a suitable text for the beginner; it is designed for the educated, knowledge-processing specialist. It attempts to show such a specialist how to do a better and more systematic job. With the exception of Chapter 2, the material presented herein is not generally available elsewhere.

The approach to designing corporate knowledge bases presented here is deliberately compatible with established techniques for database design. This compatibility has been made possible by the way in which we regard "data", "information" and "knowledge" as strictly separate, but integrated, concepts (Chapter 3). In other words, existing techniques for information analysis are used to design the information component of a knowledge base. Thus, in a sense, we see knowledge base architecture as a direct extension of existing database architecture, and have acknowledged this relationship in the design technique presented here which may be seen as a direct extension of existing techniques for database design. This text then should also be of interest to those involved in the design of conventional databases in which the management of the "rules" is a complex issue.

The design method for knowledge systems (Chapter 4) discussed in this text is presented as though for hand computation. It should be stressed that this is for the sake of exposition only. For the effective application of the method to a large problem, a support environment, or "knowledge base design assistant" is essential. Such an environment would be expected to assist with the knowledge acquisition (Chapter 6) and knowledge analysis (Chapter 7) phases by looking after all the "housekeeping" and by playing an active role in the normalization process (Chapter 5). The knowledge base engineering (Chapter 8) and knowledge base implementation (Chapter 9) phases should be fully automated. The knowledge base design assistant should also play a crucial role in knowledge base maintenance (Chapter 10). A restricted, prototype knowledge base design assistant was constructed in 1986 by Alan McNamarra as part of the Knowledge Engineering Work Bench project which was made possible by the generous support of the Australian Federal Department of Science. This prototype system has been used extensively for conducting experiments associated with the research reported herein.

In September 1988 construction commenced of a software package which supports and implements the knowledge systems design technique reported in this text. This software is being constructed by the Australian Commonwealth Scientific and Industrial Research Organisation (CSIRO) within their Division of Information Technology. This software functions as a complete Knowledge Analyst's Assistant, and is intended for serious, professional use. It is constructed so as to be independent of any particular expert systems shell or other implementation language. As well as enabling the knowledge analyst to design and maintain modules of knowledge, the software provides a prototyping facility. A full description of the operation of this software is given at the end of Chapter 10 in Section 10.8. In the first instance, enquiries should be directed to:

Knowledge Systems Design Project,
CSIRO,
Division of Information Technology,
PO Box 1599,
North Ryde, NSW, 2113,
Australia.

The software is scheduled to be available for distribution late in 1989.

We adopt two important conventions. First, new terms, as they are defined, will be presented in italics and a reference to each definition should be found in the index; italics are also used for emphasis. Second, when terms are used in the general text before they have been formally defined, in which case the reader is called upon to provide an intuitive meaning, the term will appear within quotation marks. Thus, if a technical term appears within quotation marks in the general text, then this means that the reader is not expected to know precisely what the term means, but from the context, should be able to sense approximately what the term means.

I would like to thank all those who have assisted in the development of this text. First, I would like to thank Professor Ross Quinlan of the University of Sydney who encouraged me to write the book. Second, I would like to thank the University of Technology, Sydney, for their generous study leave provisions during which the greater part of the writing was done. Third, I would like to thank the CSIRO's Division of Information Technology at North Ryde, Sydney, for welcoming me to their laboratory where most of the book was written. In particular, I would like to thank the chief of the Division who was initially Dr G. E. Thomas and subsequently Dr J. F. O'Callaghan for their hospitality. Fourth, I would like to thank Dr I. W. Montgomery, an exponent of the Binary Relationship approach to information analysis, for his assistance with the information analysis. Last, I would like to thank Dr R. M. Colomb, principal research scientist at the Division, for painstakingly reading and rereading the manuscript as it developed and for his detailed comments; I would like to acknowledge his excellent suggestions, many of which which have been incorporated into the text.

John K. Debenham,
University of Technology, Sydney
November 1988.

1 Perspective

1.1 INTRODUCTION

In this chapter we place knowledge systems in an historical perspective. First, we discuss a major development in knowledge processing machinery, namely the Japanese Fifth Generation Computer Systems Project. Second, we compare and contrast traditional hardware and software technology with knowledge processing technology. Third, we look at the recurring patterns in the history of design techniques and predict the need that knowledge systems will have for rigorous design. And last, we discuss the relevance of "expert systems" to the evolving world of knowledge systems.

1.2 FIFTH GENERATION COMPUTER SYSTEMS

The Japanese Fifth Generation Computer Systems Project (FGCS) has been one important factor responsible for the rise in interest in Knowledge Systems. The FGCS project is, of course, not the only such development. However, it was the first to be publicized on a grand scale and it has been well reported so it is appropriate for us to begin by reviewing briefly some of the goals and intentions of this substantial project.

The Japanese Fifth Generation Computer Systems (FGCS) Project has been dubbed "The Second Computer Revolution"; others have described it as the *first* computer revolution (Feigenbaum and McCorduck, 1983) and the "Third Industrial Revolution" (Sinclair, 1984). What is this project? Why is it so special? What does it mean to the professions in general? What does it mean to the information industry in particular?

During 1981 the Japanese Government conducted a substantial survey which attempted to identify the computing requirements of Japan into the 1990s. This survey concluded with four main goals (Moto-Oka, 1982):

1. to increase productivity in low-productivity areas; key target areas being:
    *   document processing;
    *   office management;
    *   decision making in management;
    *   office automation;
2. to meet international competition and contribute toward international cooperation. An important consequence is "knowledge" being seen as a commodity which can be packaged and sold;

5

3. to assist in saving energy and resources. This includes the reduction of movement of people through the installation of sophisticated, distributed knowledge-based systems;
4. to cope with an aged society. This includes the effective education of an aging society; in particular, the provision of effective computer-assisted education for the professional at home and in the office throughout that professional's career.

It is clear that all four goals have significant implications for professional life. If the four goals noted above are achieved, then the main impact on professional life implied directly by those goals will be:

1. both a substantial change in the intellectual "objects" which professionals use within their own businesses, and a substantial change in the intellectual "objects" used by the whole business community, and with which professionals will have to interact;
2. the sort of knowledge which members of professions presently possess and from which these professionals presently derive an income will become increasingly available in a mechanized form;
3. both a substantial change in the way in which professionals interact with each other and a substantial change in the way in which professionals interact with their clients and their clients' businesses;
4. the way in which professionals acquire, maintain and propagate their professional knowledge will change.

Thus, the impact on professionals within the information industry will take two forms; first, the way in which they, as professionals, go about their business will change, and second, the computer systems with which they deal will be playing a significantly different role in their clients' lives than the majority of computer systems do today.

In October 1981 the Japanese Government announced the FGCS project, and on 14 April, 1982 the Institute for New Generation Computer Technology (ICOT) was launched in Tokyo. The aim of the FGCS project is to design and build computing equipment that will satisfy the four goals identified in the survey, and noted above. The plan is for the project to be complete by 1992. The extent to which this plan is being realized on schedule is not clear. However, whether the FGCS project meets its goals or not, it is our view that considerable progress is being made by this and other projects towards the construction of knowledge processing machines of some sort. It is our view that during the early 1990s knowledge processing hardware will be widely available, and will be sufficiently powerful to threaten the professional community with substantial change.

How will fifth generation computers differ from current generation computers? The differences between the first four generations of machines are principally in the hardware, that is, in the way in which they are constructed; the basic design remains much the same. The design philosophy of traditional computers is often referred to as "Von Neumann architecture", and is named after an early pioneer in computing. Four key features of machines based on Von Neumann architecture are:

1. They have a program controller which controls the sequential operation of the program (i.e. one instruction is executed at a time).

2. They have a memory which consists of a large number of discrete memory locations. Each location is primarily intended to store a number.
3. They have a processor which is capable of performing operations on the values stored in the memory. The operations are primarily arithmetic.
4. They have input and output devices which are based principally on typed characters.

The whole architectural concept of fifth generation computers will differ radically from the Von Neumann architectural philosophy; both the architectural concept itself and the way in which this concept is realized in VLSI (i.e. "computer chips") or in ULSI (i.e. Ultra Large Scale Integration, the computer chips of the near future) will represent major advances. Key features of the new architecture follow:

1. There will be a large number of processors which may compute, in some sense in parallel, more or less independently from one another.
2. The processors will hold their own data, and, in addition, will be tightly coupled with large database machines, which will be especially designed for that purpose.
3. Each processor will be designed to perform logical deduction as its basic computational step. In addition, the processors will have access to very high speed arithmetic and other special purpose, auxiliary processors.
4. Input and output facilities will include the mechanization of "intelligent interfaces" based on work in Artificial Intelligence. These will include optical character recognition and speech recognition, as well as spoken output.

In short, the machines will provide an architecture well suited to the mechanization of intelligence. A central design decision of the FGCS project was to adopt "logic" as the kernel programming language. We will discuss "logic" in the following chapter. If the FGCS project succeeds in meeting all of its goals, it will, without doubt, constitute a quantum leap in the development of computing machinery.

What do the Japanese hope to gain from the FGCS project? The FGCS project is a vital component in Japan's decision to become the first post-industrial society. In industrialized society the wealth of nations depends on natural resources, the accumulation of money and upon weaponry. In a post-industrial society the wealth of nations will depend on information, knowledge and intelligence.

> "Japanese planners view the computer industry as vital to their nation's economic future and have audaciously made it a national goal to become number one in this industry by the latter half of the 1990s. They aim not only to dominate the traditional (Von Neumann) forms of the computer industry (Kashiwagi, 1985) but to establish a 'knowledge industry' in which knowledge itself will be a saleable commodity like food and oil. Knowledge itself is to become the new wealth of nations." (Feigenbaum and McCorduck, 1983.)

1.3 HARDWARE AND SOFTWARE

The much publicized Japanese Fifth Generation Computer Systems Project has undoubtedly been partly responsible for the rapidly increasing interest in knowledge processing among the members of the computing profession. This project has presented the profession with the promise of an architecture which differs radically from conventional hardware design and which is intended for knowledge processing. This has quite understandably generated considerable motivation for professionals to find out what "knowledge processing" is all about. It is, however important to remind ourselves that while these knowledge processing machines will no doubt bring dramatic increases in speed and decreases in cost for processing knowledge they will not possess an increase in capability over conventional architectures. That is, anything that can be done on a knowledge processing machine can be done on a conventional machine, possibly at considerably slower speed. Thus, whereas it is true to state that some knowledge processing applications which are unfeasible today will become feasible on these new architectures, it is also true to say that knowledge processing machines will not provide us with any theoretical increase in computing capability. In other words, knowledge processing machines will not transcend the capability of the classic Turing model.

We have seen that the impact of knowledge processing machines will be largely one of efficiency; in particular, the efficiency of processing "knowledge". Thus, we propose that the appropriate response to the advent of such machines is to ask, "How can we design application systems which take the greatest advantage of this new hardware?". Consideration of this question forms the greater part of the work reported here.

The Japanese Fifth Generation Computer Systems Project was also greatly responsible for the sudden increase in interest within the computing profession in the logic programming languages. After all, logic programming was announced as the kernel language of these new computers. Professionals in the information industry have been confronted with a language which has some extraordinary properties. This language admits a purely declarative semantics, and so contains no purely imperative statements such as the assignment statement. As we will see, a language which admits a declarative semantics is more suited to the representation of "knowledge" or "rules" than a conventional, imperative programming language. Logic programming is described as being a "very high level" language and yet it is to be, in effect, the machine code of these new computers. Thus, professionals have been faced with the prospect of a quantum leap in software technology of undeniably impressive dimensions.

There is no doubt that, in general, knowledge can be expressed far more simply in logic than in, say, the programming language BASIC. However, it is important to remind ourselves that the use of logic as an implementable formalism for the representation of knowledge will not, in itself, simplify the design process. In other words, just because we are using logic to implement a system, the whole business of constructing a "good" design will not be reduced to the application of a few simple rules. To draw an analogy with programming, one could argue that a programmer is likely to write better structured code when using the programming language Pascal than when using the programming language BASIC. However, it is quite possible to write equally *unstructured* code in Pascal as anything that can be represented in BASIC. That is, a programming language may reflect a design philosophy, but, if it is a general purpose language, it can't be expected to enforce the application of that philosophy.

1.4 SYSTEMS DESIGN

During the early to mid-1960s commercial applications programming had gained considerable momentum. By and large, this period is characterized by the construction of sizable pieces of software by small teams of clever, intuitive and resourceful programmers. The members of these teams had often been trained in engineering, mathematics or the sciences. It was not uncommon for the programmers of that period to have received little or no formal training in programming. It was most uncommon for them to have received any training what-soever in systems design. The software generated during this period was often constructed quickly and comparatively cheaply. Documentation of the software was typically poor. When extensive documentation was provided, it tended to present an accurate functional view of how the software worked rather than a systems view of how the software might be maintained.

In time, the maintenance of these early commercial systems became an increasing problem. As maintenance costs increased, managers realized the importance of rigorous approaches to systems analysis and design in general, and of structured techniques in particular. As a result, the majority of this early work was discarded piece by piece, and was systematically redesigned and reconstructed.

History has repeated itself in many facets of computing; the history of the introduction of design techniques is without doubt no exception. During the early to mid-1970s, large organizations were beginning to assemble large corporate databases. The intention was to make these databases available on a wide scale throughout the organization using the timesharing, and later through the distributed hardware systems of the day. Once again, the construction of this central resource was often delegated to a small team of clever, intuitive and resourceful personnel. The members of these teams had often had substantial experience in constructing programs. To them, programs were representations of algorithms or processes. However, these people had probably not been confronted before with the problem of constructing a representation or "snapshot" of large amounts of corporate data, of ensuring that this snapshot was correct, and, most important, that it remained correct as it was modified in time. These early data analysts had usually received no training in data analysis. The early databases that they designed were usually characterized by moderately neat data storage coupled to comparatively messy programs written in some host language which was often a conventional programming language such as COBOL. In a sense, these data analysts thought of these programs as "driving" the database.

In time, the maintenance of these early databases became an increasing problem. Operationally, the problem with maintenance was often as much with preserving the integrity of the database while responding to changes in circumstance as it was with extending the database to perform inherently new tasks. Within these early database systems, the principal component associated with this maintenance problem was often the programs rather than the data. This might appear to be somewhat ironical because programming tended to be the skill in which these early database designers were most proficient! As we will see later on, their difficulty was not with programming as such but with the use of an (imperative) programming language to represent rules which were typically of a non-imperative nature. As the programs within the database developed in complexity they became referred to as the "spaghetti code". As we will discuss in Chapter

3, an important feature of spaghetti code is that it consists of imperative programs which attempt to represent essentially declarative rules using an imperative formalism, that is, in a conventional programming language. As we will see, to implement one rule can entail the construction of a number of programs.

As the maintenance costs of these early database applications increased, managers were faced with very substantial problems. The databases had become key corporate resources which were vital to the everyday operation of the organization. In time, managers realized the importance of thorough database design in general and of a systematic approach to information analysis in particular. However, unlike programs, these early databases were difficult to dismantle piece by piece, so, despite escalating maintenance costs, the analytical redesign of many large, corporate databases was substantially delayed. In fact, many of these early "monolithic" databases survived until well into the 1980s.

It is our belief that history is in the process of repeating itself yet again. On this occasion the context is the construction of "knowledge systems". During the early to mid-1980s, research establishments and large corporations were experimenting with the construction of so-called "expert systems". The intention of these systems was to construct computer programs that were able to perform at the level of trained human experts in some clearly defined, restricted problem domain. The application chosen often required that the expert system had access to a corporate database, *but* applications in which the expert system was permitted to interact with the corporate database were not common. Fairly early in the history of expert systems, the criterion "that expert systems should solve problems *in the same way* as the experts themselves" gained broad acceptance.

The construction of these early expert systems was often delegated to a small team of clever, intuitive and resourceful personnel. The members of these teams had often had substantial experience in programming, systems analysis and occasionally in database design. They had usually received a substantial amount of training in the use of at least one expert systems "shell". These expert systems were constructed moderately quickly, typically at the rate of two or three rules per day, on average, to construct a demonstrable prototype. The documentation of the knowledge in these expert systems tended to be poor. When good documentation was provided, it tended to present an accurate declarative description of the knowledge represented rather than a systems view of how to maintain, modify and extend the knowledge. It is our belief that in time the maintenance of these early knowledge systems will become an increasingly serious problem (Jansen, 1988 and 1989). It is also our belief that it will only be when the design techniques for knowledge systems have learned from the experience of the design of both programs and databases that knowledge systems will be able to play an ongoing, reliable role as components in large computer systems. In our opinion, the true role for knowledge processing is as a technology which is fully integrated with both the programming and database technologies.

We have just noted aspects of the history of systems design in three domains of computing, namely programming, database and knowledge systems. In all three of these domains, as we have reported it, something has gone wrong with the design process in common use in the early years of the development of each of these three domains. Why should this be? There is one important aspect of each of these three developments that we have not yet mentioned. That is, that in their early years, the development of these three domains tended to be "software product led". The early programmers learned FORTRAN or COBOL and, by applying often considerable intelligence, learned to view problems as FORTRAN or COBOL constructs. Programming seemed to be easy: a one-step process from algorithm to program. No wonder that the programmers of the early 1960s could not see the need for elaborate and time consuming design techniques. The early database analyst learned the CODASYL or some other approach to data and, by applying often considerable intelligence, learned to view problems as CODASYL constructs: a one-step process from data to data structure. No wonder that the database analysts of the early 1970s could not see the need for elaborate and time consuming design techniques. The early knowledge analyst learned AL/X, EMYCIN or some other shell and, by applying often considerable intelligence, learned to view problems as AL/X, EMYCIN, or whatever, constructs: a one step process from knowledge to knowledge structure. No wonder the knowledge analysts of the early 1980s could not see the need for elaborate and time consuming design techniques.

We do not doubt that some may find our potted history of design techniques a little simplistic and perhaps biased. However, the fact remains that few expert, knowledge-based systems being constructed in the mid-1980s are being designed for *maintenance*. We see it as almost tautological that if such a system is in a large, complex domain and if this domain is expanding at a reasonable rate, then that system will surely become unmaintainable in due course.

We stress that we are not stating that expert, knowledge-based systems are not being designed for growth. Much work is being done on machine learning, which enables knowledge systems to modify and improve themselves. These modifications and improvements, however, tend to be restricted to adjustments to the knowledge base which lie within the scope of the original design. We believe that machine learning will not automate the knowledge base maintenance problem which, in general, includes modifications which lie beyond the scope of the original design. We should also like to stress that much, but not all, of the technique that we will present here for knowledge-base design can itself be automated.

1.5 EXPERT SYSTEMS

Many of the early, widely-reported expert systems such as MYCIN (Shortliffe, 1976), DENDRAL (Buchanan and Feigenbaum, 1978), R1 (McDermott, 1980) and PROSPECTOR (Gaschnig, 1981), were constructed to solve problems in domains which are substantially removed from the main business of commercial information processing. The effect of these widely reported "expert systems" has been to tempt data processing professionals to consider analogous applications in their own area for possible expert systems development. An example being the interest in diagnostic expert systems, for example to diagnose faults in equipment; such applications are clearly inspired by the highly publicized early work in medical diagnosis. It is fair to comment that this search for analogous application areas in mainstream computing has not always been fruitful. It is also fair to comment that the failure to identify worthwhile, analogous problems has led many professionals to conclude that, as far as their general business is concerned, expert systems are "some way down the track".

Our thesis is that a high proportion of commercial information processing (including all non-trivial database applications) have an identifiabie scope for expert (knowledge-based) systems development. In addition, we maintain that if such applications had been designed correctly as expert (knowledge-based) systems in the first place, then many of the problems which plague the information industry today (for example, the maintenance of large quantities of procedural code in database applications) could have been avoided. Also, if current commercial applications had been designed as knowledge systems initially, then the scope for further expert systems development in such applications would be clear. In other words, the scope for further knowledge systems development in traditionally constructed systems is hidden by the complex manner in which those systems handle knowledge. Thus, our general advice to practitioners is that they should not search for exotic expert systems applications until they have at least acknowledged and understood the knowledge processing which they are already doing.

1.6 SUMMARY

We have discussed the impact that we can expect knowledge systems to have on the computer professional; this will be both in the manner in which computer professionals run their own professional lives and in the types of computer systems with which computer professionals will deal. Traditional hardware and software technology has been compared and contrasted with knowledge processing technology. We have noted that developments in hardware technology will bring increased efficiency to knowledge-processing applications; also developments in software technology will not reduce the need for rigorous application systems design techniques. The history of systems design has been discussed and parallels have been drawn with the design of knowledge systems. We have observed the dangers in design being "software product led". Finally, we have discussed the perception of knowledge systems from the point of view of a computer professional who is familiar with reported developments in expert systems.

2 Logic as a knowledge language

2.1 INTRODUCTION

Logic has been chosen as the language for illustrating this text for two reasons. First, it is widely understood, and second, it has achieved a high level of exposure through its association with the Japanese Fifth Generation Computer Systems Project. However, it is important to realize that this text is not wedded to logic. If the reader has a strong commitment to some other knowledge-processing formalism, then we suggest that the reader translates the logic illustrations into that formalism. This chapter contains a tutorial introduction to logic. It has been written primarily for those readers who are not familiar with logic as a computational formalism. Those who have some understanding of logic may choose to moderate the attention given to this chapter.

Non-trivial problems in first-order predicate logic were first computed extensively in the mid-1960s. Since that time the techniques have become more sophisticated and the applications of computational logic have become more varied. Recently, the Japanese have chosen logic as the kernel programming language for their Fifth Generation Computer Systems (FGCS) project (Moto-Oka, 1982). This has caused an increased interest in logic as a computer language within the information industry.

The relevance of computational logic to our discussion of "knowledge systems design" is twofold. First, as the kernel programming language of the FGCS project, logic will be the target language for knowledge systems which are to be implemented on these fifth generation machines. Thus, an understanding of how logic is computed is all but essential to the construction of good applied, knowledge-processing software. In fact, we have adopted logic as the knowledge language in a hypothetical knowledge-processing machine which is seen as the target machine for the applications which are discussed herein (*see* Chapter 4). Second, we will use the language of logic to represent the "knowledge" in the applications discussed. Note that we are not promoting logic as an ideal "knowledge representation" language; there are many richer formalisms for that purpose including those that incorporate a representation of some form of plausible inference. However, logic is a very simple formalism and is easy to master; it is also quite sufficient to illustrate the examples discussed.

In this chapter we will refer to a number of applications of logic but will concentrate primarily on logic as a programming language and as a database language. Any

13

formalism that admits a "declarative semantics" and can be interpreted both as a programming language and as a database language is called a *knowledge language*. As we will see, logic admits a declarative semantics and can be interpreted both as a programming language and as a database language.

In this chapter we explore the computational process, known as "resolution", which drives the particular form of logic which has been chosen to be the kernel language of the FGCS project (Ueda, 1988). We will first introduce a form of computational logic based on the "resolution principle" and demonstrate its use as the basis for a question-answering system. We show that this question-answering system admits naive interpretations as both a programming language and a database language. We then show that both of these naive interpretations may be extended to give a practical programming language and a practical database language with some very interesting properties. Both of these extensions are achieved:

1. by the provision of appropriate additional computational features using special built in procedures, and;
2. by the provision of appropriate additional control features.

We discuss the properties of both of these languages, and show that they are powerful and practical tools for use in everyday information processing.

2.2 COMPUTATIONAL LOGIC

When using the language of first-order logic to represent an application, we first identify those things in the application which are to be represented by "labels". This is achieved by repeatedly decomposing the "things" in that application until the decomposition has identified the "fundamental, indivisible, real objects" in that application. In the context of an application, this decomposition process is carried out on any "thing" which contains, as a part of it, another "thing" of interest to the application. Such a fundamental, indivisible, real object is represented in the language of first-order logic by a *label*. A label is identified by a "label name". A *label name* may be any unique text string. For example, when decomposing the things in an application, the real object "item number 1234" may be classified as a fundamental, indivisible, real object, represented by a label whose name is the text string "#1234". A collection of fundamental, real objects may be associated with a *population*. For example, a collection of numbers, each representing the item number of a spare part, might be associated with the population "spare-part-number". A population is identified by a "population name". A *population name* may be any unique text string. For example, "spare-part-number" is a population name.

In addition to labels, such as #1234, the language of first-order logic admits "variables". A *variable* is a notion which represents individual objects, but no particular individual object. A variable is identified by a "variable name". A *variable name* may be any unique, non-numeric text string. We will often use the letters "w", "x", "y" and "z" as variable names. Variables may be "quantified" either as "for all values of the variable" (denoted by $\forall$), or as "for at least one value of the variable" (denoted by $\exists$). For example, "for all values of the variable named x" would be written in the language of first-order logic as "$(\forall x)$", also "for at least one value of the variable named y" would be written in the language of first-order logic as "$(\exists y)$". The operators $\forall$ and $\exists$ are called *quantifiers*. $\forall$ is called the *universal quantifier*, and $\exists$ is called the *existential quantifier*. The set of variables and the set of labels taken together are called the set of *atomic symbols*.

"Functions" are also permitted to operate on the atomic symbols in the language of first-order logic; indeed they are extremely useful. By a *function*, or strictly, an *n-adic function*, we mean a function:

$$f : \times^n T \to T$$

where T is the set of "terms". A 1-adic function is usually called *monadic*, and a 2-adic function is usually called *dyadic*. For example, suppose that the integers are atomic symbols and, as a consequence, are terms. Then f_+ is a particular dyadic function:

$$f_+ : \times^2 T \to T$$

defined by:

$$f_+(x, y) = x + y$$

that is, f_+ is ordinary arithmetic addition. A *term* is defined by:

1. The atomic symbols are terms.
2. If the set $\{t_i\}_{i=1,..,n}$ are n terms and f is an n-adic function, then $f(t_1, t_2,..,t_n)$ is a term.

Following the above example, we note that:

$$f_+(2, 3)$$
$$f_+(f_+(3, 1), f_+(-4, f_+(5, 6)))$$

are two different terms. A *constant term* is a term which contains no variables. A function is identified by a "function name". A *function name* may be any unique, non-numeric text string. We will often use "f", "g" and "h" to represent functions. Thus, for example, if "x" is a (variable) atomic symbol and "f" is a monadic function then "f(x)" is a term.

The functions in logic provide logic programming and logic database with their natural data structures of "lists" and "trees". A *list* is a data structure which may be defined recursively as:

1. $\emptyset$ denotes the "empty" list.
2. If y is a list and x is a single element, then x.y is a list with *head* the element x and *tail* the list y.

For example, a list of three elements "a.b.c" can be naturally represented using a two-argument list-building function called "list":

list(a , list(b , list (c , $\emptyset$)))

where $\emptyset$ is the empty list. In Figure 2.1 this three-element list is shown in graphic form.

Although lists are represented within the logic itself using such a list-building function, externally we will use the more convenient notation "x.y" to denote a list with single element x as head and list of elements y as tail. The important thing is that, no matter what notation is used, list structures find a natural place in logic. Likewise, binary trees may be built using a three-argument function "t". For example:

t(t(t($\emptyset$,c,$\emptyset$),b,t($\emptyset$,d,$\emptyset$)),a,t($\emptyset$,e,$\emptyset$))

where $\emptyset$ is the empty tree, is a representation of the tree shown in Figure 2.2.

A *predicate*, or strictly an *n-adic predicate*, is a function:

$$P : \times^n T \rightarrow \{ \text{TRUE, FALSE} \}$$

where T is the set of terms. The n arguments of an n-adic predicate are called a *tuple*, or strictly an *n-tuple*. A *constant tuple* is a tuple which contains no variables. If $\underline{x}$ is a tuple such that:

$$P(\underline{x}) = \text{TRUE}$$

then $\underline{x}$ is said to *satisfy* the predicate P. If a predicate could reasonably be stored as a table it is called a *relation*. Note that our notion of a relation is not the same as the notion of a "relation" in common use in set theory. Our notion is intended to model the "relation" as in relational database (i.e. a "flat file"). The above phrase "could reasonably be stored as a table" means that the relation can only have a finite number of tuples which satisfy it, and that this finite number cannot be too large. The definition of a relation is thus highly subjective; we have no difficulty with this. All that matters is that in a given application some predicates will also be relations. In fact the distinction between predicates and relations is only of interest when deciding which predicates should actually be stored and which should be deduced; this is considered in Chapter 9. However, it is clear that a predicate which is satisfied by an infinite number of tuples cannot be a relation. For example:

plus(x, y, z)

Figure 2.1 A three element list

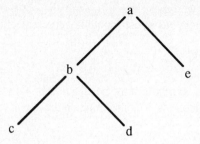

Figure 2.2 Five element binary tree

meaning x + y = z, cannot be a relation. Predicates (and relations) are identified by a "predicate name" (or "relation name"). A *predicate name* (or *relation name*) may be any unique, non-numeric text string. We will sometimes use the letters P, Q, R and S as predicate names.

In simple cases, predicates, and relations can be thought of as parses of sentences in the conventional verb-phrase noun-phrase sense. For example, "the cost of item number #1234 is $12" could be parsed as cost12('#1234') where "cost12" is a predicate representing "the property of costing $12" and the "subject" of the sentence, #1234, is written inside the parentheses. It is often convenient to abandon the elementary verb-phrase noun-phrase parse and to introduce predicates having more than one argument. An alternative representation of the above could be:

item/cost:$('#1234' , '12')

#1234 and 12 are two labels linked by the predicate "item/cost:$"; where, in general, item/cost:$(x, y) means "x is the item number of an item whose cost price is y:$". Note that the predicate name consists of an ordered list of descriptors; each descriptor refers to its corresponding argument in the predicate. We adopt the convention that the descriptors in this list are separated by " / " symbols. Each descriptor *may* be followed by a specification of the units, if any, of the arguments to which it corresponds. We adopt the convention that the specification of the units, if present, are attached to the appropriate descriptor separated by a ":". Note that when labels are written inside a predicate's parentheses, we enclose the label with single quotation marks. This requirement is optional when the label name is a purely numeric string. For example, "all items cost $12" could be represented as:

($\forall$x) item/cost:$(x , '12')

and "at least one item costs $12" could be represented as:

($\exists$x) item/cost:$(x , 12)

Note that in this example we have chosen to omit the optional dashes around the 12. Also, for example, "Every item has a cost" could be represented as:

$$(\forall x)(\exists y) \text{ item/cost:\$}(x , y)$$

It is easy to see that the $\exists$ symbols may be dispensed with and replaced by special functions called "Skolem functions". Consider again the above example:

$$(\forall x)(\exists y) \text{ item/cost:\$}(x , y)$$

assuming that each item has a unique cost, the y value will be determined by the x value, thus we can replace y by f(x), where f is a function which determines the actual cost in dollars of a given item number, to give:

$$(\forall x) \text{ item/cost:\$}(x , f(x))$$

In this case, f is an example of a *Skolem function*. If all the existentially quantified variables have been replaced by Skolem functions, then all variables present must be universally quantified. Thus, for simplicity of presentation, we omit to write the $\forall$ symbols. That is, we assume that any variable present will be a "for all" variable.

The language of first-order logic also contains *connectives* between predicates:

~   meaning "not";
∧   meaning "and";
∨   meaning "or";
→   meaning "implies"; and
←   meaning "is implied by".

Thus, "all items costing \$12 are out of stock" could be represented as:

$$\text{item/cost:\$}(x , 12) \quad \rightarrow \quad \sim \text{instock}(x)$$

where, in general, instock(x) means "x is the item number of an item which is in stock".

To summarize, the *language of first-order logic* consists of "predicates" (e.g. "P"), "labels" (e.g. #1234), "variables" (e.g. "x"), "functions" (e.g. "f") and logic "connectives"; constructs which may be assembled using the symbols of the language of first-order logic are called *sentences*, or, strictly, *first-order sentences*. The language of first-order logic does *not* admit predicates as variables, and it does *not* admit predicates applied to predicates. For example, the following two sentences are not permitted in the language of first-order logic:

for all properties P, P(x) → P(x)
P(P(x))

These two examples are permitted in *higher-order logic*. The language of first-order logic does *not* admit statements of modality such as "it is possible that...." which is permitted in *modal logic*; nor does it admit imperative sentences such as "go home" which could be represented in a *logic of commands*.

The classic problem of first-order *computational logic*, or *theorem proving*, is to determine whether a given sentence T is a "logical consequence" of a set of given first-order sentences, or *axioms*, {A1, A2,..., An}. If T is a "logical consequence" of the axioms, it is called a *theorem*. Unfortunately, this problem cannot be solved by any algorithm. There are "semi-algorithms" which, if T is a consequence of {A1, A2,..., An}, will demonstrate this *eventually*, but no time bound for the calculation *can* be found in general. On the other hand, if T is not a consequence of {A1, A2,..., An}, then the calculation may continue forever. In this sense, first-order logic is strictly not decidable; it may be described as being "semi-decidable".

To demonstrate theorem T we first construct the *goal*, Ans ← T, which may be read "T implies the answer", where Ans is a special predicate called the *Ans predicate*, or the *answer predicate*. It may be shown that deducing T from {A1, A2,..., An} is logically equivalent to deducing "Ans" from {A1, A2,..., An, Ans ← T }. After all, *if* T is derivable from {A1, A2,..., An} *then* Ans is derivable from {A1, A2,..., An, Ans ← T } because Ans ← T simply means "T implies Ans". We will consider arguments in this latter form; this has the advantage that no matter what the theorem is, the calculation is directed towards the generation of the sentence "Ans".

There are special forms of logical arguments which are decidable, an important one being the case when all the sentences have the special form:

A ← (B ∧ C ∧ D)

which is often written in shorthand form as:

A ← B, C, D

where A, B, C and D are predicates. This sentence is to be read "A is the case if B and C and D are true". Note that ← means "is implied by" and the commas mean "and". In this special form there may be at most one predicate to the left of ←; it is called the *head*. There may be any number of predicates to the right of ←; collectively they are called the *body*. No "nots" and no "ors" are permitted. From now on we restrict our discussion to sentences of this special form which are called *Horn clauses, positive clauses* or simply *clauses*. Predicates which occur in the body of a clause which are not the head predicate of that clause are called the *body predicates* of that clause. Thus, note that if the head predicate makes a recursive appearance in the body of a clause then it is not a body predicate of that clause. For example:

person/mother(x, y) ← person/parent(x, y), person/sex(y , 'female')

is an example of a clause; in this clause:

• person/mother(x, y) means "person named x has a mother named y";
• person/parent(x, y) means "person named x has a parent named y";
• person/sex(x, y) means "person named x has sex y".

A collection of clauses, all of which have the same head predicate, is called a *clause group*, or simply a *group*. Actually this is a bit of a simplification as later on we will permit groups to have "internal predicates" but these need not concern us now. For example, the following collection of clauses is a group:

person/ancestor(x, y) ← person/father(x, y)
person/ancestor(x, y) ← person/mother(x, y)
person/ancestor(x, y) ← person/ancestor(x, z), person/father(z, y)
person/ancestor(x, y) ← person/ancestor(x, z), person/mother(z, y)

The unique head predicate of each clause in a clause group is called the *head predicate* of that group; for example, person/ancestor is the head predicate of the group shown above. The body predicates of all the clauses in a clause group are collectively called the *body predicates* of that group. Note that in the above example person/ancestor is the head predicate of the group, so despite the fact that it also appears on the right of the ← symbol it is *not* a body predicate in that group. The group shown above enables information about the head predicate, person/ancestor, to be deduced from the body predicates, person/father and person/mother. We adopt the following notation for groups:

person/ancestor ⇐ person/father, person/mother

in which the single head predicate is written to the left of the ⇐ symbol and the body predicates are written to the right. A group is called a *categorical group* if it contains sufficient clauses to enable *all* the information in the head predicate to be deduced from the information in the body predicates. For example, the group given above, with head predicate person/ancestor, is a categorical group.

As we shall see, it is extensions of Horn clause logic that are used for logic programming and for logic database. In addition, Horn clause logic provides the foundation to the form of logic adopted by the Japanese as the kernel language of the FGCS project. It is a *positive logic*, that is, it is without negation; this presents problems in applications when it is required to represent "not".

The most celebrated rule of inference in computational logic is the *resolution principle* (Robinson, 1965) which derives one clause from two given clauses. (*See* Chang & Lee, 1973 for an introductory text.) The resolution principle is based on a pattern matching process. For example, if we have the two clauses:

Animal(x) ← Human(x)
Human('Socrates') ←

The first clause is true for all x. In particular, the first clause will be true if x is the constant label "Socrates":

Animal('Socrates') ← Human('Socrates')
Human('Socrates') ←

Note that the body of the first clause is the same as the head of the second clause. Thus, from these two clauses we may deduce that:

Animal('Socrates') ←

As another example, if we have two clauses:

P(x , f(x)) ← Q(x), R(x , 'a')
S(y) ← V('a' , y), P('b' , y), U(f('b'))

The first clause is true for all x and the second for all y. By setting variable x to the particular constant label b in the first clause and variable y to the particular constant term f(b) in the second clause we obtain:

P('b' , f('b')) ← Q('b'), R('b' , 'a')
S(f('b')) ← V('a' , f('b')), P('b' , f('b')), U(f('b'))

Note that the head predicate of the first clause is now the same as the second predicate in the body of the second clause. Note also that each of these two clauses contains fewer variables respectively than the original clauses; we say that each of them is an *instantiation* of the corresponding original clause. Alternatively we say that the original clauses have been *instantiated* to give these two clauses. From these two clauses we may deduce:

S(f('b')) ← V('a' , f('b')), Q('b'), R('b' , 'a'), U(f('b'))

This clause is called the *resolvant* of the two original clauses. Note that the construction of the resolvant consists of two steps. The first step is called *unification* in which variables in two clauses are given values to make the head predicate of one clause identical to a predicate in the body of the other clause; we say that these two predicates have been *unified*. The second step is called *resolution* which is the construction of a new clause by combining the two clauses which contain the two unified predicates. The resolution step amounts to simple string replacement and is easy to compute; it formally replaces the unified predicate in the body of one clause with the body of the other clause which contains the unified head predicate. We say that Horn clause T is a *logical consequence* of the set of Horn clauses {A1,A2,...,An} if T can be derived by application of the resolution principle from the set {A1,A2,...,An}.

When using the resolution principle we must first choose which two clauses are to be resolved, then we must choose which two predicates in these clauses are to be unified. For example, suppose that we have chosen the following two clauses:

P(x , f(x)) ← Q('a'), R('a' , x)
S(x) ← P(f('a') , x), P('a' , f('a'))

The head predicate of the first clause may be unified with either of the predicates in the body of the second clause: these two choices will lead to two different conclusions. Thus, application of the resolution principle requires a *control strategy* that will both choose which clauses are to be resolved and, within those clauses, which predicates are to be unified. An important general control strategy for Horn clauses is **Linear** resolution with **Unrestricted Selection** for **Horn** clauses, or LUSH, (*see* Van Emden, 1977). The term LUSH is now rarely used, but an important special case of LUSH, the SLD strategy, is referred to widely; it is essentially this strategy which is used to drive the programming language Prolog. The SLD strategy first *focuses* on the goal sentence:

Ans ← T

Then, in general, it takes the leftmost predicate in the body of the sentence in focus and attempts to resolve it with the head of one of the clauses {A1, A2,..., An} in that order. If this operation is successful, then the resulting clause becomes the new sentence in focus. If it is unsuccessful, we say that the search has *failed* and then the system *backtracks* to the previous point at which there was an alternative, untried choice of head from {A1, A2,..., An} and the strategy tries again to resolve the leftmost predicate in the body of the sentence in focus with the head of an alternative clause in {A1, A2,..., An}. The procedure halts when the sentence:

Ans ←

which has no body, has been constructed. For example, consider the following problem in which the statement numbered 4 is the theorem:

1.   P('a') ← P('b')
2.   P('b') ←
3.   Q('b') ←
4.   Ans ← P(x), Q(x)

The strategy focuses on the statement numbered 4 and attempts to resolve its leftmost body predicate with the first possible axiom, that is, with the statement numbered 1:

5.i.   Ans ← P('b'), Q('a')

The strategy now focuses on the statement numbered 5 and attempts to resolve its leftmost body predicate with the first possible axiom, that is, with the statement numbered 2:

6.i.   Ans ← Q('a')

The strategy now focuses on the statement numbered 6 and attempts to resolve its leftmost body predicate with the first possible axiom, none will work. Fail. Can the statement numbered 5 be resolved with an axiom other than the statement numbered 2? No. Fail. Backtrack. Can the statement numbered 4 be resolved with an axiom other than the statement numbered 1? Yes, with the statement numbered 2. OK, proceed.

5.ii.   Ans ← Q('b')

The strategy now focuses on the statement numbered 5 and attempts to resolve its leftmost body predicate with the head predicates of the axioms; this attempt is successful with the statement numbered 3:

6.ii.   Ans ←

And the theorem is proved.
  Given a goal sentence:

  Ans ← T

and axioms {A1, A2,..., An} we may construct a tree for this problem as follows. The root of the tree is labeled with the goal. The resolvants of the goal with each of the axioms form the first level nodes of the tree. In general, the resolvants of the i'th level nodes with the axioms {A1, A2,..., An} form the (i+1)'st level nodes. A *solution node* is a node marked with:

  Ans ←

The tree for the simple example given above is finite, and is shown in Figure 2.3. In Figure 2.3 each arc has been numbered with the number of the axiom used in that deduction. The application of the SLD search strategy to automatic theorem proving can be interpreted as searching this tree for solution nodes; its operation can sometimes be accelerated by concurrent execution (Fagin and Despain, 1984).

  The design of parallel architectures to mechanize "and-parallelism" and "or-parallelism" (Kowalski, 1982b) is a key development in the Fifth Generation Computer Systems project. Recent reports are encouraging (Ueda, 1988). An *admissible* search

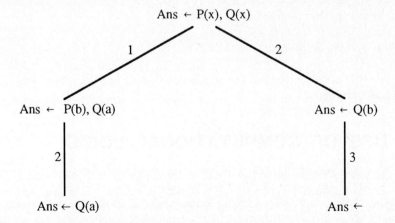

Figure 2.3 Tree for a simple resolution problem

strategy has the property that if a tree for a problem contains a solution node, then the search strategy will find that solution node eventually. Note that, under this strict definition of admissibility, the SLD strategy is not admissible (Lloyd, 1984) and (Potter and Vasak, 1985). Horn clauses together with resolution and any admissible search strategy are called *Horn clause logic*, or simply *clausal logic*.

As a practical example consider the set of "axioms":

item/cost:$(#1234 , 12) ←
item/cost:$(#2468 , 25) ←
item/cost:$(#3579 , 8) ←
item-list/price-list(∅ , ∅) ←

item-list/price-list(x.y , u.v) ← item/cost(x , u), item-list/price-list(y , v)

where item-list/price-list(x , y) means "x is a list of item numbers and y is a list of the corresponding prices". Suppose that we wish to demonstrate that "item number 3579 costs $8". We construct the goal:

Ans ←   item/cost:$(#3579 , 8)

And then use the SLD strategy to direct the search for a solution node by unifying this clause with the above set of "axioms". Taking these axioms in numbered order, the SLD strategy will first attempt to resolve the goal with axiom numbered 1, this resolution is unsuccessful. Next, the SLD strategy will attempt to resolve the goal with axiom numbered 2 and this is also unsuccessful. Next, the SLD strategy will attempt to resolve the goal with axiom numbered 3 and this is successful; the resulting resolvant is:

Ans ←

And the procedure halts which demonstrates that "item number 3579 costs $8".

A less trivial example is to show that "the price list for items 1234 and 3579 is $12 and $8 respectively" by constructing the goal sentence:

Ans ← item-list/price-list(#1234.#3579 , 12.8)

Use of the SLD strategy leads to the conclusion "Ans", and does so directly, that is, without backtracking.

2.3 USE OF COMPUTATIONAL LOGIC

During the late 1960s the principal intention for computational logic was to use it to mechanize the business of proving mathematical theorems. This goal has not been achieved except in trivial cases, the main difficulty being the control of the combinatorial explosion in the number of deductions. We find that the more we deduce, the more we can deduce and so on. Some progress has been made, however, one important advance being "connection graphs" (Kowalski, 1975). However, research in computational logic has produced some practical applications. In fact the Japanese have chosen Horn clause logic as the basis for the kernel programming language in their Fifth Generation Computer Systems project. (*See* Moto-Oka et al 1982 and Kowalski, 1982b.) This has generated considerable interest in logic as a computer language (Kowalski, 1982a) within the information industry. We will be primarily concerned here with the use of clausal logic both as a programming language and as a database language. Both of these uses of clausal logic are derived from the use of clausal logic as a question-answering language.

Logic may be used for *question-answering systems* by introducing a simple device (Green, 1969) which enables us to retrieve facts from a set of clauses. Instead of having just "Ans" on the left hand side of a goal sentence we give the "Ans" predicate arguments. For example:

Ans(x) ← item-list/price-list(#1234.#3579 , x)

reads "that x is the answer if x is the list of prices corresponding to the list of item numbers #1234.#3579". When the calculation is directed by the SLD strategy with this as the goal sentence it will terminate with:

Ans($12.$8) ←

The example just cited in question-answering could be interpreted as a simple computer program which executes the command "*calculate* the price list for items 1234 and 3579". In this program, item/cost is the name of an array containing three pairs of data items, and item-list/price-list is the name of a procedure which calculates price lists. This is an example of *pure logic programming*, or simply *logic programming*. The adjective "pure" indicates the absence of additional features which are required to enhance logic's capability as a practical programming language. We will see that such enhancements are of two types. First, the provision of specific computational features such as procedures to perform simple arithmetic. Second, the provision of control features such as find one answer only or find all possible answers. The above example of pure logic programming is naive, but from it we note the following important properties:

1. The demonstration of "partial correctness" of the program is trivial. (A program is said to be *partially correct* if, whenever it halts, it gives the correct answer.) Each line of the program may be verified independently of the rest of the program. Thus, when each line of the program has been shown to be correct, if the program halts, then it cannot give an incorrect answer.
2. The order of the statements in the program will not effect the validity of the result of the computation. In this sense, logic is a *non-deterministic* programming language, because if there is more than one correct answer, then reordering the statements of the program can have the effect that the program will find a different (correct) answer.
3. The program is not "goal dependent". The same program could be used "to find two item numbers which cost $25 and $8" by:

Ans(x) ← item-list/price-list(x , $25.$8)

to which the answer might be #2468.#3579 . The same program could also perform the bizarre calculation "to determine if there is an item whose item number is numerically the same as its cost in dollars":

Ans(x) ← item/cost(x , x)

Thus, the language does not require that arguments be designated as either "input" or "output" arguments; a language with this property is not *goal dependent*.

The question-answering example given above could be interpreted as a simple database. In this database "item/cost" is the name of a relation containing data about the cost of three items, and "item-list/price-list" is the name of a procedure that can compute information about price lists. The goal sentence may be interpreted as the command "*retrieve* the price list for items numbered 1234 and 3579". This is an example of a *pure logic database*, or simply a *logic database*. We will see that by enhancing logic in two ways we obtain a powerful database language. First, an efficient mechanism is required for the storage and retrieval of actual data. We will see that this can be achieved by coupling a conventional database system to the logic, and that this coupling can be achieved in a natural way. Second, the control mechanism will be extended to implement instructions such as "find all but without repetition" as well as other facilities required to support database usage. From this simple example we note two important properties of logic as a database language (which should be seen in addition to the properties of logic as a programming language noted above):

1.   The formalism is capable of representing an item of knowledge in one place, once and for all, regardless of what it is to be used for. Thus, with the help of a systematic approach to design, we might reasonably expect substantial reductions in maintenance costs when compared to traditional systems.
2.   The user of a pure logic database will see no difference between the retrieval of stored information and the calculation of information, such as the calculation of the price list in the above example. The system will behave just as though all the information in all relations had in fact been stored. For this reason, if "item/cost" has been stored then it will be called a *real relation*, and if "item-list/price-list" has not been stored then it will be called a *virtual relation*.

Other applications of computational logic include directing robots (Green, 1969), problem solving (Kowalski, 1979b), and expert systems (Clark and McCabe, 1982).
     The answer predicate (i.e. Ans) will find the "first" answer it can and then halt. By the "first" we mean the first answer located by the search strategy, whether it be the SLD strategy or some other. Thus, the Ans predicate is sometimes referred to as the *find-one predicate*. For example, the goal statement:

Ans(x, y) ← item/cost:$(x, y)

which reads that "for any x and y, x and y are the answer if item number x costs $y" will return:

Ans(#1234, 12) ←

if the SLD strategy had been applied to the above example. Most implementations of logic programming provide some form of *find-all predicate* which enables all correct answers to be calculated. We will employ the predicate:

tuple/find-all-list((x), y)

in which "(x)" is a tuple which is usually present in at least one of the body predicates "to the left of" this predicate in the body of a clause, and "y" is a logic programming list which is usually present in the head predicate or in at least one of the predicates "to the right of" this predicate in the body of a clause. This predicate operates as follows. When control is passed to this predicate the value of the tuple (x) is added to the list y, the predicate then "fails" and the search "backtracks" to look for the next tuple (x) *until* the search for new tuples (x) is unsuccessful. The search strategy finally halts when an exhaustive search of the search space has been completed. By this stage, the list y should contain at least one version of every tuple (x) that is a logical consequence of the axioms. For example, the goal statement:

Ans(z) ← item/cost:\$(x, y), tuple/find-all-list((x, y), z)

which reads "find a list consisting of all x and y such that item number x costs \$y"; this goal statement will activate a search which will terminate with the list containing three tuples as shown in Figure 2.4. Most implementations of logic programming contain special predicates that will achieve the same result as the tuple/find-all-list predicate but possibly in a different way.

The ability to perform for-all searches efficiently has important consequences for the effective mechanization of negation. The logical equivalence:

$$(\forall x)\sim P(x) \leftrightarrow \sim(\exists x)P(x)$$

shows that the problem of showing "that it is not the case that there exists an x such that P(x)" is equivalent to the problem of showing "that for all x it is not the case that P(x)".

x	y:\$
#1234	12
#2468	25
#3579	8

Figure 2.4 Table of costs for every item

2.4 LOGIC AS A PROGRAMMING LANGUAGE

Pure Horn clause logic may be extended to a practical programming language by introducing a set of fundamental computational procedures and by providing additional control facilities.

In order to perform arithmetic addition in pure logic, it would be necessary to represent all the rules of addition in logic as well as defining within the logic what numbers were! This would be absurd if the logic were to be executed on a computer which could perform arithmetic operations directly, efficiently and quickly. Thus, the arithmetic facilities of the machine, and other basic, low-level operations, are made available to the logic using *inbuilt predicates*. For example, the predicate plus(x , y , z), which means "x + y = z", could be provided in which case the programmer may proceed as though all the information about the predicate "plus" were actually present in the program. For example, the programmer will assume that:

> plus(1 , 1 , 2) , plus(2 , 3 , 5) and so on

are "virtually" provided. Likewise, times(x , y , z) meaning "x × y = z" could be provided. In fact the values of these inbuilt predicates are computed as required. For example, if:

> Ans(x) ← plus(2 , x , 7)

had been derived, then the computation would proceed as though:

> plus(2 , 5 , 7) ←

were present to derive:

> Ans(5) ←

and the computation would then halt. We will assume that inbuilt functions are available for the four basic arithmetic operations and that order for numbers is provided by:

> less-than(x , y)

which means "x < y", as well as an inbuilt function for arithmetic equality, and so on.

Using these inbuilt predicates we might extend the example given above by including:

> item/sell(x , y) ← item/cost(x , z), times(z , 1.25 , y)
> invoice(∅ , 0) ←
> invoice(x.y , z) ← invoice(y , w), item/sell(x , v), plus(v , w , z)

where item/sell(x , y) means "item number x sells for y dollars"; note that the above clause defining item/sell is in fact a representation of the business rule "that all items are marked up by 25 per cent". The predicate invoice(u , v) means "u is a list of item numbers and v is the total cost in dollars of those items". Note that the above clauses defining the procedures "item/sell" and "invoice" may be proved to be partially correct easily.

The inbuilt predicates "plus" and "times" are a little clumsy so we will often use instead the conventional arithmetic notation. For example, instead of the clause:

$$P(x, z) \leftarrow Q(x, y), \; plus(y, 1, w), \; times(x, w, z)$$

we will write:

$$P(x, z) \leftarrow Q(x, y), \; y + 1 = w , \; x \times w = z$$

The SLD search strategy is too simple a control mechanism to automatically execute all logic programs efficiently. To overcome this, we can either devise more intelligent control mechanisms or provide the logic programmer with additional control instructions. The construction of super-intelligent control mechanisms has been an ideal of logic programming for some while (*see* Kowalski, 1979a), and some progress has been made (*see* Potter and Vasak, 1985). In the meantime the provision of control instructions for use by the programmer is typical of logic programming languages today. In Prolog there is a "cut" operator which enables the programmer to control backtracking (*see* Chapter 4 in Clocksin and Mellish, 1981). In the hands of the inexperienced, these control operators can give rise to unnecessarily expensive computations. It should be stressed that there is considerable debate at present as to what control operators are preferable, and to what extent they should be used. No standard has been generally agreed to. It is interesting to note that IC-PROLOG (Clark, McCabe and Gregory, 1982) is comparatively free of meta-logical control operators. Needless to say, practical implementations of logic as a programming language, such as Prolog, contain many more in-built predicates and other features than have been discussed here. For example, the construct:

$$P \rightarrow Q; R$$

meaning "if P then Q else R" is an important addition to Prolog.

It is several years since the publication in 1975 of the first logic programming manual, and a wide variety of logic software is now available. More recently, logic has been assured of a significant role in the Japanese Fifth Generation Computer Systems Project, (Kowalski, 1982b, and Moto-Oka et al, 1982). It is important to appreciate the difference between "Horn clause logic" and "Prolog". By *Horn clause logic*, we mean Horn clauses together with any admissible search strategy. Prolog uses Horn clauses, together with the SLD strategy, and a particular set of built-in functions, and a particular set of control instructions which includes the "cut" operator. Note that the Japanese have adopted Horn clause logic, and not Prolog, as the essence of the kernel language in their Fifth Generation Computer Systems project. The precise variant of Horn clause logic that will be adopted as the FGCS kernel language has been the subject of considerable debate (*see* Fuchi, 1982 and Ueda, 1988).

2.5 USE OF LOGIC AS A PROGRAMMING LANGUAGE

Note that whenever we introduce a new predicate in logic programming we always state what that predicate "means": the reason for this is more than just expository. Given just the meaning of each predicate in a first-order sentence it is not only possible but usually very simple to demonstrate the partial correctness of that sentence. The partial correctness of each sentence in a logic program may be checked individually. When all sentences in a logic program have been shown individually to be partially correct, the program is partially correct. It is interesting to note that there is no need for loop invariants (*see* Gries 1981) and the like to show that logic programs are partially correct.

Logic is virtually unique as a programming language in that it admits a *declarative semantics*, that is, the statements in logic programs may be interpreted as statements of fact, in addition to the conventional *imperative semantics* in which a logic program is interpreted as a sequence of commands as determined by the control strategy used, be it the SLD, or some other strategy. Languages that admit a declarative semantics are also referred to as being *non-imperative*. An interesting feature of a programming language which admits a declarative semantics is that it cannot contain any purely imperative statement forms. The assignment statement found in conventional programming languages is purely imperative as its operation can only be explained in terms of *how* it works: thus, there can be no assignment statement, or analogue of the assignment statement in logic programming.

We have already noted that logic programming admits trivial correctness proofs, is non-deterministic and is non-goal dependent. Other important properties include the following:

1. It is very *high level* in that the programs are often "very close" to their description in natural language.
2. It is a very *simple* language with just one statement form.
3. It is a very *powerful* language in that complex programs can be written quickly and accurately with few statements.
4. There is no distinction between program and data.
5. There is no distinction between input and output of procedure arguments. Furthermore, partially completed data structures containing both labels and variables can be passed by unification from one procedure to another.
6. It is not necessary or even correct to think of a logic variable as the name for a machine storage location.
7. The imperative semantics for logic programs is "totally defined" in the sense that, unlike conventional programming languages, it is comparatively simple to explain *exactly* how a logic program will behave. A consequence of this is that it is impossible for a syntactically correct program to perform an illegal or undefined operation, such as the "array subscript out of bounds" error and the like which plague many students while learning to use conventional programming languages.

Logic programming is based on positive Horn clause logic. If negation is to be introduced, then it will have to be by the provision of a "negative" predicate or by an extension to the control mechanism.

Negation may be introduced through the provision of "negative" predicates by the programmer. If P and Q are two predicates with the property that P is true if, and only if, Q is not true, then P is said to be the *negative predicate* of Q, and vice versa. For example, in addition to the "item/cost" predicate introduced above, we might introduce its negative predicate:

$$\text{not[item/cost]}(x,y) \leftarrow x \neq 1234,\ x \neq 2468,\ x \neq 3579$$
$$\text{not[item/cost]}(x,y) \leftarrow x \neq 1234,\ x \neq 2468,\ y \neq 8$$
$$\text{not[item/cost]}(x,y) \leftarrow x \neq 1234,\ y \neq 25,\ x \neq 3579$$
$$\text{not[item/cost]}(x,y) \leftarrow x \neq 1234,\ y \neq 25,\ y \neq 8$$
$$\text{not[item/cost]}(x,y) \leftarrow y \neq 12,\ x \neq 2468,\ x \neq 3579$$
$$\text{not[item/cost]}(x,y) \leftarrow y \neq 12,\ x \neq 2468,\ y \neq 8$$
$$\text{not[item/cost]}(x,y) \leftarrow y \neq 12,\ y \neq 25,\ x \neq 3579$$
$$\text{not[item/cost]}(x,y) \leftarrow y \neq 12,\ y \neq 25,\ y \neq 8$$

where "not[item/cost]" is to be taken as a predicate name. In other words, "not[..]" is not to be taken as a higher order operator. This notation for negative predicates lies outside our convention for naming predicates. Note that:

$$\text{not[item/cost]}(\ \#6, 18\ ) \leftarrow$$

is true. After all, it is true to say that "it is not the case that item number 6 costs \$18". However, the reason for this is that there is no such thing as item number 6, and in this example there is no such thing as an item which costs \$18. Note that the definition of the predicate not[item/cost] is considerably more involved than the definition of the predicate item/cost. For many predicates it is just not practical to construct the definition of the corresponding negative predicate.

A common way of introducing negation through an extension to the control mechanism is based on the "negation as failure" principle (*see* Clark, 1978), in which a statement is assumed to be "false" if an attempt to prove it "true" fails. The goal sentence:

$$\text{Ans} \leftarrow \text{item/cost:}\$(\ \#4321\ ,\ 16\ )$$

cannot be resolved with any of the clauses in our example; it would fail, and we would assume that "it is not the case that item number 4321 costs \$16". Note that the reason for this *might* be that there is no item with item number 4321. For the negation as failure principle to work the goal must fail. There are a number of sufficient conditions for failure which lie beyond the scope of this discussion, see for example (Lloyd, 1984). For example, it should be intuitively reasonable to suggest that as long as the goal and the axioms contain a "reasonable quantity" of constants the goal will fail if it should fail. As a more subtle example, suppose that we wish to demonstrate that "no invoice could cost \$19". One way of doing this is to attempt to find one that does cost \$19 using the goal sentence:

$$\text{Ans}(x) \leftarrow \text{invoice}(\ x\ ,\ 19\ )$$

However, this goal would not fail; it would continue to compute the cost of every invoice, and would compute forever being unable to reach a conclusion. This is one reason why the SLD strategy is not admissible.

A substantial amount of logic applications programs have been written. See Santane-Toth and Szeredi, 1982 for an interesting review.

2.6   LOGIC AS A DATABASE LANGUAGE

We first summarize our expanded example which now reads:

    item/cost:$(#1234 , 12) ←
    item/cost:$(#2468 , 25) ←
    item/cost:$(#3579 , 8) ←
    item-list/price-list(∅ , ∅) ←
    item-list/price-list(x.y , u.v) ← item/cost(x , u), item-list/price-list(y , v)
    item/sell(x , y) ← item/cost(x , z), times(z , 1.25 , y)
    invoice(∅ , 0) ←
    invoice(x.y , z) ← invoice(y , w), item/sell(x , v), plus(v , w , z)

Pure Horn clause logic may be extended to a database language by providing fundamental database features and by providing additional control facilities such as those required to answer complex queries.

We will show how these fundamental database features may be provided, both when the storage mechanism is simple (e.g. arrays or indexed sequential files) and when the storage mechanism has standard database features (e.g. a full relational database) (*see* Schmidt and Brodie, 1982), having elementary database integrity checks, and so on. We will refer to whatever storage mechanism is employed as the *database engine* or DBE. The DBE may be a part of an integrated logic database management system, or it may be an auxiliary facility linked to the logic system. In their plans for Fifth Generation Database technology, the Japanese have chosen the relational database storage mechanism as their DBE. See Amamiya et al., 1982, Chakravarthy, Minker and Tran, 1982 and Lloyd, 1983 for a tutorial introduction.

When the DBE is simple, it may be coupled naturally to the logic by, for example, providing item/cost as a built in predicate. In this case the predicate item/cost would be stored in some structure within the DBE and its values retrieved on demand, in an analogous way to the computation of values by the procedure "plus" in logic programming. Data can be stored using the special "STORE-TUPLE" predicate:

    STORE-TUPLE(item/cost(#1470 , 3:$))

which would store the given data in the actual storage structure. The special predicate "DELETE-TUPLE" removes data from a storage structure, and the special predicate "REPLACE-TUPLE" replaces one data item with another. Note that these special predicates, "STORE-TUPLE", "DELETE-TUPLE" and "REPLACE-TUPLE", are not of first-order and do not admit a pure declarative semantics.

A particular form of built-in predicate is the "is-a" predicate, and its special restriction the "is-the" predicate. Suppose that the relation item/cost is stored in the DBE. It is often useful to be able to access one "column" of a relation. For example, suppose that we simply wanted to find a single, valid item number. This could be achieved by:

Ans(x) ← item/cost(x, y)

However, the presence of the variable "y" makes this form a little messy. Instead, we permit the use of an *is-a predicate* which has the form:

is-a[<descriptor>](x)

For example:

Ans(x) ← is-a[item](x)

would achieve the same result as the previous goal statement. On occasions, the descriptor in question will only apply to one label; for example, the descriptor "today's-date" will presumably only be associated with one label. In this case, to draw attention to this fact, we employ a special restriction of the "is-a predicate", namely the *is-the predicate*. To retrieve today's date we could construct the goal statement:

Ans(x) ← is-the[today's-date](x)

We will find the "is-a" and "is-the" predicates useful in Chapter 7 when we consider the analysis of knowledge.

When the DBE is supported by standard database features which include database integrity checks, these integrity checks may be made available within the logic. For example, consider flags to indicate whether or not "STORE-TUPLE", "DELETE-TUPLE" or "REPLACE-TUPLE" have been successful. These can be incorporated in the operation of these predicates by:

REPLACE-TUPLE(item/cost:$(#1470 , 3) , item/cost:$(#1470 , 4) , R)

where R is a flag-predicate, with no arguments, which will be "TRUE" if the replacement was successful, and "FALSE" otherwise. Other standard predicates include the "BEFORE" predicate where:

BEFORE(event1 , event2)

will be "TRUE" if event1 occurs before event2, and is "FALSE" otherwise.

It is easy to see that if the logic is permitted to interact with the DBE without restriction, then anomalies can occur. For example, consider the goal:

Ans(x) ← REPLACE(item/cost:$(x, 8), item/cost:$(x, 9)), x < 1999 which reads "x is the answer if x is the number of an item which cost \$8 and which has been increased to \$9 and x < 1999". When the SLD strategy is applied to this goal it will fail because the number of the only item which costs \$8 is #3579, and 3579 is not less than 1999. However, in the process of the calculation, the leftmost predicate in the goal will have been satisfied, that is, the cost of item number 3579 will have been increased from \$8 to \$9. This is undesirable as a failed goal statement should have no effect on the system whatsoever. Thus, we insist that changes may only be made to the stored information by the particular instantiation of the goal statement which succeeded in returning an answer. For example, the goal:

$$\text{Ans}(x) \leftarrow \text{REPLACE}(\text{item/cost:}\$(x, 8), \text{item/cost:}\$(x, 9)), \quad x > 3500$$

would succeed, would have returned the answer "3579", and, as a result, the cost of item number #3579 would have been increased from \$8 to \$9.

As another example consider the goal sentence:

$$\text{Ans}(x) \leftarrow \text{item/cost:}\$(x, 12), \quad \text{STORE-TUPLE}(\text{item/cost:}\$(x, 13)), \quad P(x)$$

where $P(x)$ is any predicate, with the SLD strategy. We assume that the first domain of the item/cost relation has been identified as the "key"; that is, this relation is constrained to hold at most one cost price for each item number. After the first successful resolvant, the goal statement will become:

$$\text{Ans}(\#1234) \leftarrow \text{STORE-TUPLE}(\text{item/cost:}\$(1234, 13)), \quad P(\#1234)$$

However, note that the validity of this statement is a consequence of the fact that item number 1234 costs \$12, and this statement is now attempting to assert that item number 1234 costs \$13. Thus, it is desirable that this goal should fail and the calculation should backtrack. This behavior can be enforced by "locking" the record:

$$\text{item/cost:}\$(\#1234, 12)$$

in the DBE. A *locked record* cannot be altered until it is "unlocked". In this example the record in the relation item/cost:

$$\text{item/cost:}\$(\#1234, 12)$$

would be locked when the above resolution is performed. This would prevent the relation from holding an entry for the cost of item number 1234 other than \$12. This record will then remain locked until *either* the goal is satisfied *or* the strategy backtracks to the point of the above resolution and looks, in this particular example unsuccessfully, for another matching tuple.

The data in a complex DBE would certainly have some internal structure. Suppose that a major requirement had been identified for retrieving the list of items with a given cost, and suppose that within the DBE there was a structure to facilitate this. This structure can be made available to the logic using the special predicate:

cost:$/item-list(x , y)

which would set "y" to the list of all item numbers of items costing $x. Note that this in-built predicate will have been identified at design time. A predicate of this kind is called an *inverse predicate*. In an intuitive sense this example is the "inverse" of the predicate "item/cost:$". It is important to appreciate that this inverse predicate is *not* to be treated as an "ordinary" predicate. In particular, it may only operate efficiently with the first argument as "input" and the second argument as "output". Thus, this predicate may only be capable for finding efficiently the list of all item numbers with a given price. For example:

Ans(x) ← cost:$/item-list(3, x)

will find the list of all item numbers of items which cost $3. This predicate can be used to great effect in establishing a variety of goals. For example, if this predicate was mechanized efficiently, then the goals to show that:

• there are only three items which cost $17;
• there is no item costing $19,

could be satisfied efficiently.

In Chapters 8 and 9 we will show that the systems designer has three choices for the implementation of an inverse predicate. First, if the inverse predicate is a relation, then its values may be stored as a relation in the ordinary way. Second, an inverse predicate may be defined in terms of its "original" predicate using the tuple/find-all-list predicate. For example:

cost:$/item-list(x, y) ← item/cost:$(z, x), tuple/find-all-list((z), y)

Third, an inverse predicate may be defined in terms of the other predicates in the system, some of which may themselves be inverse predicates. We have introduced the notion of inverse predicates so that the system designer has the option of considering and catering for, at the system design stage, possibly expensive for-all searches. The use of inverse predicates to improve efficiency is discussed in Debenham and McGrath, 1982.

We have already noted the inadequacy of the SLD strategy to execute logic programs efficiently: the same is true of logic database. Logic will have to be extended if it is to support fifth generation databases (Kurokawa, 1982). One such extension is described in Debenham and McGrath, 1983.

Logic is a universal database language in the sense that data description, data manipulation, transaction specification and integrity checking can all be represented in one simple formalism, logic, which also provides the essential syntax of a wide variety of powerful languages for the user interface. We note two quite different implementations of QBE (Zloof, 1977). In Neves, Anderson and Williams, 1983 QBE is implemented in Prolog; on the other hand, in Debenham and McGrath, 1983, a QBE-like language is described and actually implemented within the control mechanism, that is, by modifying the SLD strategy. (*See* also Li, D. 1984).

Many early implementations of logic as a programming language offered file and data handling facilities, but not database management system facilities such as restart and recovery which are essential for any practical application of substance.

2.7   USE OF LOGIC AS A DATABASE LANGUAGE

In our example, which is summarized at the beginning of the previous section, we have seen how predicates may be represented as either real or virtual relations. However, it is important to note that the logic itself does not dictate what is to be stored as *real relations* and what is to be calculated. This will be determined by the functional requirements of the system. Consider the rule:

item/sell(x , y) ← item/cost(x , z), times(z , 1.25 , y)

This rule could be implemented in one of five different ways:

1.   item/cost could be stored as a real relation, in which case the rule:

item/sell(x , y) ← item/cost(x , z), times(z , 1.25 , y)

defines the virtual relation item/sell.
2.   The rule could be inverted to define item/cost in terms of item/sell by:

item/cost(x , z) ← item/sell(x , y), times(z , 1.25 , y)

in which case the rule defines the virtual relation item/cost in terms of the real relation item/sell.

The functional requirements could require that both item/sell and item/cost be stored as real relations, in which case:

3.   Either the rule in 1 above or the rule in 2 above could be used as an integrity constraint to check that item/sell and item/cost are consistent after an update.
4.   The rule in 1 above could be used to update item/sell when item/cost is updated. In which case, some form of locking of files would be required.
5.   The rule in 2 above could be used to update item/cost when item/sell is updated. Again, file locking would be required.

In Debenham and McGrath, 1982, the use of logic as a language for systems design, systems implementation, applications development and systems maintenance is discussed, and a method is described for determining, in particular, whether the functional requirements of the system require that a rule is to be represented as the definition of a virtual relation or as the specification of an integrity constraint.

As we have noted, logic database management systems for commercial use are still at the experimental stage. (*See* Debenham and McGrath, 1982 for a discussion of experimental implementations in logic of two large commercial databases.) One of the conclusions drawn from those experiments was the potential for very substantial savings in maintenance costs when compared with existing, traditional implementations. One reason for this was the ease with which analysts took to the expression of the business rules in logic. The analysts in our study were greatly impressed by the simple way in which the business rules may be represented in logic no matter what they are to be used for (i.e. the formalism is not goal-dependent) and no matter how they are to be implemented (e.g. as the definition of virtual relations or as integrity constraints). If the application has been well designed, then each item of knowledge in the business rules will be represented in one place in logic. The maintenance strategy of the design technique employed should show how a change to a rule causes a simple change to the representation of the knowledge in the logic.

In addition to the properties just cited, the properties of logic as a programming language translate directly into properties of logic as a database language. Furthermore, within a logic database implementation, logic may also be used as a powerful programming language for performing complex calculations on or with the data.

Positive Horn clause logic provides the foundation for logic database. The problems with introducing negation into logic programming apply to logic database as well. In addition, a logic database may have substantial real relations stored in the DBE. These relations can provide the data for very expensive searches. Consider an attempt to establish that there is *no* item in the item/cost relation with the property that it costs \$3 and its item number is a multiple of ten:

$$\text{Ans} \leftarrow \text{item/cost}(\,x\,,\,3\text{:\$}\,),\,\text{times}(\,z\,,\,10\,,\,x\,)$$

This could initiate a very expensive search of the whole of the item/cost relation. One way of reducing the cost of searches such as this within the logic itself, is to use inverse relations such as the cost/item-list relation referred to above, (*see* also Debenham and McGrath, 1982).

2.8 SUMMARY

Of the many applications of computational logic, logic programming and logic database have attracted considerable interest in the information industry. This interest has recently increased due to the commitment of the Japanese to logic in their Fifth Generation Computer Systems Project. We have indicated how logic operates as a programming and as a database language, and have discussed some of its important properties.

③ Data, information and knowledge

3.1 INTRODUCTION

In this chapter we introduce the notion of a "functional association" which underlies our approach to knowledge systems. This notion enables us to define "data", "information" and "knowledge", and to discuss the classification of objects into these three categories. Thus, a clear understanding of sections 3.2, 3.3 and 3.4 is essential before proceeding further. Section 3.5 relates knowledge systems to conventional systems and so an understanding of this section enables our work to be seen in a correct perspective. In section 3.6 tools for modeling are introduced. Our treatment of tools for modeling information is very brief; the reader is assumed to have acquired these skills elsewhere.

Part of the general business of constructing a computer implementation of a given application is the "classification" and "representation" of the objects in that application. By the *classification* of an object we mean the business of deciding whether a given object in that application should be classified as "data", "information" or "knowledge". By the *representation* of an object, we mean the business of constructing an actual representation of that object in an appropriate formalism.

We introduce the notion of "functional association" and use it to define the terms "data", "information" and "knowledge". We comment on the general business of object classification and demonstrate that this process is strictly non-trivial. This establishes part of the need for a rigorous methodology for designing knowledge systems. We then discuss two important features of formalisms; whether or not the formalism is "information goal-dependent" and "knowledge goal-dependent". Next, we discuss precisely what we mean by "knowledge systems" and shown how "knowledge systems" are related to traditional systems. The design methodology that we propose for knowledge systems is based on the construction of a formal *model* of the application. We end the chapter by introducing formalisms for modeling "data", "information" and "knowledge".

3.2 FUNCTIONAL ASSOCIATIONS

As we have foreshadowed, we will refer to the fundamental, indivisible objects in an application as the *data* in that application.

An important structural feature of many relations is the so called "functional dependency" *from* the key domains *to* the non-key domains. In a relation, domain A is said to be *functionally dependent* on the set of domains {B} if to each tuple of values in the set of domains {B} there corresponds precisely one value in domain A, at any given time. For example, in a shared medical practice, in which at most one doctor was on duty at any time, the date and the time of day of an appointment could be sufficient to determine the doctor involved and the patient involved; that is:

    date/time/doctor/patient(dd-mm-yy, hr-min, doc#, pat#)

The identification of the first two domains of this relation as the key, implies that if we know the date and the time, then we know both the doctor and the patient. We say that the third and fourth domains of this relation are functionally dependent on a compound key consisting of both date and time taken together. Thus, a relation can represent a functional dependency between items of data. However, note that we cannot give a succinct definition of the above function; in fact, the only way that we can specify the function is by listing all tuples, concerning time, doctors and patients, which satisfy it.

    Consider the simple rule "To convert from degrees Fahrenheit to degrees Celsius, subtract 32 and divide by 1.8". This rule is also in functional form; in fact, it is a function *from* degrees Fahrenheit *to* degrees Celsius. This function is also between two items of data which are "degrees Fahrenheit" and "degrees Celsius". However it differs from the relation previously discussed in one important way; this time, we can actually define the function:

    f : (deg F) → (deg C)

in a succinct form by:

    $f(x) = (x - 32) \div 1.8$

Both of the examples just considered concern functions between items of data. The first cannot be defined succinctly in the sense that a succinct definition that will "work for all time" cannot be constructed; it is thus called an *implicit functional association*. The second can be defined succinctly and "for all time"; it is thus called an *explicit functional association*. Note that we have used the word "association" rather than "dependency" to acknowledge that the context of our discussion is more general than functional dependencies in relations.

    We introduce two relations:

    item/sale-price(item-number, item-selling-price:$)
    item/cost-price(item-number, item-cost-price:$)

where, in general, item/sale-price(x, y) means "x is the number of an item whose selling price is $y", and item/cost-price(x, y) means "x is the number of an item whose cost price is $y". Now, consider the simple rule, "selling price is 1.25 times buying price" which might be represented by the clause:

    item/sale-price(x , y) ← item/cost-price(x, z), $y = 1.25 \times z$

this rule is also in functional form. In fact it represents a function *from* the relation:

>   item/cost-price

to the relation:

>   item/sale-price

The nature of this function is quite explicit; it is succinct as it enables a large of information about the relation:

>   item/sale-price

to be deduced. Thus, it is also an explicit functional association.

We are now in a position to define what we mean by the "data", "information" and "knowledge" in an application:

1.   The *data* is the fundamental, indivisible objects in that application.
2.   The *information* is the implicit functional associations between data in that application.
3.   The *knowledge* is the explicit functional associations between items of information and/or data in that application.

Note that in this categorization there is no reference to implicit functional associations between items of information. This may appear to be an omission. Consider the following; if it is possible to specify a correspondence between all tuples that could belong to relation P and all tuples that could belong to relation R such that to each P-tuple there is a unique R-tuple, and if, at any time, to each tuple stored in P there is a (unique) corresponding tuple stored in R, then there is an implicit functional association from relation P to relation R. However, in this case we would say that relation P was a candidate, compound key for relation R, thus giving rise to a new relation constructed from P and R. In other words, there is little to be gained from considering implicit functional associations between items of information as being different from implicit functional associations between collections of items of data.

The distinction between implicit and explicit functional associations is hard to draw precisely. For example, consider the relation shown in Figure 3.1 for which the general rule "that if a $\leq$ 4 then b = 2 $\times$ a" always holds. Thus, the first three lines of the current contents of the relation are instances of this general rule, and the other lines represent the exceptions to this general rule. Is this an implicit or an explicit functional association? After all, it can be represented in clausal logic as:

> $R(x, y) \leftarrow \leq(x, 4), y = 2 \times x$
> $R(5, 6) \leftarrow$
> $R(8, 3) \leftarrow$
> $R(9, 4) \leftarrow$

a	b
1	2
3	6
4	8
5	6
8	3
9	4

Figure 3.1 Part implicit, part explicit association

Thus, no matter which way we consider it, this functional association is "part implicit" and "part explicit". We will not try to resolve this apparent dilemma because it is our belief that, in practice, functional associations tend to be principally implicit or principally explicit. In other words, we suggest that if a functional association is under consideration which has both a substantial implicit part and a substantial explicit part, then perhaps the functional association should be decomposed into two, or more, subassociations each of which is either clearly implicit or clearly explicit.

3.3 THE OBJECT CLASSIFICATION PROBLEM

It may appear, on the basis of intuition and the exploration of simple examples, that the facts in an application will have a natural interpretation as either data, information or knowledge. In other words, it may appear that, in practice, "object classification" is a fairly trivial matter. *Object classification* is the business of deciding whether an object in the application should be represented as data, information or knowledge. We now show that object classification is far from trivial. As a direct consequence, we also show that there is no a priori classification of objects in an application as "data", "information" or "knowledge". We will see that the classification of an object as "data", "information" or "knowledge" is, in fact, part of the design process and amounts to a fundamental design decision.

The observations of the previous paragraph have substantial implications for the maintenance of knowledge systems, because they establish a clear requirement for the designer of a system to convey to those responsible for maintenance how the objects have been classified. To put the matter simply, if it is required to change the system during maintenance, then there must be some form of indication as to whether the change should be made to the data, to the information or to the knowledge. As we will see in the next chapter, data, information and knowledge are represented in different formalisms, and can be stored in different parts of a machine architecture. Thus, it is essential that a maintenance programmer knows where to find the representation of a fact which has to be altered.

Expert systems are often referred to as "knowledge-based" systems. In this connection, the phrase "knowledge-based" is in contrast with the phrase "information-based", that is knowledge and information are seen as being distinct; but precisely what is "a piece of real knowledge", and what is "a piece of real information"? If we are presented with some fact from the external world, how do we classify it as knowledge, information, data, or perhaps something else? We will illustrate this problem by analysing the sample fact "the interest rate on savings accounts is 5 percent" in six different ways.

Analysis 1

Suppose that the analyst has decided that "the interest rate on savings accounts" is a fundamental, indivisible object. Then the sample fact would be classified as data; it could be represented by the label:

5

this label could be associated with a population named:

interest-rate-on-savings-accounts:%

Thus, in Analysis 1, the sample fact has been classified as data, represented as a label and associated with a population. In this example, we might also introduce the constraint that this population can have at most one label associated with it at any one time.

Analysis 2

Suppose that the analyst has decided that "interest-rate" and "account-type" are fundamental, indivisible objects, and are thus items of data. Furthermore, suppose that the analyst has decided that the sample fact is an implicit functional association between these two data items. Thus, the sample fact would be classified as information; it could be represented by the tuple:

('savings' , '5')

this tuple could be grouped with other similar tuples in a relation:

account-type/interest-rate(account-description , rate:%)

Thus, in Analysis 2 the sample fact has been classified as information, represented as a tuple and grouped with other, similar tuples in a relation. Note that as the above relation has its first argument as the key, this constraint will ensure that, in particular, there can be at most one tuple in the relation which represents the interest rate on savings accounts.

Analysis 3

Suppose that the analyst has decided that, as in Analysis 2, "interest-rate" and "account-type" are fundamental, indivisible objects and so, in addition, is "account number". Thus, the analyst has identified three data populations. Furthermore, suppose that the analyst has identified two different implicit functional associations between these three populations. These implicit functional associations are represented by the two relations:

account/interest-rate(<u>account-number</u> , rate:%)
account/account-type(<u>account-number</u> , account-description)

and are thus items of information. Furthermore, suppose that the analyst has decided that the sample fact is an explicit functional association between these two information items. The sample fact would then be classified as knowledge; it could be represented by the clause:

account/interest-rate(x , '5') ← account/account-type(x , 'savings')

This clause could be grouped with other similar clauses in a clause group. Thus, in Analysis 3, the sample fact has been classified as knowledge, represented as a clause, and grouped with other, similar clauses in a group. The analyst may wish to attach a knowledge constraint to this clause group which specifies that there can be at most one clause referring to each account type.

Analysis 4
Suppose that the analyst has decided that "account-number", "account-type", "mean-balance" and "interest-payable" are fundamental indivisible objects and are thus items of data. Furthermore, suppose that the analyst has identified three different implicit functional associations, in the sample fact, between these items of data. These three implicit functional associations are represented by the three relations:

account/account-type(<u>account-number</u> , account-description)
account/mean-balance(<u>account-number</u> , mean-balance:$s)
account/interest(<u>account-number</u> , interest:$s) .

and are thus items of information. Furthermore, suppose that the analyst has decided that the sample fact is an explicit functional association between these three information items. The sample fact would then be classified as knowledge; it could be represented by the clause:

account/interest(x , y) ← account/account-type(x , 'savings'),
        account/mean-balance(x , z), y = z × (5/100)

This clause could be grouped with other similar clauses in a clause group. Thus, in Analysis 4 the sample fact has been classified as knowledge, represented as a clause, and grouped with other, similar clauses in a group. The analyst may wish to attach a knowledge constraint to this group as in Analysis 3.

Analysis 5
Suppose that the analyst has identified the same populations and the same relations as in Analysis 4. However, instead of using these to represent the sample fact as a clause, the analyst uses these relations to actually store the information implied by the sample fact for every savings account in the application. For example, suppose that account number

1234 happens to be a savings account with mean balance $200, then there would be the following entries in the relations:

    account/account-type('1234', 'savings')
    account/mean-balance('1234', '200')
    account/interest('1234', '10')

These three tuples would be grouped with similar tuples for all other savings accounts in the application. Thus, in Analysis 5, which uses exactly the same populations and relations as Analysis 4, the sample fact is stored implicitly as a set of tuples. In addition, the sample fact could also be stored as an information integrity constraint to ensure that the stored information is consistent. Note that the first argument is the key in each of these three relations; this will ensure that, in particular, each account number identifies an account which has a unique account type.

Analysis 6
Suppose that the analyst has noted that accounts are identified by their "account-no.", and that each account has an "interest-rate". The analyst identifies an implicit functional association between these two notions and defines the relation:

    account/interest-rate(<u>account-number</u> , rate:%)

Suppose that the only savings accounts in the application have account numbers 1234, 2468 and 3579, then the sample fact may be represented as:

    account/interest-rate('1234' , '5')
    account/interest-rate('2468' , '5')
    account/interest-rate('3579' , '5')

Thus, in Analysis 6, the single, sample fact has been represented as a *set of tuples*.

We have seen that a simple sample fact can be classified and represented accurately in a variety of different ways. The way in which it is represented will depend in part on the way in which it is classified. Thus, we see that a distinction between the knowledge, the information and the data in an application must be related to the analysis technique used and the way in which it is applied. In particular, any effective method for the identification of the data, information and knowledge in an application must refer directly to the analysis method and the way in which it has been employed.

We have seen that the distinction between data, information and knowledge is a product of the analysis method and the way in which it is applied; it is not a distinction which exists independently in the real world. In other words, it is incorrect to identify:

•   that which *can* be represented by labels as "data";
•   that which *can* be represented by tuples as "information"; and
•   that which *can* be represented by clauses as "knowledge".

This has been illustrated by the above example. In addition, we now consider the matter of representing constraints which has so far been ignored deliberately in the present discussion.

Consider the domain integrity rule: "All account numbers must lie between 1000 and 4999". This can be represented in clausal logic as a clause group:

invalid(x) ← account-no.(x) , x < 1000
invalid(x) ← account-no.(x) , x > 4999

Clausal logic can be interpreted as a general purpose programming language so it is clear that any computable, "static" domain integrity rule can be expressed in clausal logic. A *static constraint* is a constraint which specifies how something must be; the statement, "all account numbers must lie between 1,000 and 4,999" which restricts the form of an account number, is an example of a static constraint. In contrast with static constraints, an *update constraint*, or *dynamic constraint*, is a constraint which specifies how something may be altered; for example, "the interest rate on savings accounts never changes by more than 1 percent at a time", which restricts the amount of change to the interest rate on savings accounts, is an example of an update constraint.

Consider the relation integrity rule: "The interest on an account is always less than the mean annual balance". This can be represented as:

invalid(x, y, z) ← account/mean-balance(x , y),
    account/interest(x , z), y ≤ z

Again it is clear that any computable, static relation integrity rule can be expressed in clausal logic.

To summarize, we have seen that the distinction between the data, information and knowledge in an application must be expressed in terms of the analysis method and the way in which it is applied. It is incorrect, for example, to equate the knowledge in an application with those objects in the application which may be represented in clausal logic.

3.4 GOAL DEPENDENCY IN FORMALISMS

It should be clear that labels and populations provide a formalism in which data may be represented; tuples and relations provide a formalism in which information may be represented; and clauses and groups provide a formalism in which knowledge may be represented. We now explore the "goal-dependent" features of tuples and relations as a formalism for representing information, and both traditional programming languages and Horn clause logic as formalisms for representing knowledge. We have already noted that relations often represent a natural "information flow" from the key domain(s) to the non-key domain(s). In general terms, a formalism is said to be *goal-dependent* if an attempt to extract facts using it can only be conducted naturally in "one direction". This notion should become clearer in the discussion which follows.

3.4.1   Relations for information

One important feature of the relation as a formalism is that it is "non-information-goal-dependent" in a sense which we now explain. In practice, relations often have a natural "key" domain. For example, in a finance house application the relation:

account/interest-rate(account-number , x:%)

could be used to store the daily interest rate payable on each account. Note that account number determines the interest rate, but not vice versa. The account-number domain is thus identified as the *key domain*. The key domain of a relation is the subject of an *information-(functional-) dependency* between the domains; in other words, this functional dependency is *from* the key domain(s) *to* the non-key domain(s).

Assuming that a database management system provides a modest level of query processing, and that the relation quoted above is represented in such a database management system, this relation could be used to satisfy the following forms of query:

1.   to find the daily interest rate payable on a given account;
2.   to find one (or all) account numbers whose daily interest rate payable is some given value;
3.   to find those account numbers whose daily interest rate payable is numerically equal to the account number.

In queries of type 1 above, the first argument of the relation will be used as the "functional input" and the second argument as the "functional output". In queries of type 2 above, the second argument of the relation will be used as the "functional input" and the first argument as the "functional output". In queries of type 3 above, both arguments are used in a pattern-matching process and thus play both "functional input" and "functional output" roles. Thus, we conclude that relations, together with a modest database management system, provide a "non-(information-) goal-dependent" formalism in the following sense. A formalism is said to be *information-goal-dependent* if the data items occurring in expressions represented in the formalism are assigned either "information-functional input" or "information-functional output" roles. The relation, which represents functional associations between data objects, has no a priori assignment of the roles "functional input" and "functional output" to its arguments, and thus is a non-(information-) goal-dependent formalism. In other words, despite the fact that relations represent a natural functional dependency, when we wish to retrieve facts from a relation, we are not bound to follow that functional dependency.

3.4.2   Imperative formalisms for knowledge

Two important features of a formalism for knowledge representation are whether the formalism is "information goal-dependent" and "knowledge goal-dependent". We will illustrate these two notions by first discussing the representation of knowledge in traditional, imperative formalisms and then, in the following section, the representation of knowledge in declarative formalisms such as Horn clause logic.

Many traditional database management systems employ relations as an information storage formalism. However, as we will see, relations cannot, in general, represent rules. For example, consider the rule "the daily interest on accounts is determined by multiplying the account balance by the account interest rate (percent)" which, in effect, tells us how to calculate values for the tuples in the relation:

account/interest-pay(<u>account-number</u> , amount:$)

if we know the values of the tuples in the two relations:

account/interest-rate(<u>account-number</u> , rate:%)
account/balance(<u>account-number</u> , amount:$)

In traditional database management systems, rules are typically represented in a formalism which closely resembles a conventional, imperative programming language, such as COBOL or Pascal. For example, to use this rule to calculate the daily interest payable on a given account, we might construct the procedure:

function interest-pay(account-number)
retrieve account/interest-rate(account-number , y)
retrieve account/balance(account-number , z)
interest-pay := z × (y ÷ 100)
end

where the ":=" sign above represents conventional assignment. Note that this procedure implements the knowledge in our business rule in a directed, functional way. The functionality is *from* "account-number" *to* "interest-pay". For example, the above functional implementation of this rule would not be of *direct* use in either of the following tasks:

• to find one, or all, account numbers whose daily interest payable is some given value;
• to find the accounts whose account number and daily interest payable are numerically equal.

Both of which can be performed directly on the basis of the knowledge expressed in the original rule. Thus, we observe that conventional programming languages provide an information-goal-dependent formalism; after all, in the above example, "account-number" is the "functional input" and "interest-pay" is the "functional output".

To conclude, we have noted in the previous section that the representation of real information often contains a natural, clearly identifiable, functional association; this functional association is often acknowledged by identifying the key in a relation. In which case that relation is said to represent a natural information-(functional-) dependency in the data. We have noted that relations, as a formalism for representing the functional associations between items of data, are non-(information-) goal-dependent. We have also noted in this section that imperative languages similar to traditional programming languages are employed by conventional database management systems to represent rules; as a formalism for the representation of rules, these languages are an information-goal-dependent formalism. Thus, in a very real sense, relations and imperative formalisms are not compatible with each other for the storage and manipulation of information.

3.4.3   Declarative formalisms for knowledge

We now consider the use of declarative formalisms, such as Horn clause logic, for the representation of knowledge. Consider the following example, if, in a finance house, "interest on accounts is defined to be the product of the account balance and the account interest rate (percent)" then this statement may be represented as a functional association using the (single clause) clause group:

$$\text{account/interest-pay}(\text{ w , x:\$ }) \leftarrow \text{account/interest-rate}(\text{ w , y:\% }),$$
$$\text{account/balance}(\text{ w , z:\$ }), \text{ x = z } \times (\text{ y } \div 100) \qquad \text{[A]}$$

This clause could be used directly to satisfy the following forms of query:

1. to find the daily interest payable on a given account;
2. to find one, or all, account numbers whose daily interest payable is some given value;
3. to find the accounts whose account number and daily interest payable are numerically equal.

As in our previous discussion of relations, in queries of type 1 above, the first argument of the predicate:

account/interest-pay

will be used as the "functional input" and the second argument as the "functional output". In queries of type 2 above, the second argument of the predicate will be used as the "functional input" and the first argument as the "functional output". In queries of type 3 above, both arguments are used in a pattern matching process and so both play "functional input" and "functional output" roles. Thus, we conclude that, like relations, clausal logic provides a non-(information-) goal-dependent formalism. Thus, in a very real sense, relations and declarative formalisms *are* compatible with each other for the storage and manipulation of information.

However, the above clause contains a "knowledge-(functional-) dependency". A Horn clause identifies a *knowledge- (functional-) dependency* between the predicates in the clause; this functional dependency is *from* the body predicates *to* the head predicate. For example, in clause [A] above note that the information in:

account/interest-pay

is deduced from the information in:

account/interest-rate

and in:

    account/balance

as well as from rules for simple arithmetic. Note that the above clause was constructed as a response to the business rule "interest on accounts is defined to be the product of the account balance and the account interest rate (percent)". Note also that this business rule contains no particular knowledge functional dependency; the business rule does *not* contain any explicit implication that clause [A] represents *all* that the business rule has to say. For example, perhaps the business rule also implies that:

$$\text{account/interest-rate}(\text{ w , y:\% }) \leftarrow \text{account/interest-pay}(\text{ w , x:\$ }),$$
$$\text{account/balance}(\text{ w , z:\$ }), x = z \times (y \div 100) \qquad \text{[B]}$$

and that:

$$\text{account/balance}(\text{ w , z:\$ }) \leftarrow \text{account/interest-pay}(\text{ w , x:\$ }),$$
$$\text{account/interest-rate}(\text{ w , y:\% }), x = z \times (y \div 100) \qquad \text{[C]}$$

It is important to realize that groups [B] and [C] are *not* logical consequences of group [A]. Thus, if groups [B] and [C] are implied by the given business rule then they should be stated in addition to group [A].

A formalism for knowledge is said to be *knowledge-goal-dependent* if the data and information items occurring in expressions represented in the formalism are assigned "knowledge-functional input" and "knowledge-functional output" roles. We have already noted that clausal logic provides a non-(information-) goal-dependent formalism. However, note that in clause [A] above, the predicates:

    account/interest-rate
    account/balance

are in a very real sense the "knowledge-functional input" predicates whose values are used by the clause to calculate the values of the "knowledge-functional output" predicate:

    account/interest-pay

Thus, we conclude that clausal logic is a knowledge-goal-dependent formalism. In other words, we have seen how clausal logic is incapable of representing directly a sentence which contains no particular knowledge-functional dependency.

In summary, we have seen that, unlike the imperative programming languages employed by conventional database management systems to represent rules, Horn clause logic is *not* an information-goal-dependent formalism. However, Horn clause logic *is* a knowledge-goal-dependent formalism.

Knowledge-dependencies (in clauses) differ from information-dependencies (in relations) in two important ways. First, it is usually far from obvious from the "raw facts" as to which (knowledge) dependency is actually intended. Second, it is usually far from obvious as to which of the intended knowledge dependencies will subsequently be required as an operational component of the overall system. These two observations together, in effect, imply that analysing knowledge as an activity is substantially more complex than analysing information and data. Furthermore, they imply that we should not see the "clause group" as a satisfactory fundamental unit for knowledge acquisition. We will later propose that the "cluster" is the appropriate basic unit for gathering knowledge. We will show that, in general, "clusters" are *not* a knowledge-goal-dependent formalism.

In the table given in Figure 3.2, we summarize the goal-dependency properties of three formalisms. These three formalisms are:

- imperative programming languages ("imperative");
- declarative Horn clause logic ("declarative"); and
- "clusters" which will be introduced later in this chapter.

3.5 KNOWLEDGE SYSTEMS

We will now comment on the nature of "knowledge systems". In particular, we will now discuss the relationship between "knowledge systems" and conventional systems, and the relationship between "knowledge systems" and expert systems.

First, we discuss some basic jargon concerning systems. By and large, computer systems are designed to respond to stimuli (or, if you prefer, to give "answers" to "queries"). We refer to the range of types of stimuli to which a system is designed to respond as the *query types*. Many computer systems are designed to accommodate changes in circumstance (or, if you prefer, to "receive updates"). We refer to the range of types of changes that the system is designed to accommodate as the *update types*. The notions of query type and update type are intended to capture the "everyday" demands placed on the system. Beyond the scope of the query and update types, with which the system is designed to cope, there will be more substantial "maintenance operations" which will usually be performed by skilled personnel.

	Information goal-dependent	Knowledge goal-dependent
Imperative	yes	yes
Declarative	no	yes
Clusters	no	no

Figure 3.2 Goal-dependency properties

Two important characteristics of a system are the "form" of the query types and the "scope" of the update types. The *form of a query type* is said to be:

- **data** if that query type can be answered using knowledge and information to deduce data values from the values of certain labels;
- **information** if that query type can be answered using knowledge, information and data to deduce values of certain tuples; and
- **knowledge** if that query type can be answered using knowledge, information and data to deduce certain rules.

The *scope of an update type* is said to be:

- **data** if the facts in the update type can be represented in the system through changes to labels;
- **information** if the facts in the update type can be represented in the system through changes to tuples; and
- **knowledge** if the facts in the update type can be represented in the system through changes to clauses.

We refer to systems in which the knowledge is encoded in a conventional programming language: the information is either stored explicitly in simple storage technology or implicitly in a conventional programming language, the data is stored in simple storage technology, the form of the system query types is information and data, and the scope of the system update types is data, as *data processing systems* as shown in Figure 3.3.

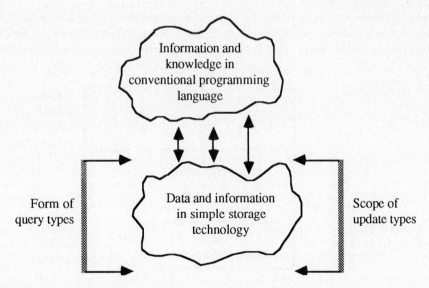

Figure 3.3 Data processing system

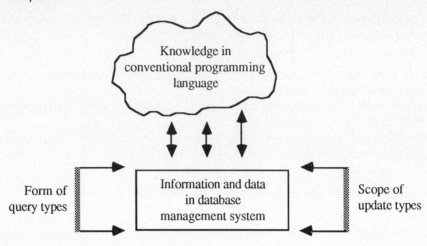

Figure 3.4 Information-based system

We refer to systems in which the knowledge is encoded in a conventional programming language, which employ a database management system for information and data storage, in which the form of the system query types is information and data, and the scope of the system update types is information and data, as *information-based systems*, or *conventional database systems* as shown in Figure 3.4.

We refer to systems in which the knowledge is encoded in a knowledge language, which employ a database management system for information and data storage, in which the form of the system query types is information and data, and the scope of the system update types is information and data and possibly limited knowledge, as *deductive database systems*, as shown in Figure 3.5.

We refer to systems in which the knowledge is encoded in a knowledge language, which employ a database management system for information and data storage, in which the form of the system query types is knowledge, information and data, and the scope of

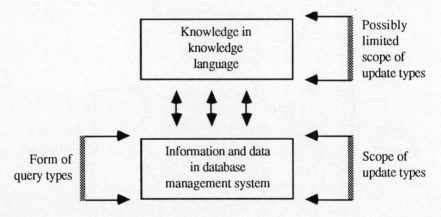

Figure 3.5 Deductive database system

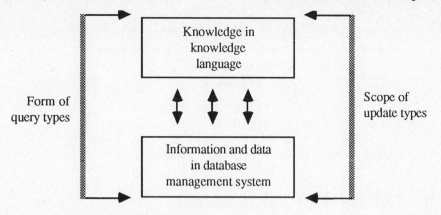

Figure 3.6 Knowledge-based system

the system update types is knowledge, information and data, as *knowledge-based systems*, or simply *knowledge systems*, as shown in Figure 3.6.

Thus, we see that knowledge systems are more than just conventional database systems in which the host programming language has been replaced by a knowledge language. A knowledge system will, in general, be designed to support query and update types that interact with the knowledge component as well as the information and data component(s). For example, a knowledge system can be expected to *explain how* it has derived a piece of information; on the other hand, a deductive database system would not necessarily be expected to do this.

We now discuss the relationship between "knowledge systems" and "expert systems". We think of expert systems as computer systems which attempt to perform similar tasks as knowledge systems but, for an expert system, the knowledge has usually been extracted directly from an expert and has been deliberately represented "as it is". Thus, in an expert system the knowledge has not been analysed, modeled and normalized. So, in a sense, we think of expert systems as prototype knowledge systems. We maintain that many of the criteria which are often quoted as defining the effective scope of expert systems technology should not apply to knowledge systems. For example:

- expert systems are often built to perform in the manner of a particular trained human expert; a knowledge system should not be constrained in this way. In fact, normalized knowledge should be "modular" in the sense that it can easily be placed alongside knowledge extracted from another source.
- expert systems do not usually interact with large corporate databases; a knowledge system should be designed with sufficient care and precision for it to be able to interact fully with all existing resources.
- expert systems usually perform tasks which are clearly "contained"; a knowledge system should be based on carefully modeled and normalized knowledge which should enable it to expand across boundaries between formally separated tasks.

With the exception of the above, "expert systems" and "knowledge systems" mean pretty much the same thing. "Expert systems", being related to the knowledge of a

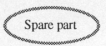

Figure 3.7 Representation of thing-population

particular expert, has something of a pioneering flavor, whereas "knowledge systems" has something of a systems architectural flavor. However, we do not wish to involve ourselves in a discussion as to which is the correct name, "knowledge" or "expert"; perhaps "expert knowledge-based systems" is a suitable compromise.

3.6 TOOLS FOR MODELING

We now discuss the three notations that we will use for modeling an application. These three notations are: a notation for data, a notation for information and a notation for knowledge.

3.6.1 Modeling data

Populations represent fundamental, indivisible objects which are *not* tangible, physical objects. We have noted that populations are sometimes associated with "sets of labels". We now refine and extend the notion of a population somewhat. The population "spare part number", which is clearly associated with a particular set of labels (i.e. the actual set of spare part numbers) is called a *name-population*. On the other hand, the population "spare part" which just refers to the abstract thing "spare part", and thus is *not* associated with a particular set of labels, is called a *thing-population*. We will shortly introduce the notation of Binary Relationship (B-R) modeling (Nijssen and Halpin, 1989). For the sake of those who are familiar with the B-R approach, a name-population corresponds to the B-R concept of a "LOT", and a thing-population corresponds to the B-R concept of a "NOLOT".

We represent a thing-population by a heavy oval shape, for example the diagram in Figure 3.7 might represent the thing-population "spare part".

A thing-population may be associated with a number of name-populations. For example, the thing-population "spare part" may be associated with the two name-populations "spare part name" and "spare part number". With each thing-population we identify a particular name-population which has the property that each label in this name-population uniquely identifies each thing in the thing-population, this name-population is

Spare part number

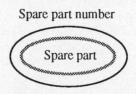

Figure 3.8 The identifying population

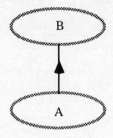

Figure 3.9 Sub-type relationship

called the *identifying population*. For example, with the thing-population "spare part" we might identify the name-population "spare part number" whose labels might be the set of numbers from 1,000 to 4,999. We represent this identifying population as another oval shape which is drawn outside the first with a slightly thinner line:

     The only structure in data that interests us is the "type hierarchy". If, as a general rule, all labels associated with population A are also associated with population B, then we say that population A is a *sub-type* of population B. The collection of all sub-type relationships is called the *type hierarchy*. It should be clear that the type hierarchy will have a lattice structure in general. Thus, we represent the type hierarchy in a natural way by denoting that population "A" is a sub-type of population "B" as shown in Figure 3.9 where the arrows are always drawn from the bottom of the page to the top of the page. In established approaches to data analysis it is not uncommon for the sub-type relationship to be restricted to being between thing-populations only. We will adopt this restriction here.

3.6.2 Modeling information

Information is implicit functional associations between items of data. For example, "spare parts have a cost" could be interpreted as an implicit functional association between the thing-population "spare part" and the thing-population "cost". With the thing-population "spare part" we associate the identifying name-population "spare part number"; the labels in the population "part number" are any number between 1,000 and 4,999. With the thing-population "cost" we associate the identifying name-population "dollars". We use the B-R modeling notation for information, and this example could be represented as shown in Figure 3.10. This notation can be read from left to right as "spare parts have a cost", or from right to left as "the cost of a spare part". Note that there is a double arrow over the "have a" box; this denotes that "spare part determines cost". Note that the

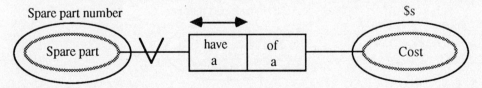

Figure 3.10 B-R diagram

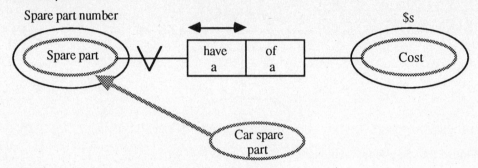

Figure 3.11 B-R diagram with sub-type relationship

reverse is not necessarily true. In other words, the double arrow establishes an information functional dependency *from* spare part *to* cost. Note also that there is a wedge drawn between spare part and the "have a" box; this denotes that *all* spare parts are involved in this functional association; that is, it denotes that *all* spare parts have a cost.

It is usual to show any sub-type relationships between thing-populations on the information diagram. For example, if "car spare part" was a sub-type of "spare part" then this fact could be included on the diagram shown in Figure 3.10 to give the diagram shown in Figure 3.11. Note that the thing-population "car spare part" is not shown with an identifying name-population in Figure 3.11: it is presumed that "car spare part" inherits the identifying name-population of the thing-population "spare part", namely "spare part number". Alternatively, we could introduce the new name-population "car spare part number" in which case the diagram would be as shown in Figure 3.12.

3.6.3   Modeling knowledge

Knowledge is (computable) explicit functional associations between items of information and/or data. Extending the above example, "the selling price for spare parts costing less than $20 is the cost price marked up by 30 percent, and the selling price for spare parts costing $20 or more is the cost price marked up by 25 percent". The information in this

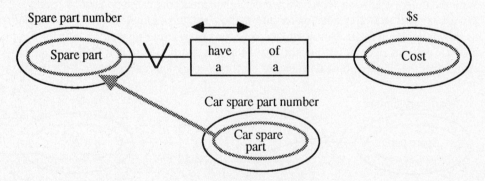

Figure 3.12 Sub-type with identifying name-population

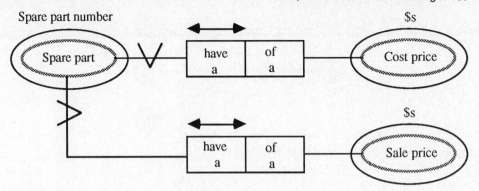

Figure 3.13 Information in the example

example can now be represented as shown in the diagram in Figure 3.13. However, this example also contains some knowledge. The knowledge in this example can be represented using a "dependency diagram". The dependency diagram for this example is shown in Figure 3.14. The dependency diagram notation should be read as "the information in the relation:

 spare-part/sale-price:$

may be deduced from the information in the relation:

 spare-part/cost-price:$

using the group named [A]".

As we will see, as the line shown in Figure 3.14 is not annotated in any way this indicates that *all* such information may be deduced using group [A], and that, when used in conjunction with the find-all mechanism of logic, the group will calculate each matching tuple once and only once. The group associated with the dependency diagram shown in Figure 3.14 is:

$$\text{spare-part/sale-price}(\,x, y\,) \leftarrow \text{spare-part/cost-price}(\,x\,, z\,),$$
$$z < 20\,,\ y = z \times 1.3$$
$$\text{spare-part/sale-price}(\,x, y\,) \leftarrow \text{spare-part/cost-price}(\,x\,, z\,),$$
$$z \geq 20\,,\ y = z \times 1.25 \hspace{3cm} \text{[A]}$$

Spare-part/sale-price   [A]   Spare-part/cost/price

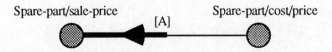

Figure 3.14 Knowledge in the example

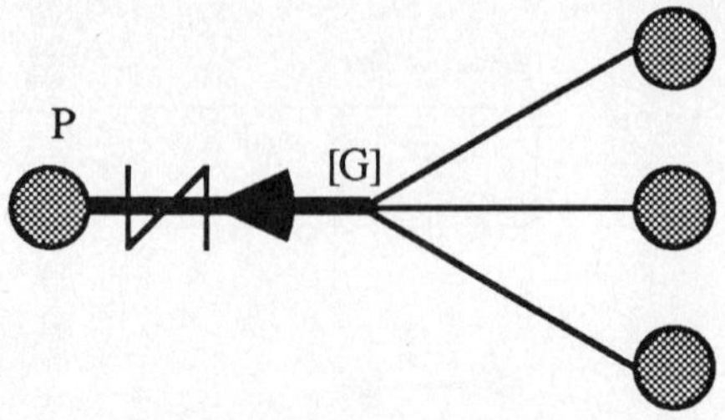

P

[G]

Figure 3.15 Diagram for a non-categorical group

In general, a *dependency diagram* for a group with group name [G] and head predicate P is a directed tree. In this tree there is a node labeled [G]. There is a directed arc from this node labeled [G] to a node labeled P. There is a node for each body predicate; these nodes are labeled with a body predicate name. There is a directed arc from each node labeled with a body predicate to the node labeled [G]. By convention, the nodes of the dependency diagrams are labeled with the names of thing-populations. Thus, dependency diagrams could form the basis of an abstract modeling tool for knowledge but this lies beyond the scope of our discussion here. In other words, our present interest in dependency diagrams is purely as a pragmatic tool for knowledge systems design.

If the group is *not* a categorical group then the arc from the node marked [G] to the node marked P is marked with a "flash" as shown in Figure 3.15.

For example, the group:

spare-part/sale-price(x, y) ← spare-part/cost-price(x , z),
   $z \geq 20$, $y = z \times 1.25$ [A']

is not categorical. Its dependency diagram is shown in Figure 3.16.

If the group is *not* a unique group then the arc from the node marked [G] to the node marked P is marked with a "bar" as shown in Figure 3.17.

For example, the group:

spare-part/sale-price(x, y) ← spare-part/cost-price(x , z),
   $z = 20$, $y = z \times 1.25$
spare-part/sale-price(x, y) ← spare-part/cost-price(x , z),
   $z < 20$, $y = z \times 1.3$
spare-part/sale-price(x, y) ← spare-part/cost-price(x , z),
   $z \geq 20$, $y = z \times 1.25$ [A'']

Spare-part/sale-price   Spare-part/cost-price

[A']

Figure 3.16 Dependency diagram for non-categorical example

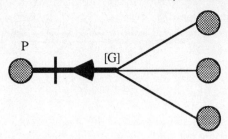

Figure 3.17 Diagram for non-unique group

is not a unique group. Its dependency diagram is as shown in Figure 3.18. Remember that if, in a group, the head predicate P makes an additional recursive appearance in the body of a clause in the group, then P does *not* count as a body predicate in that group.

In Chapter 2 we introduced the special find-all predicate:

tuple/find-all-list

In particular we showed that this predicate could be used to define inverse predicates. For example:

cost-price/item-list(x, y) ← item/cost-price(z, x), tuple/find-all-list((z), y)

The dependency diagram for a group which employs the:

tuple/find-all-list

predicate does *not* show this predicate on the diagram; instead the diagram shows a "wedge" on all arcs to body predicates whose behavior must be compatible with the find-all mechanism. Therefore, in this example the dependency diagram would be as shown in Figure 3.19. Note that the "wedge" is drawn across the line at the "item/cost-price" end; this means that if the "item/cost-price" predicate is to be provided as "input" to this group, then it must be defined in such a way that it is compatible with the find-all mechanism.

In Chapter 2 we also introduced the "is-a" predicate and the "is-the" predicate; these two special predicates are *not* shown on the dependency diagram. In Chapter 3 we introduced the concept of "internal predicates"; internal predicates are *not* shown on the dependency diagram. This raises the theoretical possibility of a dependency diagram with

Spare-part/sale-price   Spare-part/cost-price

[A']

Figure 3.18 Dependency diagram for non-unique example

Cost-price/item-list   Item/cost-price

Figure 3.19 Dependency diagram for inverse predicate

no "body"; although it is difficult to see how this might occur in practice. However, for completeness, a dependency diagram with no body is shown as in Figure 3.20.

Consider the statement "the selling price for spare parts with a part number less than 9,999 is the product of the cost of the spare part and the mark-up-factor, where the mark-up-factor is determined by the type of the spare part". This rule could be represented by the single clause group:

> spare-part/sale-price(x, y) ← spare-part/cost-price(x, z),
> x < 9999,   spare-part/part-type(x, v),
> part-type/mark-up-factor(v, w),   y = (z × w)   [B]

the dependency diagram for this group is shown in Figure 3.21. Note that the arc to the root node:

> spare-part/sale-price:$

has been marked with a flash because we have not been told that *all* the information in:

> spare-part/sale-price:$

can be obtained in this way.

In Chapter 6 we will discuss "modal operators". In simple terms, we will permit predicates to be the subject of expressions of probability, certainty, likelihood and so on. For example, we will admit clauses of the form:

> **with certainty p**[school-leaver/prof(x, y)] ← person/father(x, z),
> **with certainty q**[father/school-leaver/prof(z, x, y)],
> p = 0.5 × q^2

which represents the rule "the degree of certainty with which a school leaver will take up a given profession is half of the square of the degree of certainty that that school leaver's father believes that his child will take up that profession". It is easy to see that this rule

Figure 3.20 Dependency diagram for "body-less" predicate

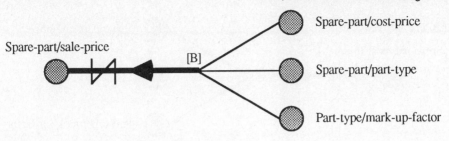

Figure 3.21 Dependency diagram for group [B]

could also be represented as a Horn clause by adding an extra argument to two of the predicates:

school-leaver/prof/certainty(x, y, p) ← person/father(x, z),
father/school-leaver/prof/certainty(z, x, y, q),
$p = 0.5 \times q^2$

Both of these forms are valid representations of the rule. However, if the analyst is using an expert systems shell which provides an in-built mechanism for manipulating degrees of certainty, then we prefer the first of these two forms. In this case, the range of possible degrees of certainty are shown directly on the dependency diagram. This is achieved in the following way: each node is annotated with a pair of ranges of certainty in the format Cert[...]:[...]. This pair is written with one member of the pair "closer" to the centre of the dependency diagram. For each node, the member of the pair which is "closest" to the centre of the dependency diagram represents the range of possible certainty factors in "input" mode, and the member of the pair which is "furthest" from the centre of the dependency diagram represents the range of possible certainty factors in "output" mode as shown in Figure 3.22. This notation may seem clumsy, but the wisdom behind it will become clear when we discuss cluster group diagrams for modal clause groups.

We will now introduce the "cluster". A *cluster* for a collection of predicates consists of a set of groups where each group has one of the predicates from the collection as head

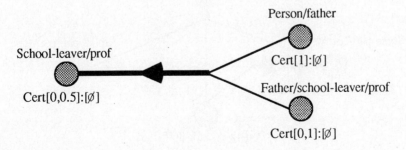

Figure 3.22 Dependency diagram for modal example

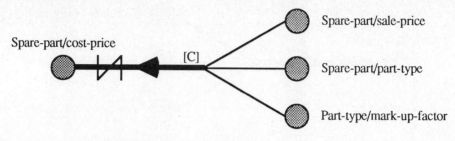

Figure 3.23 Dependency diagram for group [C]

and the body of each group will be a subset of the collection of predicates. For example, consider the set of predicates as in [B] above:

    spare-part/sale-price
    spare-part/cost-price
    spare-part/part-type
    part-type/mark-up-factor

In addition to group [B] it would be no surprise to find that:

    spare-part/cost-price(x, z) ← spare-part/sale-price(x, y),
                spare-part/part-type(x, v),
                part-type/mark-up-factor(v, w),   y = (z × w)   [C]

The dependency diagram for this group is shown in Figure 3.23.

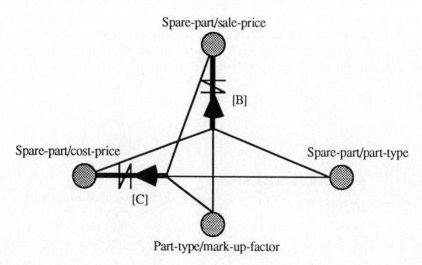

Figure 3.24 Cluster group diagram

Furthermore, we would not expect that the predicate spare-part/part-type could be deduced from the other three predicates unless "mark-up-factor" determined "type" which, we will assume, is not the case. Finally, we assume that the predicate type/mark-up-factor cannot be deduced from the other three. At first glance it might appear that the predicate type/mark-up-factor could be defined by:

$$\text{part-type/mark-up-factor}(\,v, w\,) \leftarrow \text{spare-part/part-type}(\,x, v\,),$$
$$\text{spare-part/cost-price}(\,x, z\,),$$
$$\text{spare-part/sale-price}(\,x, y\,),\quad y = (\,z \times w\,)$$

but this group will only work if there is at least one part number in the system for each type. Hence, we reject it. Thus, the cluster for these four predicates consists of the two groups [B] and [C]; we call this cluster "[D]".

It is often useful to represent the knowledge-dependency structure of an entire cluster; this may be achieved in an obvious way by drawing the "cluster group diagram". The *cluster group diagram* shows all the groups in the cluster on one "dependency" diagram. For the cluster [D] above, the cluster group diagram is shown in Figure 3.24. If, furthermore, it is required to represent the way in which these knowledge-dependencies are established, then this can be achieved by simply quoting the clauses which make up the groups in the cluster.

The cluster group diagram contains an unnecessary amount of information for use in system design. Thus, we introduce the "cluster diagram" for a given cluster. Given a cluster for a collection of predicates, the *cluster diagram* is a directed graph. There is a node for each predicate which is marked with that predicate's name. There is a single "central node" which is marked with the cluster's name. We usually draw the central node

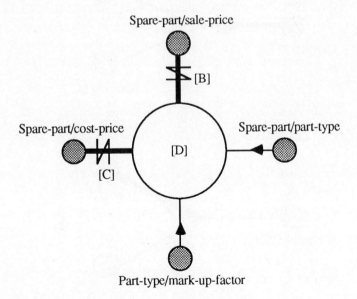

Figure 3.25 Cluster diagram

as a large circle. There is an arc between the central node and each of the nodes which are marked with a predicate's name. In addition, these arcs are marked as follows: If the arc is connected to a predicate which is the head of one of the groups in the cluster, then the arc is marked with the name of that group and with a "flash" or a "bar" if the group is so marked. Otherwise, the arc is marked with an arrow *from* the predicate node *to* the central node. For example, the cluster diagram for the above example is shown in Figure 3.25. The cluster diagram represents an "executive view" of the knowledge-dependencies in the component groups.

To construct the cluster group diagram for groups involving modal operators, we simply take the set theoretic union of the annotations on the component dependency diagrams. For example, if the only two dependency diagrams in a cluster were as shown in Figure 3.26, then the cluster group diagram would be as shown in Figure 3.27.

To construct a cluster diagram for groups involving modal operators, we proceed in exactly the same way as above. For example, the cluster diagram for the modal cluster diagram shown in Figure 3.27 would be as shown in Figure 3.28. As we will see later on, we regard clusters, or cluster diagrams, as knowledge modules which may be "plugged together" to form the kernel of a knowledge system.

We are particularly interested in two properties of clusters; they are "complete" clusters and "consistent" clusters. If a cluster for a collection of predicates consists of categorical groups, such that for each predicate in that collection there is one group with that predicate as its head, then the cluster is called a *complete cluster*. For example, cluster [D] is *not* complete because it does not contain a categorical group with "spare-

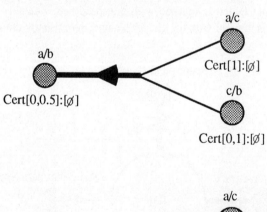

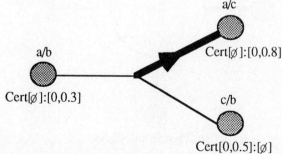

Figure 3.26 Two modal diagrams from the same cluster

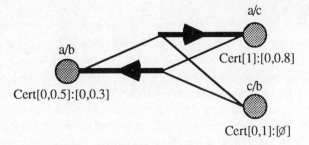

a/c

Cert[1]:[0,0.8]

a/b

Cert[0,0.5]:[0,0.3]

c/b

Cert[0,1]:[∅]

Figure 3.27 Modal cluster group diagram

part/part-type" as head, and it does not contain a categorical group with "part-type/mark-up-factor" as head. The idea behind a *consistent* cluster is that the knowledge in such a cluster should not permit the derivation of a contradiction. The demonstration of consistency is extremely complex in general. Instead, we introduce the notion of "information model consistency". To demonstrate "information model consistency", we associate a set of tuples with each predicate; these tuples are seen as satisfying that predicate at some particular time. All of these tuples, associated with each predicate in the cluster, are called an "information model of the cluster". A cluster is called *information model consistent* if, for each predicate, this associated set is precisely the set which can be deduced from the group in the cluster which has that predicate as head. This notion of consistency is very clumsy but, nevertheless, it can be computed. Its principal weakness is that it depends on the construction of a good information model of the cluster. This notion of consistency demonstrates that the groups in a cluster are consistent with a particular model only of the information in that cluster.

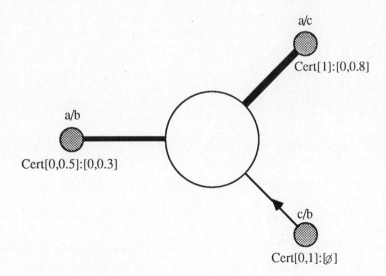

a/c

Cert[1]:[0,0.8]

a/b

Cert[0,0.5]:[0,0.3]

c/b

Cert[0,1]:[∅]

Figure 3.28 Modal cluster diagram

3.7 SUMMARY

We have discussed the notion of "functional association" and have used it to define "data", "information" and "knowledge". We have investigated the object classification problem and have concluded that any effective method for the identification of the data, information and knowledge in an application must refer directly to the analysis method and the way in which it has been used. The goal dependencies in formalisms have been explored; in particular, it has been argued that relations, as a formalism, are compatible with Horn clauses but not with traditional, imperative languages. Furthermore, it has been shown that Horn clauses are a "knowledge goal-dependent formalism". We have placed knowledge systems in perspective with conventional systems, and have contrasted knowledge systems with expert systems. And last, we have introduced the necessary tools for modeling data, information and knowledge.

4 The knowledge systems design problem

4.1 INTRODUCTION

This chapter attempts to make precise the meaning of a "good" knowledge system by specifying a particular architecture on which such a system is presumed to be implemented. This specification is a little tedious in places, particularly in Section 4.3. If the reader is not concerned with the level of detail reported here, then some omissions can be made. In any case, the reader is advised to pay close attention to sections 4.2, 4.4, 4.5.2, 4.5.3, 4.6 and 4.7.

The subject of this text is principally the problem of designing application systems which take full advantage of the architecture of knowledge processing machines. In order to give full meaning to the statement of this problem, we must state precisely what constitutes a "knowledge processing machine architecture" and in this chapter we will discuss such an architecture. We first review key features of a proposal for a knowledge processing architecture. Then we give an outline definition of our knowledge processing machine (*KPM*) architecture; this is achieved by giving an outline specification of the low-level language that such a machine will be designed specifically to represent and process efficiently. Next, we summarize the essential features of the KPM's conceptual architecture. Then we consider the use of the KPM's core languages. The "object representation problem" is considered, and finally the "knowledge systems design problem" is stated.

4.2 FIFTH GENERATION MACHINES

Much has been published on proposed architectures for fifth generation knowledge processing machines. (See, for example, Amamiya et al., 1982.) One key feature of these proposals is that there will be a "knowledge processing" module in which the fundamental computational step will be resolution. Another key feature is that there will be an "information processing" module which will be specifically designed to store and manipulate relations. These two modules, the "knowledge processing" and the "information processing" modules, will be tightly integrated. This integration will be achieved to some extent in the actual fabrication; that is, at the chip level. On the basis of these observations on fifth generation machines, an important, core component of such a machine could be represented as shown in Figure 4.1.

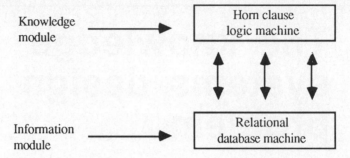

Figure 4.1 Basic fifth generation architecture

The basic problem facing the application systems designer of a knowledge system is, given one of these fifth generation machines, to design application systems which take full advantage of the new architecture of that machine. The problem that we address in this text is that of constructing a systems design methodology which will substantially mechanize the generation of systems, so that these systems will take full advantage of this new architecture. As we have seen in Chapter 3, one important, non-trivial problem that such a methodology must address is to determine whether a real fact in the application should be implemented in the knowledge module or in the information module.

The goal of our design methodology is to at least partially mechanize the generation of application systems which take full advantage of knowledge processing machine architectures. Thus, it is necessary that we state what, for our purposes, constitutes a "knowledge processing machine". To do this, we will shortly give an outline definition of a hypothetical architecture which we refer to as the *KPM* (i.e. **K**nowledge **P**rocessing **M**achine). Note that we are *not* concerned with the complete functional specification of such an architecture; we are not even concerned with the presentation of an abstract, schematic view of the architecture. We are concerned with the (moderately informal) definition of the capabilities of the KPM architecture. This will be achieved by specifying parts of the low-level language that such an architecture will be specifically designed to represent and process. As we will see, the KPM "machine language" comprises three separate component languages. These three component languages will be referred to as the *KPM core languages*, or simply as the *core languages*.

4.3 THE KPM CORE LANGUAGES

We now give an outline description of that part of the KPM machine language which relates directly to the "KPM core" (i.e. that part of the architecture concerned purely with "internal processing"). In other words, we are not interested, for example, in the communications and interface languages. The parts of the KPM machine language which are concerned with "internal processing" consist of three separate languages which are referred to as the *KPM core languages*, or simply as the *core languages*. The three core languages are called the *data language*, the *information language* and the *knowledge language*. In Chapter 3 we considered object classification and concluded that objects do not have a classification as data, information or knowledge which is independent of the use of a particular design technique. Thus, care must be taken not to associate the term "data" directly with that which can be represented in the "data language", likewise for "information" and "knowledge". For the time being, the phrases "data language", "information language" and "knowledge language" should be taken to refer only to the languages which we are about to discuss; in other words, it should not be assumed as yet that these phrases have any necessary connection with "data", "information" and "knowledge".

Our description of the statements in the KPM core languages will be brief, and we will try to avoid substantial reference to concepts which are adequately dealt with elsewhere. Most of the statements that we introduce are predicates which will be employed by logic programs. The remainder of this section contains a rather tedious description of some of the KPM's low level commands. These descriptions are presented here to ensure that the reader thinks of the KPM as a "real" machine. However, the descriptions do not make stimulating reading. The reader is cordially advised to skim through the remainder of this section which outlines the three KPM component languages. The main points to be gleaned from the remainder of this section are summarized in the following Section "4.4 The KPM conceptual architecture".

4.3.1   The data language

The data language supports a type hierarchy. (See Date, 1986 for a discussion on "types".) For example, suppose that in an application we choose to represent the concept of "employee", "manager", "worker" and "secretary". Suppose also that all managers, workers and secretaries are employees, and that all secretaries are workers. Then we say that secretary is a sub-type of worker, and, in turn, worker and manager are a sub-type of employee. We might show this type hierarchy on a diagram in an obvious way as shown in Figure 4.2.

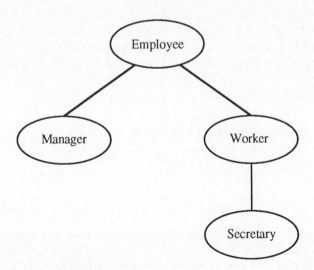

Figure 4.2 Example of a type hierarchy

Herein, types are identified by a unique *type name* which is any unique, non-numeric text string in which spaces have been replaced by -'s. Types are created by:

    CREATE-TYPE(<name>)

where <name> is the type name. The predicate CREATE-TYPE is set to TRUE if this operation is successful. Types may be related by the "sub-type" relation, using the statement:

    CREATE-SUB-TYPE(<name1> , <name2>)

where <name1> is the name of the type which is to be a sub-type of the type whose name is <name2>. The predicate CREATE-SUB-TYPE is set to TRUE if this operation is successful. A type which has been created may be removed by the statement:

    DESTROY-TYPE(<name>)

where <name> is the name of the type to be destroyed. The predicate DESTROY-TYPE is set to TRUE if this operation is successful. In particular, the DESTROY-TYPE operation will not be successful if there are any sub-type relationships associated with that type. Likewise, a sub-type relationship which has been created may be destroyed by:

    DESTROY-SUB-TYPE(<name1> , <name2>)

where <name1> is the name of the type which is a sub-type of the type whose name is <name2>, and this sub-type relationship is to be destroyed. The predicate DESTROY-SUB-TYPE is set to TRUE if this operation is successful.

The data language contains instructions for "labels". A *label* will represent any individual object which the analyst has decided is not to be decomposed into smaller objects. A *label* may be any unique text string. By convention, for a label, we separate the words in the text string with -'s. If such a text string represents a quantity in some units then an indication of these units *may* be added to the string using the form:

    <text string>:<units>

Thus, the following could be examples of labels:

    123,-Sydney-Street,-Melbourne,-VIC-3456
    24:$
    36:%

The data language contains instructions for "populations". A *population* may be identified with a set of labels which are said to "belong to" or to "be identified with" that population. If a label is one of a group of labels in a population, then it must satisfy the "constraints" of that population. A population is identified by a "population name". A *population name* may be any unique, non-numeric text string. We create a population name by the statement:

> CREATE-POP(<name>)

where <name> is the population name. The predicate CREATE-POP is set to TRUE if this operation is successful. When a population has been created, types may be assigned to it by the statement:

> ADD-TYPE-POP(<pop-name> , <type-list>)

where <pop-name> is the population name, and <type-list> is a list of types to be attached to that population. The predicate ADD-TYPE-POP is set to TRUE if this operation is successful. Once types have been assigned to populations, they may be un-assigned by the statement:

> REMOVE-TYPE-POP(<pop-name> , <type-list>)

where <pop-name> is the population name, and <type-list> is a list of the types to be removed from that population. The predicate REMOVE-TYPE-POP is set to TRUE if this operation is successful. Labels which are grouped in a population inherit the types of that population. If a function is from some domain to a population as range, then the function inherits the type of the population in its range. For example, consider the function:

$$ f : A \times B \rightarrow P $$

where P is a population with type T; the function f is also said to have type T.

If the labels which belong to a population are all quantities in the same units, then the units may be added to the population name separated by a ":" as for labels above.

The following could be examples of population names:

> home-address
> job-description
> item-cost:$
> student-mark:%

A population name may be deleted by the statement:

> DESTROY-POP(<name>)

where <name> is the population name. The predicate DESTROY-POP is set to TRUE if this operation is successful. In particular, the DESTROY-POP operation will not be successful if there are any labels in the system which belong to that population. In other words, to delete a population name we must first ensure that all labels in that population have been deleted.

To identify a label with a population, we use the statement:

STORE-LABEL(<population>(<label>))

where <label> is the label and <population> is the population name. The predicate STORE-LABEL is set to TRUE if this operation is successful.

To see if a label is already identified with a population, we use the statement:

RETRIEVE-LABEL(<population>(<label>))

where <label> is the label and <population> is the population name. The predicate RETRIEVE-LABEL is set to TRUE if the label <label> is already stored in the population named <population>. In addition, we may wish to retrieve one (or all) of the labels grouped in a given population. This may be achieved in logic programming by a single (or repeated) reference to:

RETRIEVE-LABEL(<population>(<variable>))

where <variable> is a logical variable name and <population> is the given population name. The predicate RETRIEVE-LABEL is set to TRUE if this operation is successful. In particular, when there are no more labels to be retrieved, the predicate will be set to FALSE.

If we wish to change a label which has been identified with a population we use the statement:

REPLACE-LABEL(<population>(<label1>) , (<label2>))

where <population> is the name of the population with which the original label, <label1>, has been identified, and <label2> is the new label which is to replace <label1>. The predicate REPLACE-LABEL is set to TRUE if this operation is successful.

If we wish to delete a label which has been identified with a population we use the statement:

DELETE-LABEL(<population>(<label>))

where <population> is the name of the population, and <label> is the name of the label which is to be deleted from that population. The predicate DELETE-LABEL is set to TRUE if this operation is successful.

A wide variety of constraints may be specified for labels and populations. The constraint language within the data language consists of Horn clauses augmented, if necessary, by special predicates. If a population has units attached to it, then all labels grouped together in that population must have the same units attached to them. If a label occurs in two populations, then those two populations must have "compatible types". By *compatible types* we mean that at least one type attached to one of the populations either is equal to or is a subset of at least one type attached to the other population. If a population consists of labels which represent numerical values, then constraints on allowed values of those labels may be specified, such as upper and lower bounds for the labels. If a population consists of labels which represent text strings, then constraints on the syntax and possibly semantics of the strings may be specified. Constraints may be specified to restrict the form and number of labels that can be grouped in a population and an important special case is when the population is restricted to containing one label only. In addition, constraints may be specified which restrict the way in which a label may be changed by the REPLACE-LABEL statement. It is not necessary for our purposes here to give a detailed specification of the constraint definition and maintenance languages.

4.3.2   The information language

A *constant tuple* is any tuple which contains no variables. Thus, a constant tuple inherits a list of types from its constituent labels and constant terms. (Recall that functions inherit their type from their range. Terms have the same type as the main function in that term.) Constant tuples which have the same list of types may be grouped together to form a *relation*. A constant tuple is identified by the list of labels in that constant tuple. The information language contains instructions for tuples and relations. An important part of the definition of a relation is the specification of the component populations of the tuples which make up that relation. These populations are usually called the *domains* of the relation. By convention, we identify each domain by the appropriate name-population. Relation names consist of a list of population names separated by /s; this list consists of the thing-populations which correspond to the name-populations associated with each domain. For example, the following could be used to identify relations:

> item/cost(<u>item-number</u>, item-cost:$)
> employee/address(<u>employee-name</u>, employee-address)

It is important to appreciate that a specification of the component populations (or "domains") of a relation may not convey all that there is to know about the meaning of that relation. For example, there may be a number of ways in which the populations "item" and "cost" may be related. Thus, this notation for identifying relations may not be adequate; if this is so, then the list of domains separated by /s will have to be augmented in some way to ensure that each relation name is unique and meaningful. For example, in an application it might have been noted that all employees understudy the work of another employee. Let us assume that the analyst has only identified the population "employee", then the "understudy" relation will have the form:

> employee/employee

which is clearly not a very meaningful description of the relation "to understudy".
   A relation (or "stored predicate") may be created by the statement:

> CREATE-REL(<name> , <domain-list>)

where <name> is the name of the relation, and <domain-list> is an ordered list of the populations in that relation. The predicate CREATE-REL is set to TRUE if this operation is successful.

A relation may be deleted by the statement:

DESTROY-REL (<name>)

where <name> is the name of the relation. The predicate DESTROY-REL is set to TRUE if this operation is successful. For example, this operation will *not* be successful if there are any tuples in the relation. That is, only an empty relation can be destroyed by this command.

To identify a constant tuple with a relation, we use the statement:

STORE-TUPLE(<relation>(<value1>,...,<valueN>))

where <relation> is the name of the N-adic relation in which the N-tuple is to be stored, and <value1>,...,<valueN> are the N labels which constitute the N-tuple. The predicate STORE-TUPLE is set to TRUE if this operation is successful.

To retrieve a constant tuple from a relation, we use the statement:

RETRIEVE-TUPLE(<relation>(<exp1>,...,<expN>))

where <relation> is the name of an N-adic relation from which the N-tuple is to be retrieved, and each of the <exp1>,...,<expN> are either un-instantiated logical variables, instantiated logical variables, general terms or labels. The predicate RETRIEVE-TUPLE is set to TRUE if this operation is successful. If this operation is successful, then the N-tuple <exp1>,...,<expN> will be fully instantiated and will equal a constant tuple stored in the relation whose name is <relation>. If repeated reference is made to a RETRIEVE-TUPLE statement in logic programming by the backtracking mechanism or by parallel processing, then the N-tuple <exp1>,...,<expN> will be set to the "next" matching constant tuple on each successful execution of the RETRIEVE-TUPLE statement. When there are no further matching tuples in the relation, the predicate RETRIEVE-TUPLE will be set to FALSE. When a constant tuple has been retrieved through the execution of a logic program which references the RETRIEVE-TUPLE statement, it is usually necessary to "lock" the retrieved constant tuple until the goal is satisfied or that RETRIEVE-TUPLE statement fails. A *locked tuple* cannot be altered until it is unlocked.

To replace a constant tuple in a relation with another constant tuple, we use the statement:

REPLACE-TUPLE(<relation>(<old-tuple>), (<new-tuple>))

where <relation> is the name of the relation, <old-tuple> is the name of the constant tuple in that relation which is to be replaced by the constant tuple <new-tuple>. The predicate REPLACE-TUPLE is set to TRUE if this operation is successful.

To remove a constant tuple from a relation we use the statement:

DELETE-TUPLE(<relation>(<value1>,...,<valueN>))

where <relation> is the name of the N-adic relation in which the N-tuple <value1>,...,<valueN> is stored. The predicate DELETE-TUPLE is set to TRUE if this operation is successful. The predicates STORE-TUPLE, RETRIEVE-TUPLE, REPLACE-TUPLE and DELETE TUPLE are not first-order (see Bowen and Kowalski, 1982 for a discussion of non-first-order operators).

A "key" may be defined for a relation. A *key* is an ordered subset of the set of domains in that relation such that the set of labels in that subset in any given constant tuple in that relation is unique for that constant tuple in that relation. The value of a key is thus determined by the values of the domain or domains which make up the key. For example, "first-name" and "surname" may be the two domains which make up the key in a relation. In which case:

first-name/surname

is called a *compound domain*, or *compound population*; a value of the two domains in this compound domain is called a *compound label*. In this example:

John/Smith
Mary/Jones

might be two compound labels.

Keys are used to define key constraints and, in addition, they may be employed to guide the physical storage and retrieval mechanism. A key is defined by the statement:

CREATE-KEY(<relation> , <domain-list>)

where <relation> is the name of the relation, and <domain-list> is the ordered list of domain names which are in that relation; in this list those domains which are to be included in the key of that relation are underlined. The predicate CREATE-KEY is set to TRUE if this operation is successful. A key may be modified by the statement:

REPLACE-KEY(<relation> , <domain-list1> , <domain-list2>)

where <relation> is the name of the relation, and <domain-list1> and <domain-list2> are lists of the domains in that relation; in <domain-list1> the domain names of the old key are underlined, and in <domain-list2> the domain names of the new key are underlined. The predicate REPLACE-KEY is set to TRUE if this operation is successful. A key may be deleted by the statement:

DELETE-KEY(<relation> , <domain-list>)

where <relation> is the name of the relation, and <domain-list> is the list of domain names of that relation in which the key domains are underlined; this key is to be deleted as the key of that relation. The predicate DELETE-KEY is set to TRUE if this operation is successful.

In addition to the implementation of the instructions described above, the KPM will implement commands for *processing* tuples and relations, (*see*, for example, Date, 1986). The extent to which these high level commands for information processing are actually implemented does not concern us. All that matters, as far as we are concerned, is that tuples and relations can be processed efficiently and that we can estimate the time that such processing will take.

A wide variety of constraints may be specified for tuples and relations. The constraint language within the information language consists of Horn clauses augmented, if necessary, by special predicates. First, all labels occurring in constant tuples are required to satisfy the constraints of the populations which make up the domains of that relation to which the constant tuple belongs. Thus, constraints for tuples and relations inherit the full power of constraints for labels and populations. All constant tuples are required to satisfy *key constraints* which require that the specified key in a relation is unique. We may also specify "transitive constraints". A *transitive constraint* requires that a fixed subset of the domains of each constant tuple in one relation is also present in (or, more generally, bears some specified relationship to) another fixed subset of the domains of at least one constant tuple in another relation. A simple example of a transitive constraint is that "all spare part numbers occurring in the spare-part/buy relation must also occur in the spare-part/supplier relation". We also specify general constraints on the form of the constant tuples in a relation and the ways in which those constant tuples can change.

4.3.3   The knowledge language

A clause is identified by a "clause name". A *clause name* may be any unique, non-numeric text string. A *(clause) group* consists of a set of clauses all of which have the same head predicate. For example, using the predicates:

item/sell(<u>item-number</u>, sell-price:$)
item/buy(<u>item-number</u>, buy-price:$)

the following collection of clauses constitutes a group:

item/sell:$(x, y) ← item/buy:$(x, z), z < 10:$, y = z × 1.5
item/sell:$(x, y) ← item/buy:$(x, z), z ≥ 10:$, y = z × 1.4

This group can be represented as:

item/sell ⇐ item/buy

On occasions, a group of Horn clauses with a single head predicate is not sufficiently powerful by itself to define the head predicate in terms of the body predicates. On such occasions it is often possible to increase the expressive power of a group by introducing "internal predicates". An *internal predicate* is a subsidiary head predicate in a group which is of purely computational significance; an internal predicate is not recognized as a head predicate or as a body predicate of that group. Suppose the predicate sell/item-list(x, y) means that "y is a list of all item numbers which sell for price $x", and that the predicate sell-list/item-list(x, y) means that "x is a list of selling prices and y is a corresponding list of all item numbers each of which sells for one of these prices". Then consider the group:

> sell-list/item-list($\emptyset$, $\emptyset$) ←
> sell-list/item-list(x.v, w) ← sell-list/item-list(v, u),
>   sell/item-list(x, z), append(u, z, w)
> append($\emptyset$, x, x) ←
> append(x.y, z, x.w) ← append(y, z, w)

In this group, the predicate "append" only has computational significance, and is thus an internal predicate. In fact, "append" simply joins two lists together; append(x, y, z) means "list z is the concatenation of lists x and y". In other words, the above set of clauses is a group with head predicate:

> sell-list/item-list

and body predicate:

> sell/item-list

This group can be represented as:

> sell-list/item-list ⇐ sell/item-list

A group is identified by a "group name". A *group name* may be any unique, non-numeric text string. A group may be created by the statement:

> CREATE-GROUP(<group> , <head>)

where <group> is the name of the group, and <head> is the name of the unique predicate which is to be the head predicate of the constituent clauses in the group. The predicate CREATE-GROUP is set to TRUE if this operation is successful.

A group may be deleted by the statement:

> DESTROY-GROUP(<group>)

where <group> is the name of the (clause) group which is to be destroyed. The predicate DESTROY-GROUP is set to TRUE if this operation is successful. For example, this operation will not be successful if there are any clauses in the group; in other words, only an empty group may be deleted.

To identify a clause with a (clause) group we use the statement:

> STORE-CLAUSE(<group> , <clause>)

where <group> is the name of the (clause) group with which the clause named <clause> is to be identified. Note that the head predicate of the clause named <clause> must be the same as the head predicate of the group named <group>. The predicate STORE-CLAUSE is set to TRUE if this operation is successful.

To replace a clause in a group with another clause we use the statement:

REPLACE-CLAUSE(<group> , <old-clause> , <new-clause>)

where <group> is the name of the (clause) group, and <old-clause> is the name of the clause which is to be replaced by the clause whose name is <new-clause>. The predicate REPLACE-CLAUSE is set to TRUE if this operation is successful.

To remove a clause from a (clause) group we use the statement:

DELETE-CLAUSE(<group> , <clause>)

where <group> is the name of the (clause) group from which the clause named <clause> is to be removed. The predicate DELETE-CLAUSE is set to TRUE if this operation is successful.

In addition to the implementation of the instructions described above, the KPM will implement commands for *processing* clauses and groups. In particular the KPM will either implement directly a RESOLVE command, which constructs the resolvant of two clauses, or, perhaps, some high level command to evaluate the Ans predicate, and, perhaps, some commands which lie between these two extremes. The extent to which these high level commands for knowledge processing are actually implemented does not concern us. All that matters as far as we are concerned is that clauses and groups can be processed efficiently, in particular the evaluation of the Ans predicate can be processed efficiently, it is also important that we can estimate the time that such processing will take.

A wide variety of constraints may be specified for clauses and groups. The constraint language within the knowledge language consists of Horn clauses augmented, if necessary, by special predicates. First, all predicates occurring in clauses are required to satisfy any constraints which apply to those predicates. Thus, constraints for clauses and groups inherit the full power of constraints for tuples and relations. In addition, there is a wide variety of constraints which restrict both the form of clauses and (clause) groups as well as constraints which restrict the way in which clauses and (clause) groups may be changed.

4.4   THE KPM CONCEPTUAL ARCHITECTURE

We now summarize the principal architectural features of the KPM which are concerned with "internal processing" as they have been identified by our description of the portions of the three core languages. The architecture contains three "conceptual" components which are specifically designed for processing "data", "information" and "knowledge" respectively. A *conceptual component* of the KPM architecture refers to the machine architecture necessary to support a set of related operations; in other words, conceptual components are functional divisions of the architecture and not physical divisions. We have defined "data", "information" and "knowledge" in Chapter 3.   Data is the fundamental, indivisible objects in an application, and can, in fact, be represented naturally in the data language. Information is the implicit functional associations between data in an application, and can, in fact, be represented naturally in the information language. Knowledge is the explicit functional associations between information and/or data in an application, and can, in fact, be represented naturally in the knowledge language. As we have seen, we must be careful not to identify "data", "information" and "knowledge" with the three components of the KPM. The "data processing component" is specifically designed to process labels and populations, as well as constraints on those labels and populations. The "information processing component" is specifically designed to process tuples and relations, as well as constraints on those tuples and relations. The "knowledge processing component" is specifically designed to process clauses and groups, as well as constraints on those clauses and groups. In addition, the architecture will contain conceptual components for performing routine arithmetic and other operations, and components for input and output operations; these conceptual components are vital to the performance and function of the architecture but do not interest us in the present context of our discussion.

An essential feature of the data, information and knowledge conceptual components is that they are all tightly integrated. The information conceptual component will be tightly integrated with the data conceptual component so that the "data" occurring in the "information" may be processed efficiently. Likewise, the knowledge conceptual component will be tightly integrated with both the information and the data conceptual components so that the "data" and "information" occurring in the "knowledge" may be processed efficiently. For similar reasons, as some constraints for tuples and relations may refer to the labels and populations in those tuples and relations, the information constraints component will be tightly coupled with the data constraints component. Likewise, the knowledge constraints component will be tightly coupled with both the

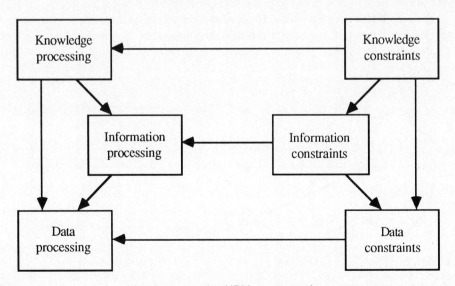

Figure 4.3 Interrelationships between the KPM conceptual components

information constraints component and the data constraints component. Thus, the inter-relationships between the conceptual components of the KPM architecture which interest us herein may be represented as shown in Figure 4.3. These six conceptual components, namely the knowledge, information and data, processing and constraints, components, are collectively referred to as the *KPM core*, or simply as the *core*.

Thus, the problem facing the application systems designer is, given an architecture similar to that of the KPM, in which the performance of the individual components can be quantified, to design application systems which take full advantage of such an architecture. Ignoring constraints for the time being, an important sub-problem is to decide whether objects in the application should be classified as "data", "information" or "knowledge". The classification problem is represented in Figure 4.4.

As we have seen in Chapter 3, the classification problem is non-trivial. As Figure 4.4 implies, we regard the business of constructing a physical object in the KPM which corresponds to an object in the application as a process which contains two important steps. The first important step is *object classification,* or simply *classification*, in which the object is classified as a candidate for representation in either the data, the information or the knowledge language. The second important step is *object representation*, or simply *representation*, in which the object is represented in that language.

4.5   USE OF THE KPM

The general problem that we have at hand is how to use the three core languages effectively. In other words, the problem is that of mapping a given application into a "good" implementation expressed in these three languages. We now take a brief digression and consider this problem in reverse; that is, we investigate the sorts of objects "in the real world" that the constructs of the core languages correspond with naturally. In other words, we will now investigate the "use" of the KPM.

In our discussion we will refer to any "thing" in an application that may be represented as a part of a computerized model of that application as an *object*. We now

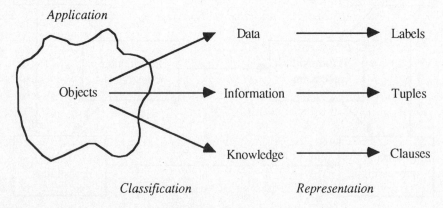

Figure 4.4 The classification problem

consider the different sorts of objects that can be naturally represented and manipulated in the three component languages. The component languages are the data language, the information language and the knowledge language.

4.5.1 Use of the data language

Labels can be used to represent the fundamental, indivisible, real objects in our application. A typical example of such an object is "a part number"; the label for that part number might be #2468. Thus, a label identifies an object in the application which is indivisible in the sense that, in that application, we are just not interested in dissecting it into components. For example, "123-Sydney-Street,-Melbourne,-VIC-3456" might be a label for an "address" object. In this example application, we assume that we are just not interested in dissecting the concept of "address" into components "street", "town", "state", "post-code" and so on. In which case an "address" is a fundamental, indivisible object. We may represent such an item in our KPM directly, and can achieve this with a *label*. As a fundamental design decision, labels have been adopted as the low-level representation language in our KPM for items which have been classified as "data". Thus, the data language, which is based on labels, provides the facility to represent and manipulate representations of "fundamental, indivisible objects".

By extension, we also require our architecture to be able to cope sensibly with a collection of labels of the same "type". For example, we might have a collection of "address" labels. Such a collection has been referred to as a *population*. Populations are identified by a *population name*. In this example, the population might be identified as the "address" population. Thus, the data language, which includes populations, provides the facility to represent and manipulate representations of "collections of fundamental, indivisible, real objects".

In practice, we might require that a variety of constraints be specified for labels and populations. We might require that every label in a population should have a specific property; for example, the labels in our "address" population might be required to contain no more than sixty characters each. We might require that the population itself should have a specific property; for example, our "address" population might be required to contain less than one thousand labels. As we will see in due course, the handling of constraints makes the business of the storage and manipulation of labels and populations strictly non-trivial.

To summarize, a component of the KPM has been specifically designed to store and manipulate individual labels, and to store and manipulate collections of these labels (i.e. "populations"). In addition, our architecture is capable of representing and applying efficiently a variety of constraints on labels and on populations. The conceptual portion of the KPM architecture which provides all of these functions is called the *data base component*. We make no apology for giving "data base" yet another meaning as the term already has a very broad usage. However, to avoid confusion we adopt the convention that our notion is spelt as two words, that is, *data base*, and that the notion in common usage is spelt as one word (i.e. *database*).

4.5.2 Use of the information language

Following our example above,

employee   home-address
(#1234   ,   123-Sydney-Street,-Melbourne,-VIC-3456   )

could be used to represent that the home address of employee number 1234 is "123 Sydney Street, Melbourne, VIC 3456". Two or more labels coupled in this way, to represent some association between two or more fundamental, indivisible real objects, are referred to as a *constant tuple* . As a fundamental design decision, tuples have been adopted as the low-level representation language for such associations between objects in our KPM. Thus, our information language, which is based on tuples, provides the facility to represent and manipulate representations of "associations between two or more fundamental, indivisible objects".

By extension, we also require our architecture to be able to cope sensibly with a collection of constant tuples each of which represents the similar functional associations between different individual items. For example, we might have a collection of constant tuples representing the home address for each member of an organization. Such a collection has been referred to as a *relation*. Relations are identified by a *relation name*. Our example relation is identified by the name "employee/home-address" as is:

employee/home-address(employee-number , address-description)

The "columns" in a relation are called *domains*. Our above example has two domains, namely "employee-number" and "address-description". Thus, our information language, which includes relations, provides the facility to represent and manipulate representations of "collections of associations between two or more fundamental, indivisible objects".

In practice, we might require that a variety of constraints be specified for tuples and relations. We might require that each label in some domain have a specified property. We might require that each combination of labels occurs at most once in some subset of the domains; in which case, that subset of domains might be identified as the *key*.

To summarize, a component of our KPM architecture has been specifically designed to store and manipulate individual constant tuples, and to store and manipulate collections of constant tuples (i.e. "relations"). In addition, our architecture is capable of representing and applying effectively a variety of constraints on tuples, domains and relations. The conceptual portion of the architecture which provides all of these functions is called the *information base component.*

The information content in expertise is often in vague, summary form. We now address the problem of interfacing the "precise" information in the relations in the information base with the often "soft" information of an expert. For example, in the piece of expertise "Companies with a comparatively high net asset backing are ripe for takeover" the phrases "comparatively high" and "ripe for" are vague and undefined. Nevertheless, this is often the form in which valuable expertise is presented to the knowledge analyst. Let us now investigate how such vague expertise may be related to precise information.

Suppose in a banking application we have the relations:

> customer/income(<u>customer-number</u> , $s-per-annum)
> customer/mean-cash-on-hand(<u>customer-number</u> , $s)

in which the annual income and mean current account balance over twelve months, respectively, are represented. We associate the new "condensed population" "income-bracket" (with labels "high", "medium" and "low") with income, and the new "condensed population" "cash-on-hand-bracket" (with labels "high", "medium" and "low") with mean-cash-on-hand. A domain which is, in effect, an abbreviated summary of another domain is called a *condensed population*. Then we construct two "condensed relations":

> customer/income-bracket(<u>customer-number</u> , bracket)
> customer/cash-on-hand-bracket(<u>customer-number</u> , bracket)

A *condensed relation* is a relation at least one of whose domains is a condensed population. We are now in a position to represent "Middle income earners are likely to have high amounts of cash on hand" in logical form:

> **if** customer/income-bracket(x , 'middle')
> **then** **is-likely**[customer/cash-on-hand-bracket(x , 'high')]

where "is-likely" is a second-order operator which, presumably, would be defined in terms of some implementation of plausible inference. This statement could also be represented in the condensed relation:

> income-bracket/likely-cash-on-hand-bracket(bracket , bracket)

which might contain, for example, the tuples:

> ('high' , 'low')
> ('middle' , 'high')
> ('low' , 'middle')

Condensed relations may either be deduced from, or induced from, existing information. In other words, they may either be summaries of or generalizations of existing information. Condensed populations and condensed relations often provide the link between the (usually) imprecise language of expertise, and the (usually) precise language of the information base.

Thus, we have seen how the information language may be used to represent ordinary "hard" associations between populations. In addition, by using condensed domains and relations, the information language may be used to represent "soft", or "expert", associations between populations. Note that our classification 'low', 'middle' and 'high' may appear to be soft but is in fact "hard"; in contrast, the "is-likely" operator is genuinely "soft".

4.5.3 Use of the knowledge language

Extending our example above, the Horn clause:

> employee/weekly-travel-loading(x , y:$s) ←
>   employee/works-in(x , 'factory'),
>   employee/home-address(x , z),
>   address/location/distance(z , 'factory' , w:kms),
>   y = w × 2.4   [A]

could be used to represent that "the weekly travel loading in dollars allocated to employees who work in the factory is 2.4 times the distance in kilometres from their home address to the factory". We note that clauses are representations of associations between relations and (in general) populations. As a fundamental design decision, we have adopted Horn clause logic as the low-level representation language for those items which have been classified as "knowledge" in our KPM. Thus, the knowledge language, which is based on clauses, provides the facility to represent and manipulate representations of "associations between relations and populations".

The clause [A] in the above example, tells us about the weekly travel loading for those employees who work in the factory. We may require additional clauses to specify the weekly travel loading for other employees who do not work in the factory. Thus, we require that our architecture be able to cope sensibly with a collection of clauses, each of which contains the same predicate as its head; in this example the head is "employee/weekly-travel-loading". Such a collection is referred to as a *clause group*, or simply as a *group*. The unique predicate at the head of each clause in a clause group is called the *head predicate* of that group. The body predicates of all the clauses in a clause group are collectively called the *body predicates* of that group. Thus, the knowledge language, which includes groups, provides the facility to represent and manipulate representations of "collections of associations between relations and populations".

Two properties of groups are of particular interest to us; we will describe some groups as "categorical" and some as "unique". A group is called a *categorical group* if it contains sufficient clauses to enable *all* the information in the head predicate to be deduced from the body predicates. For example, the group just consisting of clause [A] (see above) might not be categorical, but if the additional clause:

> employee/weekly-travel-loading(x , y:$s) ←
>   employee/works-in(x , 'office'),
>   employee/home-address(x , z),
>   address/location/distance(z , 'office' , w:kms),
>   y = w × 1.3

were added, then the resulting group might be categorical. A group is called a *unique group* if, when used in conjunction with the find-all mechanism of logic, it calculates each matching tuple once and only once. For example, a group in which a clause is repeated twice is likely to be not unique. In practice, non-unique groups are often signs of bad (logic) programming, and should be identified as non-unique; they should be recoded, if possible, to form unique groups.

In practice, we might require that a variety of constraints be specified for clauses and groups. We might require that each variable have a specified property; for example, we might specify that the weekly travel loading must always be a positive quantity. We might require that no matter how the weekly travel loading is to be calculated, the "2.4" factor may *only* be applied to those who work in the factory.

To summarize, a component of our KPM architecture has been specifically designed to store and manipulate individual clauses, and to store and manipulate collections of clauses (i.e. "groups"). In addition, our architecture is capable of representing and applying efficiently a variety of constraints on the groups as well as on the clauses in the groups and on the relations, tuples, populations and labels within the clauses. The conceptual portion of the architecture which provides all of these functions is called the *knowledge base component*.

We now discuss the relationship between the structure of the information base and an expert's expertise. In the banking example considered at the end of the previous section, if a particular customer "#1234" is in the information base as:

customer/income('1234' , '24,000:$')

where $24,000 is classified as "middle income bracket", then we may conclude that "Customer number 1234 is likely to have high amounts of cash on hand". In particular, note that from hard, precise information we have been able to deduce soft, probabilistic information. The information structure of this example is important. This condensed relation links condensed populations from the non-key fields of two relations with shared key domain. Using the notation of Binary Relationship modeling (*see* Verheijen and Van Bekkum, 1982) which has been discussed briefly in Chapter 3, this may be represented by the diagram shown in Figure 4.5. The important fact to note in this diagram is that the expertise links the condensed version of two domains which are not themselves linked

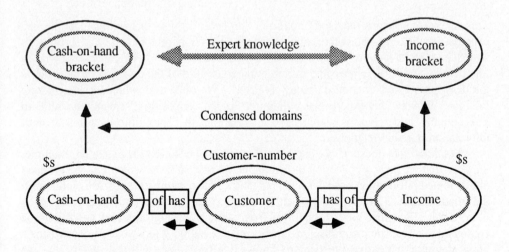

Figure 4.5 B-R diagram showing the role of expert knowledge

directly by an association which is expressible in relations. A role for expertise within the context of an existing information base is to provide links of this form, and, more important, links between domains which have a less intimate association than in the above example. Thus, in general, we expect expertise to enrich the existing "association structure" of the information base in a way that strictly lies beyond the expressive power of the hard information represented in relations. We illustrate this shortly. Note that the expertise represented in a knowledge system will perform other roles as well, for example, to resolve conflicting evidence.

We now extend the example discussed above, and introduce the three relations:

customer/job-type(<u>customer-number</u> , description);
married-customer/spouse(<u>customer-number</u> , customer-number);
customer/risk(<u>customer-number</u> , bracket);

where "married-customer" and "spouse" are sub-types of "customer", the first relation links customer to a job description, the second links customers whose spouses are also bank customers to their spouse's customer number, and the third links customers to the population "credit risk bracket" (this population has labels "high", "medium" or "low"). The expertise "Customers who have professional jobs, and have a spouse in a professional job in the middle income bracket, are probably low credit risks" may be expressed in logic in terms of these relations:

> **if**   customer/job-type(x , 'professional') **and**
> customer/spouse(x , y) **and**
> customer/job-type(y , 'professional') **and**
> customer/income-bracket(y , 'middle')
> **then probably**[customer/risk(x , 'low')]

This statement contains the "soft" notion of "probably". Note that in this example, the expertise has linked together five references to four different relations. The expertise thus straddles a wide breadth of information in the sense that, for example, there is no functional association expressible as a relation consisting of the domains "a customer's job description" and "a spouse's salary bracket". We refer to this breadth as *semantic breadth*. We view this expertise as building a "bridge" across this "semantic breadth" to link domains and relations which have no relationship expressible in terms of hard information stored in relations.

We now take these ideas one step further, and describe an extended example. Suppose that we have a collection of information bases, some of which may be grouped in distributed information base clusters, and that we have identified expertise within each information base. Further, suppose that we then acquire items of "meta-expertise", each item to the effect that bits of expertise from some of the information bases may be combined to effect some complex chain of expert reasoning. Then we have constructed a large, complex but orderly distributed knowledge base. We will see shortly that the components in such a knowledge base are clearly identifiable as "data", "information", "knowledge" and "meta-knowledge" (i.e. associations between items of knowledge). The foundation for this distributed knowledge base is a collection of existing information bases.

It is our view that the databases which are central to the present information processing needs of an organization will also play a central role in supporting the development of knowledge processing. In other words, we do not believe that the arrival of knowledge processing is going to shift the "centre of gravity" of computing significantly within a typical, large organization. If the existing, mainstream databases are to provide the foundation for knowledge processing development then there is a clear requirement to first organize the expertise already represented within them. When that expertise has been identified, normalized, labeled, constrained, and represented declaratively and explicitly, then an appropriate environment will have been created in which knowledge systems will grow naturally.

Thus, we have seen how the knowledge language may be used to represent ordinary "hard" associations between relations and, in general, populations. In addition, by using condensed domains and relations, and by introducing second-order, probabilistic predicates to represent plausible inference, the knowledge language may be used to represent "soft", or "expert", associations between relations and populations.

4.6 THE OBJECT REPRESENTATION PROBLEM

We have discussed the problem of object classification in the previous chapter. Once an object has been classified, the next step is to represent that object. The conceptual architecture of the KPM has been introduced in Section 4.4. The *core* of the KPM is represented on the diagram in Figure 4.6. Note that this diagram presents the KPM conceptual architecture as hierarchic with three distinct tiers. In Section 4.3 we introduced languages for each of these three tiers. Thus, the analyst will be presented with three distinct, low-level machine languages (i.e. the *core languages*) for representation. These are:

1. a language based on labels and populations for representing, manipulating and constraining that which has been classified as "data", namely the *data language*;
2. a language based on tuples and relations for representing, manipulating and constraining that which has been classified as "information", namely the *information language*; and
3. a language based on clauses and groups for representing, manipulating and constraining that which has been classified as "knowledge", namely the *knowledge language*.

The *object representation problem* is the problem of determining *how* an object will be represented in the KPM core languages.

4.6.1 Data representation in the data language

The *data* items in an application are the fundamental, indivisible objects in that application. These objects can be of essentially two different kinds. The distinction

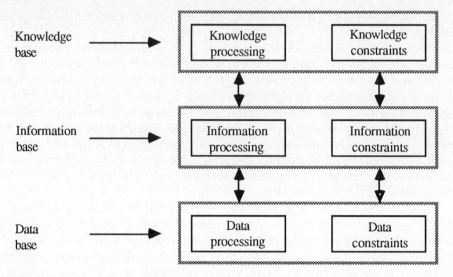

Figure 4.6 The core of the KPM

between these two kinds of object is determined by whether or not the object corresponds to a particular, indivisible, tangible, physical object. For example, "spare-part-no.-1234" may correspond to a particular spare part; on the other hand, "spare-part" is an abstract notion with a clear meaning, but does not correspond to a particular, indivisible, tangible, physical object. Items of data which correspond to a particular, indivisible, tangible, physical object are represented by a label in the data language. The objects which do *not* correspond to a particular, indivisible, tangible, physical object are represented by a population in the data language. Thus, for example,

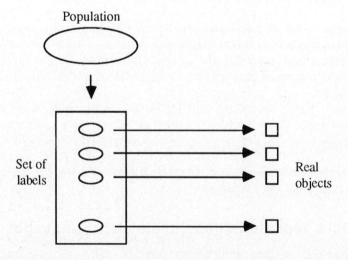

Figure 4.7 Indirect association between a population and a set of real objects

we may have a population "part-number" and associated with, but separate from, this abstract notion, we may have a set of part number labels each of which corresponds to an actual part number. As another example, we might have a label "8-8-1988" representing a real date, in addition we might have the abstract notion of "today's date". Assuming that today's date is August 8, 1988, we would then have the single label "8-8-1988" associated with the population "today's date".

We have seen that a population will sometimes be associated with a set of labels which "belong to" that population. Each label corresponds to a real, particular, indivisible object in the application. Thus, some populations are indirectly associated with a set of real objects in the application. This is shown on the diagram in Figure 4.7.

In Section 3.6.1 we distinguished between two types of population; these are name-populations which *are* associated with a set of real objects, and thing-populations which are *not* associated with a set of real objects. If, in an application, the set of real objects so associated with one population will always be a subset of the set of real objects so associated with another population, then the first population is said to be a *subtype* of the second population. For example, in some application, the set of real objects associated with the population "engineer" may always be a subset of the set of real objects associated with the population "employee". Likewise, the set of real objects associated with the population "trainee" may always be a subset of the set of real objects associated with the population "employee". In which case we would say that "engineer" and "trainee" were subtypes of the population "employee".

Subtype relationships between populations may be represented directly in the data language. As the subtype relationship is established by set theoretic inclusion we would expect the subtype structure of an application to form an algebraic "lattice". (See any good book on algebra for the definition of a *lattice*.)

An important component of the data base is the *data constraints* on the labels associated with each population in the data base. Data constraints may be static or dynamic. Common static constraints for data include:

- upper and lower bounds for the length of a string which is a label name;
- upper and lower bounds on the size of a numeric quantity which is a label name.

Common dynamic constraints for data include:

- bounds on the difference between the size of an old and a new numeric label name.

We have defined the items of data in an application to be the particular, indivisible objects in that application. We have also defined the data language of the KPM. Thus, we now ask, can we always represent the "data" in an application in the KPM "data language"? The answer is clearly "Yes" *unless* we have an infinite amount of data in the application. The number of different labels available for a particular application is clearly finite but are not restricted to any particular finite number. It is usual to refer to a set of this nature as being *finite but unbounded*. Thus, to be rather pedantic, we should note that our data language is only effective for applications in which it is required to refer to a finite, but possibly unbounded, number of different items of data.

4.6.2 Information representation in the information language

The *information* items in an application are the *implicit* functional associations between items of data. These functional associations can be of essentially two different kinds. The distinction between these two kinds of functional association is determined by whether or not the functional association represents an association between two or more tangible, physical objects. For example, "spare parts have a cost" may be interpreted as a functional association from the abstract notion of a "spare part" to the abstract notion of "cost"; on the other hand, "spare part number 1234 costs $12" may be interpreted as a functional association *from* a label associated with a real spare part *to* a label associated with a real cost. Labels are associated with particular, indivisible, real objects; functional associations between labels, are represented by tuples in the information language. Populations are *not* associated with particular indivisible real objects; functional associations between populations are represented by relations in the information language. For example, "spare parts have a cost" might be represented by the relation:

    spare-part/cost(part-number, part-cost:$)

The fact "spare part number 1234 costs $12" might then be represented as a tuple:

    (#1234, 12:$)

which could be associated with the above relation.

An important component of the information base is the *information constraints* on the tuples associated with each relation in the information base. Information constraints may be static or dynamic. Common static constraints for information include:

- the specification of a key for a relation;
- the specification of a transitive constraint for a pair of relations.

Common dynamic constraints for information include:

- bounds on the difference between the sizes of numeric labels in a tuple in a relation.

We have defined the items of information in an application to be the implicit functional associations between items of data in that application. We have also defined the information language of the KPM. Thus, we now ask, can we always represent the "information" in an application in the KPM "information language"? When we considered this question for "data" we laid down the restriction that in an application we can only refer to a finite, but possibly unbounded, number of different items of data. If the number of different items of data is finite, then there can be at most a finite number of distinct, implicit functional associations between these items of data, provided that we do not permit the unbounded repetition of domains in a relation: this is unlikely to be required in any case. Thus, subject to this extra restriction, we note that we can always represent the "information" in an application in the KPM "information language".

4.6.3 Knowledge representation in traditional systems

The knowledge items in an application are the *explicit* functional associations between items of data and/or information. These functional associations are of essentially two different kinds. The distinction between these two kinds of functional association is determined by whether or not the functional association actually enables a particular set of labels or tuples to be derived. For example, "sale price is determined by a rule on the basis of cost price" may be interpreted as a functional association *from* the relation:

> item/buy

to the relation:

> item/sell

but this functional association does not enable us to derive any tuples which satisfy the relation:

> item/sell

On the other hand, "the sale price of washing machine parts is the cost price marked up by 25 percent" is a rule which actually enables us to derive some tuples in the item/sell relation. Items of knowledge which are functional associations which actually enable a particular set of labels or tuples to be derived are usually represented by programs in traditional systems. The functional associations which do *not* enable a particular set of labels or tuples to be derived are not usually represented explicitly in traditional systems at all. For example, the statement "the sale price of an item is determined solely by the cost price of that item" specifies a functional association from:

> item/buy

to:

> item/sell

This functional association would not be represented explicitly in most traditional systems.

4.6.4 Knowledge representation in the knowledge language

We now discuss the ability of the KPM knowledge language to represent knowledge. *Knowledge* has been defined as the explicit functional associations between items of data and/or information. As we have already noted, these functional associations are of two kinds. The functional associations which do *not* enable a particular set of labels or tuples to be derived are represented by groups in the knowledge language. For example, "sale price is determined by a rule on the basis of cost price" could be represented by the group:

   item/sell ⇐ item/buy

Items of knowledge which are functional associations which enable a particular set of labels or tuples to be derived are represented by clauses in the knowledge language. For example, "the sale price of an item costing less than $10 is the cost price of that item marked up by 20 percent" may be interpreted as a functional association from the relation:

   item/buy

to the relation:

   item/sell

This functional association *does* enable a particular set of tuples to be derived. Thus, this functional association could be represented by a clause:

   item/sell(x, y) ← item/buy(x, z), z < 10:$, y = z × 1.2

An important component of the knowledge base is the *knowledge constraints* on the clauses associated with each group in the knowledge base. Knowledge constraints may be static or dynamic. Common static constraints for knowledge include:

- the specification of those predicates that *must* occur as body predicates for a group. For example, the requirement that the relation:

   item/buy

   must occur in the body of a particular group which has the relation:

   item/sell

   as head, is an example of a static constraint for knowledge.

- the specification of the "form" of any calculation that is represented in a group. For example, the requirement that if a group is used to calculate daily-interest on a bank account, then the interest-rate and the balance for that account must be retrieved before an attempt is made to calculate the daily-interest, is an example of a static constraint for knowledge. Note that this constraint would prevent "variable undefined" errors in a conventional programming language, and possibly endless backtracking in a logic programming language.

Common dynamic constraints for knowledge include:

- bounds on the difference between the size of the numeric constants in a clause in the group. For example, the requirement that the "1.2" factor in the clause quoted above could not be altered by more than 0.1 per day, is an example of a dynamic constraint.

We have defined the items of knowledge in an application to be the explicit functional associations between items of information and/or data in that application. We have also defined the knowledge language of the KPM. Thus, we now ask, can we always represent the "knowledge" in an application in the KPM "knowledge language"? We have considered this question for "data" and have laid down the restriction that in an application there can only be a finite, but unbounded, number of different items of data. We have also considered this question for "information" and have laid down the restriction that the unbounded repetition of domains in relations is prohibited. Clausal logic may be interpreted as a general purpose programming language, thus, the KPM language will be capable of representing explicit functional associations between items of information and/or data provided that those functional associations are computable. (See any good book on "Computability" or "Automata" for a definition of *computable*.)

4.7 THE KNOWLEDGE SYSTEMS DESIGN PROBLEM

A system specification usually refers to the most common query and update types and, for each type, will specify a maximum bound on the amount of time that that type should take to process. The time bounds provide the system designer with a set of constraints within which a feasible system may, or may not, be possible to construct using the available machinery. It is also usual to give the system designer expected frequencies of presentation of each query and update type; this information should enable the system designer to derive an "optimal" implementation.

As we have seen, knowledge systems will support query and update types that interact directly with the knowledge, information and data in the system. Thus, the knowledge systems designer should expect to be told the maximum permissible response times and the expected frequency of each common query and update type. The problem of designing a "good" system is to a certain extent concerned with the generation of a system that satisfies the time bounds and operates with the least overall "cost".

We now state the *Knowledge Systems Design Problem*, which is:

> *Given a fully specified machine, based on the KPM architecture, for which the performance characteristics of the three "levels" of processing are known (i.e. the "data", "information" and "knowledge" levels), to construct a design methodology which, when applied to the given application, will generate and maintain a computer system representation of that application which is, in some sense, optimal.*

The remainder of this text is concerned substantially with the development of a proposal for solving this problem.

The knowledge systems design problem has been partly solved by our discussion on object classification and object representation. After all, an intelligent software engineer should be able to design a "good" system for the KPM. However, just as with information systems, the problem with knowledge systems is not so much "designing a good one" as "designing one which can be maintained". Thus, we choose to interpret the word "optimal" above in this second sense; that is, our goal is to optimize the whole cost of designing, implementing, operating *and* maintaining the system throughout its operational life.

An important part of our solution to the knowledge systems design problem is the construction of a "model" of the application. This model will play a vital role in the initial design of the system and will form the basis of the whole business of maintaining the system.

4.8 SUMMARY

We have seen that the proposed fifth generation machine architecture has two important components for processing; these are a "knowledge processing" module, which is based on Horn clauses, and an "information processing" module, which is based on relations. We have introduced the KPM in some detail by actually quoting some of the machine level instructions that this imaginary machine might be expected to execute. The KPM machine language is in three portions; these portions are the "data language", the "information language" and the "knowledge language". We have discussed the conceptual components of the KPM architecture which are required to implement this machine language efficiently. The use of the KPM core languages has been considered, the object representation problem has been addressed, and, finally, the knowledge systems design problem has been stated.

5 Normal forms

5.1 INTRODUCTION

In this chapter we specify precisely what constitutes a good model of an application. The material in this chapter is of vital importance but makes fairly dry reading. On first reading, the reader may choose to move fairly quickly through this material; in which case the reader is advised to pay close attention to both Section 5.2 and Section 5.5.1 at least.

We will first establish the importance of normal forms to knowledge systems. Then the well known normal forms for information are reviewed; these are called the "classical" normal forms. We will introduce new normal forms for data, information, knowledge and "selections". Finally, the compatibility of these new normal forms is discussed.

The basic, guiding principle for normal forms is that in a normalized model each atomic thing identified in the application should be represented in one place in the model and in one place only. The importance of observing this principle in the construction of models for conventional database systems is well known. We now show that the cost of failing to observe this principle in the construction of models of knowledge systems can be even more serious.

In practice, knowledge is usually explicit functional associations between items of information; in other words, the representation of explicit functional associations between items of data tends to be less common. Thus, ignoring explicit functional associations between items of data for the moment, we note the hierarchy: knowledge associates items of information, and information associates items of data. This hierarchy is shown in Figure 5.1. As we shall now see, failure to identify the data items correctly greatly complicates the information, and this, in turn, greatly complicates the knowledge. In other words, there is a "multiplier effect" as the effect of poor data analysis passes up the above hierarchy.

Things	Associate	Represented by	Grouped in	Stored in
Data	--	Labels	Populations	Data base
Information	Data	Tuples	Relations	Information base
Knowledge	Information/data	Clauses	Clause groups	Knowledge base

Figure 5.1 The association hierarchy

Suppose that, in the construction of a knowledge system, a single data object is represented in two places, either as two labels or as two populations. Then any relation that contains a representation of that data object will have to do so twice. For example, consider a single data object which is accidentally represented twice as the two populations:

A   A'

This duplication will give rise to duplication in any relationship involving A and another population. Suppose that A occurs in three binary relations P, Q and R. Then we might have:

P(A,B)   Q(C,A)   R(A,D)
P'(A',B)   Q'(C,A')   R'(A',D)

Thus, we see that if a single data object is represented as two populations then a complete representation of the information in the application will contain a pair of relations for each reference to that data object. Now consider the effect that this will have on the knowledge.

First, the knowledge should contain statements which establish the identity of the representation of the two populations A and A':

is-a[A](x) ← is-a[A'](x)
is-a[A'](x) ← is-a[A](x)
P(x,y) ← P'(x,y)
P'(x,y) ← P(x,y)
Q(x,y) ← Q'(x,y)
Q'(x,y) ← Q(x,y)
R(x,y) ← R'(x,y)
R'(x,y) ← R(x,y)

Second, predicates which are defined in terms of the six predicates quoted above will introduce further duplication. For example,

$T_1(x,y)$ ← P(x,v), Q(v,w), R(w,y)

could also appear in any of the seven different forms:

$T_2(x,y)$ ← P'(x,v), Q(v,w), R(w,y)
$T_3(x,y)$ ← P(x,v), Q'(v,w), R(w,y)
$T_4(x,y)$ ← P(x,v), Q(v,w), R'(w,y)
$T_5(x,y)$ ← P(x,v), Q'(v,w), R'(w,y)
$T_6(x,y)$ ← P'(x,v), Q(v,w), R'(w,y)
$T_7(x,y)$ ← P'(x,v); Q'(v,w), R(w,y)
$T_8(x,y)$ ← P'(x,v), Q'(v,w), R'(w,y)

Furthermore, if more than one of these forms had been introduced, then they, in turn, could give rise to duplication in any knowledge expressed in terms of them, and so on, and so on. Looking back over what has been discussed, note the chaos that can result from the duplicate representation of a single item of data. Note also that this potential chaos is more extensive in the knowledge than it is in the information. Hence, the need is established for the principle "one atomic object in the application being represented in one place and in one place only" to be enforced. In addition, we note the vital need for a good analysis of the data and information to be complete before an attempt is made to express the knowledge.

5.2 THE CLASSICAL NORMAL FORMS

The basic guiding principle behind the specification of normal forms for data, information, knowledge and systems is that in a "good" model (but not necessarily in a good implementation) of an application, each relevant, atomic "thing" identified in that application will be represented in that model *in one place and in one place only*.

Normal forms for information are well established (*see* Codd, 1971 and Kent, 1983). An important motivation for these classical normal forms is that normalization should help to prevent update anomalies. We now give a loose but illuminating interpretation of those "classical" normal forms.

Information, as we have defined it, is implicit functional associations between items of data. Thus, a specification of normal forms for information will be concerned with ensuring that each real, implicit functional association in the application is represented in one place and in one place only in a model of that application. A real, implicit functional association may be represented using a relation as a function passing from those domains in the relation which make up the key to the non-key domains. Thus, the problem of modeling the information in an application is the problem of representing "well" the real, implicit functional associations in the application using relations. This is shown in Figure 5.2 where ρ is the "representation mapping". Note that in this example the "real"

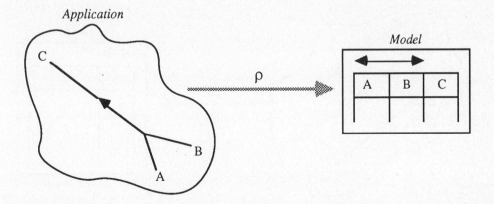

Figure 5.2 Relations represent "real" explicit functional associations

functional association in the application is represented as a functional association *from* the two key domains *to* the single non-key domain in the relation. The classical normal forms are principally concerned with the functional structure of the represented functional associations.

The first classical normal form asserts that the representation of a functional association between a collection of real objects must itself be a function. In particular, the represented function can only have single objects as values. That is, for example, when a "real" functional association is represented in the relation [A,B,C,] shown in Figure 5.2, then it will be represented as a tuple which consists of precisely one label in each domain. In the example shown in Figure 5.3 there are three labels in population B corresponding to the label a_2 in population A; thus, this example contravenes the first classical normal form.

The second classical normal form asserts that in the representation of an implicit functional association, the functional association must not contain another "sub" functional association which is *from* a subset of what is to be represented as the key domains *to* the non-key domains. The situation shown in Figure 5.4 violates second normal form. Note that in this example, C is functionally dependent on B.

The third classical normal form asserts that in the representation of a functional association, the functional association must not contain another "sub" functional association which is *from* a set of non-key domains *to* another non-key domain. The situation shown in Figure 5.5 violates third normal form. Note that in the application, B and C are functionally dependent on A, and C is functionally dependent on B.

The fourth and fifth classical normal forms assert that in the representation of a functional association, the functional association must not contain another "sub" functional association between what is to be represented as the key domains. A relation P is in fourth normal form if it is not possible to group its key domains into three compound domains so that for some relations Q and R the if-and-only-if clause:

$$P(x, y, z) \leftrightarrow Q(x, y), R(y, z)$$

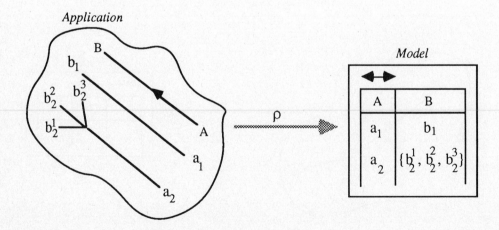

Figure 5.3 First "classical" normal form

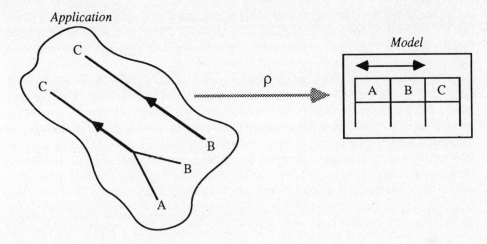

Figure 5.4 Second "classical" normal form

defines precisely all the tuples in relation P. If relation P contravenes fourth normal form, then it should be replaced by the two relations Q and R. A relation P is in fifth normal form if it is not possible to group its key domains into three compound domains so that for some relations Q, R and S, the if-and-only-if clause:

$$P(x, y, z) \leftrightarrow Q(x, y), R(y, z), S(z, x)$$

defines precisely all the tuples in relation P. If relation P contravenes fifth normal form, then it should be replaced by the three relations Q, R and S. The details of the fourth and fifth classical normal forms need not concern us here. All that matters is that fourth and fifth normal forms are concerned with the structure of the key.

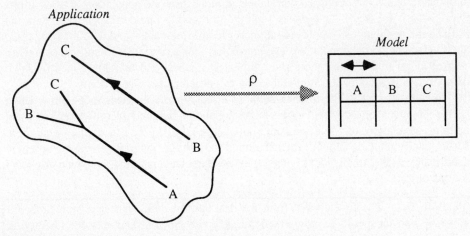

Figure 5.5 Third "classical" normal form

Thus, taken together, the second, third, fourth and fifth normal forms simply assert that a relation should represent one and only one "real", implicit functional association which will be between those objects which are represented as the key domains and those objects which are represented as the non-key domains.

As we have noted, the classical normal forms are principally concerned with the functional structure of the represented implicit functional associations. Thus, as they stand, the classical normal forms amount to tests which determine whether a representation is "good" after that representation has been constructed. Alternatively, the classical normal forms can be seen as the specification of a goal for a discipline of information and data analysis; that goal being the automatic generation of normalized models of information systems. For example, B-R modeling, which is used to illustrate this text, is more than a notation for modeling "two columned" relations. B-R modeling is a discipline of information analysis which leads the analyst to identify objects in the application, and implicit functional associations between those objects, which, when represented, tend to be in normal form.

We now discuss how these ideas have a natural extension to knowledge. It is, however, also worth noting that meaningful normal forms for data can also be phrased.

5.3 NORMAL FORMS FOR DATA

The data in an application is the fundamental, indivisible objects in that application. Thus, the representation of the data in an application in a model is concerned with the representation not of functional associations, as for information and knowledge, but of objects. However, the basic principle of each "atomic thing" identified in the application being represented in the model in one place, and in one place only, still applies.

Each fundamental, indivisible object which is a "tangible, physical object" is represented by a *label*. Each fundamental, indivisible object which is *not* a "tangible, physical object" is represented by a *population*. Labels of the same type are identified with a population.

A set of fundamental, indivisible, tangible, physical objects of the same type may be in one to one correspondence with labels in more than one population. For example, objects which are (real) "employees" may be in a one to one correspondence with the labels in the populations "employee-number", "employee-name" and with the compound labels in the compound population "age/hair-color". This poses no difficulty as we regard "employee" as a thing-population, and "employee-number" and "employee-name" as two different objects which will be represented by two different name-populations.

Recall that for each thing-population we select a particular name-population which has the property that each label in this name-population uniquely identifies each thing in the thing-population, this selected name-population is called the *identifying population*. Hence, each real data object which belongs to a thing-population will be uniquely identified by a label in this identifying population, that label is called the *identifying label* (for that object).

Principle D.1. The first normal form for data simply states that each (fundamental, indivisible) object should be represented uniquely either by one and only one identifying label, or by one and only one identifying population.

This principle merely asserts the existence and uniqueness of the identifying labels and identifying populations. This may appear to be a trivial principle but, as we have seen in Section 5.1, the cost in failing to observe this principle can be very high.

Principle D.2. This normal form for data states that if an identifying label (or population) is used to represent an object then no subset of that label (or population) should be sufficient to identify that object.

For example, in an application where we are interested in the "real" object "postal address" but not in the "real" objects "street number", "street name", "suburb", "state" and "post code", then, strictly speaking the label:

123,Smith-Street,Whitetown,NSW-2468

can be used to identify "address" and satisfies principle D.1. However it does not satisfy principle D.2 because "state" can be removed as it is determined by "postcode" and the "postcode" could be removed if it were determined by "suburb". The contravention of principle D.2 in this example is potentially serious. After all, the label quoted contains two topographic facts which are not necessary for the identification of the given address. If the postcode boundaries were redrawn, then all such labels would have to be checked for consistency with the new boundaries. In other words, this choice of label contains an unnecessary, implicit reference to the postcode boundaries. This reference could prove dangerous if those boundaries were to change.

Principle D.3. This normal form is concerned with compound identifying populations. Principle D.3 requires that it should not be possible to replace all or part of a given compound identifying population with fewer populations on which those given populations are functionally dependent in the classical sense.

For example, in an application where we are interested in employees, employee number, hair color and age it might be the case that age and hair color were sufficient to identify each employee, but that age or hair color separately would not be so sufficient. Then the choice of the compound population "age/hair-color" as the identifying population for the population "employee" satisfies principles D.1 and D.2. However, it would not satisfy principle D.3 if the concept "employee-number" had been identified and both "age" and "hair-color" were functionally dependent on "employee-number". This principle merely attempts to ensure that the "simplest" label, or population, is chosen for the identifying label, or population.

Note that principles D.2 and D.3 effectively prevent any superfluous or over-elaborate labels from being used. This should ensure that each label refers genuinely and efficiently to the object to which it was intended to refer, and only to that object.

5.4 NORMAL FORMS FOR INFORMATION

Our first principle for information simply insists that the data occurring in the information is in normal form. The reader may care to reconsider this principle after having read Section 5.7 "Compatibility of the Normal Forms".

Principle I.0. The labels and populations occurring in the predicates and relations should be in (data) normal form.

The four structural principles that we propose for information are of two types. The first two concern the presence of unnecessary arguments in the predicates, and the second two concern predicates which may be decomposed into disjuncts or conjuncts of two or more predicates. These principles should be seen in addition to the classical normal forms for information discussed in Section 5.2.

Principle I.1. There should be no "redundant domains" in the specification of a predicate.

For example, consider the predicate:

$$P(x , y , z)$$

which means "$(x + y) - y = 2 \times z$"; in this predicate the second domain is "redundant". A *redundant domain* is a domain in a predicate with the property that the values of that domain have no effect on the truth or falsity of the predicate. The value in this principle should be clear. However, it is important to note that the identification of redundant domains is not always a trivial affair. For example, consider the predicate:

company/balance-sheet/interest-rate/rating

which for a given company, whose books are presented as a balance sheet, gives a company "rating" as a good or bad investment, "interest rate" is the value of the current bank interest rate. Suppose that the knowledge used to make this judgement does not, in fact, refer to the interest rate, then "interest-rate" is a redundant domain. If the knowledge had been complex then the identification of this redundant domain could have been difficult.

Principle I.2. A real object should not be represented "explicitly" or "implicitly" in more than one domain in the specification of a predicate.

For example, consider the predicate:

$$P(x , y , z)$$

which means "x is an element, y is a list with first element x, and z .....". In this predicate x occurs explicitly in the first argument and implicitly in the second argument.

Thus, the predicate violates this principle. This principle can be difficult to check. Consider the predicate:

company/balance-sheet/interest-rate/rating

as in the previous example, but suppose that "interest-rate" was used in the knowledge to estimate the "rating", and that "interest-rate" was also buried implicitly in the definition of "balance sheet". Then this predicate would have violated this principle. To see the importance of this principle, a reference to this predicate which contained a reference to a particular balance sheet based implicitly in an 8 percent bank interest rate and an explicit reference to a bank interest rate of 9 percent would be inconsistent and could thus give rise to undesirable behavior.

Principle I.3. A predicate should not be decomposable into the conjunction of two or more predicates with fewer arguments.

For example, consider the predicate:

$P(w , x , y , z)$

which means "$z = (x + y) \times w$". This predicate may be decomposed into the conjunction of:

$Q(x , y , u)$ **and** $R(u , w , z)$

where $Q(x,y,u)$ means "$x + y = u$" and $R(u,w,z)$ means "$u \times w = z$". This principle is more important than it might at first appear. If, as in the above example, predicate P could be decomposed into the conjunct of predicates Q and R, then the knowledge implicit in Q and the knowledge implicit in R have both been buried within the single predicate P. If, for example, the meaning of Q should be changed, then the meaning of P will have to be adjusted as well. This principle thus favors the use of many predicates with few arguments. The value in using binary predicates for modeling information in database design has been well documented, (*see*, for example, Verheijen and Van Bekkum, 1982).

Principle I.4. A predicate should not be decomposable into a conditional disjunct of two or more predicates.

For example, consider the predicate:

$P(x , y , z)$

which means "if $x > 0$ then $x + y = z$ otherwise $x \times y = z$". In this example, the predicate P does not represent an atomic relationship between its logical variables. Instead we should define P by the clause group:

$P(x , y , z) \leftarrow >(x , 0), Q(x , y , z)$
$P(x , y , z) \leftarrow \leq(x , 0), R(x , y , z)$

where predicates Q and R are as in the previous example. The comments made about the importance of I.3 apply equally to this principle.

5.5 NORMAL FORMS FOR KNOWLEDGE

The knowledge in an application is the explicit functional associations between the items of information and/or data in that application. It is interesting to see that there are normal forms for knowledge, as expressed in Horn clauses, which are analogous to the classical normal forms for information, as expressed in relations. In what follows we assume that the knowledge has been represented as a set of (clause) groups.

There are two sorts of "function" which are inherent in the representation of knowledge using Horn clauses. Both of these "functions" are simply logical implication. The first sort of function is the function defined by the functional association *from* the body predicates in a clause (or group) *to* the head predicate in a clause (or group). The second sort of function is the function defined by resolution (*see* Chapter 2) *from* the clauses in a group *to* the set of clauses derivable by resolution from the group. Thus, the first sort of function can be thought of as being related to the declarative interpretation of the group, and the second sort of function can be thought of as being related to the imperative interpretation of the group. We will present our normal forms for knowledge in two distinct classes. The first class contains normal forms for both clauses and groups and is primarily concerned with the function defined by the "declarative" functional association. The second class contains normal forms for groups only and is primarily concerned with the "imperative" functional association defined by resolution.

It is instructive to reflect on important differences between (information) functional associations as represented in tuples and relations, and (knowledge) functional associations as represented in clauses and groups. In a very real sense, groups are the analogues of relations. A relation contains a total specification of a functional association *from* the key domains *to* the non-key domains. Similarly, a group contains a total specification of a functional association *from* the body predicates *to* the head predicate; thus, the body predicates of a group are the analogue of the key of a relation. Despite the fact that a relation provides a template for storing tuples, and a group can be seen as a template for storing clauses, clauses are not the analogue of tuples; in fact, they are structurally different. A tuple is composed of (constant) labels, and represents one atomic fact; in contrast, a clause often contains variables and represents all or part of a general rule. In this sense, the analogue of a tuple would be a "constant instance" of a clause in which all the variables have been replaced by labels. Nevertheless, we have clauses which may contain variables to deal with; and, as we have just remarked, clauses represent all or part of the functional association from the body predicates of the group to the head predicate of the group.

5.5.1 Normal forms for clauses and groups

The first class of normal forms for knowledge contains normal forms for the clauses in a group and some normal forms for groups themselves. The first two normal forms are concerned respectively with the normality of the information in a clause and with the correct use of labels in a clause. In the remaining normal forms the underlying function is the "declarative" functional association; that is, logical implication from the body of the clause (or group) to the head of the clause (or group). In what follows we will refer to the notion of an "information subset". If the clause:

$$P(\,x,y\,)\ \leftarrow\ Q(\,x,y\,)$$

is true, then the predicate Q is said to be an *information subset*, or *I-subset*, of the predicate P.

Principle K.1.0. The predicates occurring in a clause should be in (information) normal form.

The reader may care to reconsider this principle after having read the Section 5.7 "Compatibility of the Normal Forms".

Principle K.1.1. No clause should contain a reference to a particular label unless the possibility of having to subsequently replace that particular label with another label is inconceivable.

For example, the fact "the selling price of items is 1.2 times the buying price" could be represented by:

$$\text{item/sell-price}(\,x,y\,)\ \leftarrow\ \text{item/buy-price}(\,x,z\,),\ y = z\times 1.2$$

This clause violates the normal form K.1.1. Instead, the fact should be broken into two facts, "the mark-up factor is 1.2", and "the selling price of items equals the buying price multiplied by the mark-up factor". The first fact could be represented as a name-population called "mark-up-factor" which would be constrained to be associated with one label only; at present, the label associated with this population is "1.2". The second fact could then be represented as the clause:

$$\text{item/sell-price}(\,x,y\,)\ \leftarrow\ \text{item/buy-price}(\,x,z\,),$$
$$\text{is-the[mark-up-factor]}(\,w\,),\ \ y = z\times w$$

This clause does not violate the normal form K.1.1. This normal form is very important. If it is not observed, then the knowledge may contain a number of explicit or implicit occurrences of the label "1.2"; if the mark-up rate were to change, then all of these occurrences would have to be altered. An example of the occurrence of a constant label in a clause which does not violate this normal form follows. Suppose that the above fact had been broken into two facts, "the mark-up rate is 20 percent", and "the selling price of items is the buying price increased by the mark-up rate percent". The first fact could be represented as a name-population called "mark-up-rate:%" which would be constrained to be associated with at most one label; at present, the label associated with this population is "20:%". The second fact could then be represented as the clause:

item/sell-price(x, y) ← item/buy-price(x, z),
is-the[mark-up-rate:%](w),   y = z × (1 + w/100)

This clause contains the label "100"; however, this label could only change if the units of mark-up-rate ceased to be "percent", and, as a consequence, this clause does not violate this normal form.

Principle K.1.2. (This is similar in sentiment to the classical second normal form.) There should be no "redundant" predicates in the body of a clause (or a group). A *redundant predicate* is a predicate in the body of a clause (or a group), which, if it were deleted, would make no difference to the validity of the clause (or group).

For example, given the clause:

A(x, y) ← B(y, z), C(z, x), D(x, y)   [*]

if the clause:

A(x, y) ← B(y, z), C(z, x)

enabled exactly the same tuples to be derived for predicate A as [*] then [*] should be replaced with this form. Important examples of redundant predicates are predicates that are "duplicates", "irrelevant" or can be removed on the strength of an I-subset clause. A trivial example of the violation of this normal form by the presence of a *duplicate relation* is the double presence of relation B in the clause:

A(x̲ , y) ← B(x̲ , z), B(x̲ , z), C(z̲ , y)

An example of the violation of this normal form by the presence of an *irrelevant relation* is the clause:

A(x, y) ← B(y, z), C(z, x), D(u, v)

in which the relation D is irrelevant provided that for some particular values of u and v, D(u, v) is always true, and is asserted as being true elsewhere. Note that the relation D is clearly irrelevant because the variables u and v are not shared with the other predicates in the clause. An example of the use of an I-subset clause is the use of the I-subset clause:

A(x̲ , y) ← B(x̲ , y)

to simplify:

C(x̲ , y) ← A(x̲ , y), B(x̲ , y), D(x̲ , y)

then the $A(\underline{x}, y)$ can be removed from the second clause. This is an example of *reduction by an I-subset clause*. To see the importance of this principle, let us re-consider the first example introduced above. Suppose that when the clause:

$$A(x, y) \leftarrow B(y, z), \; C(z, x), \; D(x, y)$$

was asserted that the clause:

$$A(x, y) \leftarrow B(y, z), \; C(z, x)$$

was not asserted but was, in fact, true, then the truth of the first clause may well be unnecessarily effected if the meaning of predicate D should change slightly, for example, the predicate D may always be false, then the validity of the first clause could well be in question. In other words, the presence of predicate D in the first clause is nothing less than a "time bomb" which could give considerable and unnecessary trouble later on.

It is interesting to note that we cannot generalize reduction by I-subset clauses to reduction by clauses which contain a single relation together with other knowledge in their body, as the knowledge in such a clause will be propagated by the reduction process. This is often undesirable. For example,

$$\text{item/sell(} \underline{\text{item-no.}} \text{ , sell-price)} \leftarrow \text{item/buy(} \underline{\text{item-no.}} \text{ , buy-price)},$$
$$\text{sell-price} = \text{buy-price} \times 1.25$$

should not be used to reduce:

$$\text{item/profit(} \underline{\text{item-no.}} \text{ , profit)} \leftarrow \text{item/buy(} \underline{\text{item-no.}} \text{ , buy-price)},$$
$$\text{item/sell(} \underline{\text{item-no.}} \text{ , sell-price)}, \; \text{profit} = \text{sell-price} - \text{buy-price}$$

to produce:

$$\text{item/profit(} \underline{\text{item-no.}} \text{ , profit)} \leftarrow \text{item/buy(} \underline{\text{item-no.}} \text{ , buy-price)},$$
$$\text{profit} = \text{buy-price} \times 0.25$$

which is dangerous as a change in the mark-up rate would then have to be entered in more than one clause. This contravenes one of the fundamental principles of a good representation "that each item of knowledge should be represented in one place only". In fact, we will see that this example contravenes principle K.1.3. Thus, our normal form only permits reduction by I-subset clauses.

> **Principle K.1.3.** (This is similar in sentiment to the classical third normal form.) This important principle insists that the knowledge in one clause (or group) cannot be buried within another clause (or group).

Given two different clauses (or groups):

$$a \leftarrow [B] \quad \text{and} \quad c \leftarrow [D]$$

where "a" and "c" are the head predicates, [B] and [D] denote the body of each clause (or group) respectively, {B} and {D} denote the set of body predicates in those clauses (or groups) respectively, and $c \notin \{B\}$. If:

$$\{D\} \subseteq \{B\} \quad \text{and} \quad a \leftarrow [E]$$

are valid, where $\{E\} = \{c\} \cup \{F\}$ and $\{F\} \subset \{B\}$, then:

$$a \leftarrow [B]$$

violates this principle and should be replaced by:

$$a \leftarrow [E]$$

For example, if we have the clause:

account/balance(x, y) ← account/revenue(x, w),
     account/expenses(x, z), y = w - z

and the clause:

account/tax-payable(x, y) ← account/revenue(x, w),
     account/expenses(x, z), t = w - z, y = t × 0.2

then the second clause should be replaced by the clause:

account/tax-payable(x, y) ← account/balance(x, z), y = z × 0.2

as long as this clause is, in fact, correct. A weaker, but easier to grasp statement of this principle is that it should not be possible to use the knowledge in one clause (or group) to replace one or more predicates in the body of another clause (or group) with the head predicate of the first clause (or group). For example, consider the two clauses:

A(x, y) ← B(y, z), C(z, u), D(u, x)   [$]
E(z, x) ← C(z, u), D(u, x)

if clause [$] could be phrased as:

A(x, y) ← B(y, z), E(z, x)

then it should be phrased this way. This is a very important normal form, and is one which is often violated unwittingly in practice. In the first example above, the knowledge "that the balance of an account is the difference between the revenue and the expenses" has been buried within the second clause. If this knowledge should change, then both the first and the second clause would have to be changed. Note, however, that the third clause is quite independent of this piece of knowledge.

Principle K.1.4. (This is similar in sentiment to classical fourth normal form.) This normal form is concerned with the complexity of the bodies of the clauses (or groups). A clause (or group) is said to satisfy principle K.1.4 when it is not possible to represent it as two clauses (or groups) both of which contain fewer body predicates, of no greater arity, than the initial clause (or group), so that any predicates introduced to achieve this form are both natural and meaningful in the application.

Consider the clause:

$$A(\underline{x}, y) \leftarrow B(\underline{y}, z), C(\underline{z}, w), D(\underline{w}, y)$$

This representation may be replaced by the clause:

$$A(\underline{x}, y) \leftarrow E(\underline{y}, w), D(\underline{w}, y)$$

where:

$$E(\underline{y}, w) \leftarrow B(\underline{y}, z), C(\underline{z}, w)$$

by introducing the predicate E whose arity may be no greater than that of the predicates in terms of which it is defined; it is essential that:

$$A(\underline{x}, y) \leftarrow E(\underline{y}, w), D(\underline{w}, y)$$

be a *natural* way of phrasing the original clause. If this can be achieved, then the knowledge in the initial clause (or group) is clearly in "two dissectable parts", where the division into the two clauses (or groups) identifies these parts. It is clear that not all clauses (or groups) can be reduced in this way; for example, consider the clause:

$$A(\underline{u}, v) \leftarrow B(\underline{u}, v), C(\underline{u}, w), D(\underline{v}, w),$$
$$E(\underline{u}, x), F(\underline{v}, x), G(\underline{w}, x)$$

In this clause, the complex cross-linking of variables prevents the clause from being decomposed in the way described. It is clear that when reducing clauses to this normal form there will often be a choice of which new predicates to introduce. The criterion used is to only choose new predicates which are natural and meaningful. This principle is just as important as K.1.3. This principle requires that a complex body of a clause (or group) be simplified as much as possible without complicating the information. The general idea is that the knowledge required to define predicate E, which was extracted from predicate A, may well be present in other predicates as well as A. If this is the case, then future modifications to predicate E will have to be made in one place rather than in many places. However, if the new predicates introduced do not find a natural place in the application, or if the clauses cannot be re-expressed naturally using the new predicates, then this principle should not be applied.

5.5.2 Normal forms for groups

The second class of normal forms for knowledge contains normal forms for (clause) groups. The underlying function is the function defined by logical implication from the clauses in the group to the set of clauses derivable from the group by resolution. Each (clause) group has a unique head predicate which is the head predicate of each of the clauses in that group; the other predicates in the group are called the *body predicates* (or, *body relations*).

Principle K.2.0. The clauses in a clause group should satisfy the previously stated principles for clauses.

Principle K.2.1. There should be no redundant clauses in a clause group. A *redundant clause* in a given clause group is a clause which, if it were deleted, would make no difference to the set of clauses which could be derived from that clause group by resolution.

For example, any clause of the form:

$$P(x, y) \leftarrow P(x, y)$$

would be redundant in any group in which it were not the only member. Alternatively, in the group:

$$A(\underline{x}, y) \leftarrow B(\underline{y}, x)$$
$$A(\underline{x}, y) \leftarrow B(\underline{y}, x), C(\underline{x}, y)$$

the second clause is redundant. The removal of redundant clauses is important. If a group contains a redundant clause and if modifications are made to the redundant clause only, then the consistency of the group could well be at risk.

Principle K.2.2. Any clause derivable from the clauses in a clause group using resolution should have a unique derivation.

An important consequence of this principle is that it should not be possible to derive by resolution one clause in a clause group from the remainder. An alternative version of this principle may be expressed as follows. Each (clause) group amounts to a specification of the necessary knowledge to deduce all tuples which satisfy the head predicate given all the tuples which satisfy the other body predicates. Thus, a natural requirement for a group is that it preserves "relational behavior" in the sense that if the body predicates are "real, well-behaved" predicates then the head predicate should be a "virtual, well-behaved" predicate. By a "well-behaved" predicate we mean that when the clause is used by the "find all" mechanism, each tuple satisfying the head predicate must be generated once and only once. We will see later on the importance of the compatibility between the structure of a group and the "find all" mechanism of the implementation. However, the fundamental importance of this principle is due to the observation that if a clause can be derived from a group in two or more ways, then these two or more derivations may employ different clauses in the group. If this is so, then modifications to some of the clauses could lead to an inconsistent group. For example:

item/cost('pencil', 0.4:$) ←
item/cost('book', 1.2:$) ←
item/cost('pen', 0.7:$) ←
item/sell(x , y:$) ← item/cost:$(x, z:$), y:$ = z:$ × 1.2
item/sell('book', 1.44:$) ←

It is clear that modification to the second, fourth or fifth clause above could render the group inconsistent.

Principle K.2.3. It should not be possible to replace two or more clauses in a given group with fewer clauses which may be derived by resolution from the clauses in the given group.

A non-trivial example of the importance of this principle may be shown by consideration of the Quicksort program discussed in (Van Emden, 1977):

Sort(x1.x2 , y) ← Part(x1 , x2 , u1 , u2),
                    Sort(u1 , v1), Sort(u2 , v2), Cat(v1 , x1.v2 , y)
Sort(nil , nil) ←
Part(x1 , z.x2 , z.u1 , u2) ← ≤(z , x1), Part(x1 , x2 , u1 , u2)
Part(x1 , z.x2 , u1 , z.u2) ← >(z , x1), Part(x1 , x2 , u1 , u2)
Part(x , nil , nil , nil) ←
Cat(u.x , y , u.z) ← Cat(x , y , z)
Cat(nil , y , y) ←

In this program, Sort(x , y) means "list y is a sorted version of list x", Part(w, x, y, z) means "list x is partitioned into two lists y and z; list y contains those elements less than or equal to element w, and list z contains the remainder", Cat(x, y, z) means "list z is the concatenation of the two lists x and y". The predicate ≤ is the standard "less than or equal to" predicate, and the predicate > is the standard "greater than" predicate, both of which are assumed to be implemented in the programming language. The first two clauses form a clause group defining Sort. The third, fourth and fifth clauses form a clause group defining Part. The last two clauses form a clause group defining Cat. These three clause groups together form the program. Consider the following "similar" specification of the "Sort" group:

Sort(nil , nil) ←
Sort(x.nil , x.nil) ←
Sort(x1.x2.x3 , y) ← Part(x1 , x2.x3 , u1 , u2),
                       Sort(u1 , v1), Sort(u2 , v2), Cat(v1 , x1.v2 , y)

the first clause in the Quicksort program above may be deduced, using resolution and automated theorem proving (Chapter 2), from this clause group. In addition, that deduced clause can replace the second and third clauses in this example. Thus, the clause group in this example violates the principle K.2.3.

Principle K.2.4. If a (clause) group can be split into two or more subsets so that whenever it is invoked, a subset only of the non-unit clauses in the clause group will be employed in satisfying the goal, then such a clause group violates this principle; in this case, new head predicates should be introduced for each such subset.

For example, in the following clause group suppose that *either* the first two *or* the last two clauses would be employed to satisfy the head predicate A:

$$A(\,x\,,y\,) \leftarrow \,>(\,x\,,1\,), \ B(\,x\,,z\,), \ C(\,z\,,y\,)$$
$$A(\,1\,,3\,) \leftarrow$$
$$A(\,x\,,y\,) \leftarrow \,<(\,x\,,0\,), \ D(\,x\,,z\,), \ C(\,z\,,y\,)$$
$$A(\,0\,,-4\,) \leftarrow$$

then the principle requires that two predicates, E and F, say, be introduced:

$$E(\,x\,,y\,) \leftarrow B(\,x\,,z\,), \ C(\,z\,,y\,)$$
$$E(\,1\,,3\,) \leftarrow$$
$$F(\,x\,,y\,) \leftarrow D(\,x\,,z\,), \ C(\,z\,,y\,)$$
$$F(\,0\,,-4\,) \leftarrow$$

and that clause group A be re-expressed as:

$$A(\,x\,,y\,) \leftarrow \,\geq(\,x\,,1\,), \ E(\,x\,,y\,)$$
$$A(\,x\,,y\,) \leftarrow \,\leq(\,x\,,0\,), \ F(\,x\,,y\,)$$

It is interesting to note that this principle corresponds to the removal of reckless uses of the **if**..**then**..**else**.. construct from conventional control structures. Note that when the initial form of the above example is interpreted imperatively by the SLD strategy, it is difficult to describe the precise state of affairs when control is passed from the clause group with head predicate A to the clause group with head predicate C. On the other hand, when the second version of the above example is interpreted imperatively, control is passed from group E to group C only if $x \geq 1$ at the time control left group A.

5.6   NORMAL FORMS FOR SELECTIONS

In a knowledge base, the relations which are naturally associated with updates, that is, those relations into which raw (information) updates may be directly inserted, are called *update relations*, or, *update predicates*. Likewise, the relations which are naturally associated with queries, that is, those relations from which information is extracted to satisfy queries, are called *query relations*, or, *query predicates*. A collection of groups which enables all the tuples which satisfy the identified query predicates to be deduced from the tuples in the update predicates is called a *selection*. In this section we discuss normal forms for selections. It is assumed that a number of groups have been identified in the course of building a system, and that some of them have been chosen to be part of a selection. The remaining identified groups will not be used by this selection. It is also assumed that each group has a *cost* attached to it.

Principle S.0. The groups in a selection should be in (group) normal form.

Principle S.1. The set of groups which comprise a selection should be "minimal", that is, it should not be possible to satisfy the query predicates with another set of groups of lower total cost.

The importance of this principle extends beyond the interests of simple economy. If a selection does not consist of a minimal set of groups, then modification to some of the groups may well lead to an inconsistent selection.

5.7 COMPATIBILITY OF THE NORMAL FORMS

When developing a Binary-Relationship model of data (*see* Nijssen and Halpin, 1989) it is standard practice to convert n-ary relations, where $n > 2$, to n binary relations. This may be achieved by introducing new, hybrid data objects. For example, if it had been noted that "machine-type", "operator-name" and "shift-number" were sufficient to determine the "cost-per-hour" of a given operator operating a given machine in a given shift, then we could represent this functional association by the relation:

(machine-type, operator, shift, cost-per-hour)

in which the first three domains constitute the (compound) key. This relation could be reduced to four binary relations by introducing a new, hybrid thing-population "operation" which has an identifying name-population called "operation-number" which uniquely determines every domain in the above relation. Thus, the single relation may be replaced by:

(operation, machine-type)
(operation, operator)
(operation, shift)
(operation, cost-per-hour)

Note that the information (i.e. the relations) has been simplified at the expense of complicating the data (i.e. the populations). Moreover, one could argue that the resulting set of five populations contradicts the spirit of the normal forms for data in that we now have a population, namely operation-number, which may not correspond to any of the originally identified data concepts which were perfectly sufficient to describe the application.

It is interesting to note that the ideas discussed in the previous paragraph for data and information have direct parallels for information and knowledge. In the discussion of principle K.1.4 (above), the clause:

$$A(\underline{x}, y) \leftarrow B(\underline{y}, z), C(\underline{z}, w), D(\underline{w}, y)$$

was replaced by the pair:

$$E(\underline{y}, w) \leftarrow B(\underline{y}, z), C(\underline{z}, w)$$
$$A(\underline{x}, y) \leftarrow E(\underline{y}, w), D(\underline{w}, y)$$

This was made possible by the introduction of a new, hybrid relation named E. Thus, we see that the knowledge has been simplified at the expense of complicating the information.

Just as it is sometimes not possible to simplify the information without complicating the data in that information, so it is sometimes not possible to simplify the knowledge without complicating the information in that knowledge. For example, as we noted in our discussion of principle K.1.4 (above) it is not always possible to simplify a clause consisting of binary relations by introducing new binary relations. For example, consider the clause:

$$A(\underline{u}, v) \leftarrow B(\underline{u}, v), C(\underline{u}, w), D(\underline{v}, w),$$
$$E(\underline{u}, x), F(\underline{v}, x), G(\underline{w}, x)$$

in which the complex cross-linking of the variables prevents the simplification of this clause with the introduction of new binary predicates. However, the number of predicates in this clause could be reduced by introducing, for example, a new predicate H:

$$H(\underline{u}, \underline{v}, x) \leftarrow C(\underline{u}, w), D(\underline{v}, w), G(\underline{w}, x)$$

Thus, once again, the knowledge has been simplified at the expense of complicating the information.

Thus, we conclude that the normal forms for data, information and knowledge are simply not compatible. In particular, attempts to reduce the number of domains in the predicates can have the effect of complicating the data, and attempts to reduce the number of predicates in a clause can have the effect of complicating the information. We propose that the whole business of normalization should be viewed as a problem involving the balancing of conflicting interests. For this to be achieved in a satisfactory way, costs must be associated with various simplification procedures so that a satisfactory "optimal" solution can be reached. A solution to this "normalization problem" will have to address quantitatively the corresponding benefits of simple data, simple information and simple knowledge, and will have to balance these conflicting interests in determining the final, optimal solution.

5.8 SUMMARY

We have seen the need for normal forms by observing the potential added cost to a knowledge system by a simple duplication in the representation of the data. The classical normal forms have been reviewed, and their role in the construction of "good" representations of information has been noted. We have introduced new normal forms for data, information, knowledge and selections, and have discussed the compatibility of these normal forms.

6 Knowledge acquisition

6.1 INTRODUCTION

In this chapter we introduce our method of "knowledge acquisition". This method is fairly easy to understand but requires considerable practice before it can be effectively employed. In a real interview it is all too easy to let the domain expert influence the direction of the question sequence. Knowledge acquisition takes place in "real time" so if the analyst is to control this process, the questions must flow naturally; there is not time for pauses to think, "What is the next step in the method?". In this way the reader is encouraged to practice the technique and to learn to regard the "knowledge acquisition process" as the application of a fairly rigid discipline. The method has only been mastered when the discipline becomes subconscious behavior.

We will outline our method for "knowledge acquisition" which, as we will see, covers the whole business of extracting facts from the domain expert and representing those facts in some language that is both precise and comprehensible to the domain expert. The language that we employ is called the "language of the application model". We will discuss the different ways that a given fact can be represented and investigate the transformation of one representation to another. Then we introduce the "individual requirements" which are three simple tests that any fact has to pass to be acceptable; the "individual requirements" act as a simple filter on presented facts. Our technique for "knowledge elicitation" is described: "Knowledge elicitation" is concerned with guiding the discussion between the knowledge analyst and the domain expert. A simple worked example which illustrates the use of the technique in building an application model is presented. Finally, we introduce the "data model" which is extracted from the application model; the "data model" provides a specification of the "data base" of the knowledge system.

6.2 THE ROLE OF THE APPLICATION MODEL

Knowledge acquisition is the first phase in the construction of a knowledge system. The goal of the knowledge acquisition phase is to construct a complete, consistent, correct and non-redundant model of the application which is comprehensible to the domain expert and which is in a sufficiently precise form to enable a trained person to translate it unambiguously into some implementable formalism. This model will be referred to as the *application model*. From the application model we will extract the *data model* which provides a specification of the data base of the knowledge system.

116

The role of the application model in the design and maintenance of a knowledge system is crucial. The ultimate goal in building the application model is to construct a precise, concise and complete statement of "all that is relevant in" the application. The application model should make perfect sense both to the analyst who knows little of the background to the application area, and to the domain expert from the application area who knows little about knowledge analysis. As far as the latter is concerned, the application model represents the most highly refined picture of the application that he or she is expected to understand; thereafter, the system building process will be in the hands of the analyst and a team of technical staff. Thus, for the analyst, the application model represents the final opportunity for the gathered facts to be checked for correctness before they are represented in some formalism and eventually become an implemented system. The application model is not discarded once the system has been implemented; it is the kernel of the whole design *and maintenance* process; it forms the lynch pin of the maintenance strategy. To support knowledge systems maintenance, the application model should at all times consist of an accurate description of the knowledge with which the system has been built. Changes in the application will first be represented as modifications to the application model; these changes will be the first formal step in any maintenance operation. The application model is intimately linked with the three "system" models, which are the "data model", the "information model" and the "knowledge model". The three system models provide a formal description of the structure of the knowledge system, and can be used as a specification for an implementation of the system in any expert system "shell" or suitable language. As we will see, these four models interact with each other during the execution of maintenance operations on the knowledge system.

There are many formalisms in use today which could be used to provide a language in which application models could be phrased. However, we have rejected them for two main reasons. The first reason is that we are not aware of a formalism which is disposed naturally and equally to data, information and knowledge. In other words, many formalisms tend to at least imply that a gathered fact, once represented in the formalism, should be classified either as data, as information or as knowledge. The second reason is that formalisms tend to complicate and retard communication between the analyst and the domain experts. Thus, in general, we prefer the "informalism" of some form of stylized natural language.

The whole process of constructing the application model, and the derived data model, is called *knowledge acquisition*. The essential business in the development of the application model is the acquisition of facts from the domain expert; this often takes place during an initial sequence of interviews. Alternatively, some of the facts may be available in written form or may have been generated by some induction process. These facts, as they are acquired, are each required to satisfy some "individual requirements" which will be described shortly. Once the individual requirements have been satisfied, the facts are then phrased in the language of the application model. When the analyst believes that a sufficient quantity of facts have been gathered, an attempt may be made to construct at least part of the system. In so doing, the principle of "one statement in the application model being represented in the chosen, implementable formalism in, at most, one place" is adhered to strictly; this is ensured by the "knowledge analysis" phase which is discussed in Chapter 7. During the system building process it is not uncommon for the analyst to discover inconsistencies and gaps in the gathered knowledge and with the help of the domain expert, these are corrected. In other words, knowledge acquisition is not a sequence of steps that are performed once, and once completed, exclusive attention will be given to the subsequent phases; the analyst will revisit the knowledge acquisition phase many times during the design process and at least once during any non-trivial maintenance operation. When some form of implemented system is available, some of the gathered facts will have been represented in that (prototype) system; these facts are together referred to as the *live application model*. The remaining facts, which are not presently being employed, will be referred to as the *dormant application model*. The dormant application model will consist of bundles of facts that have not been used at all, together with portions of bundles from which one or more statements have been extracted for use in the prototype. The "live" and "dormant" models are shown in Figure 6.1. The dormant application model is retained as a reservoir of "spare facts" which could, at a later stage, prove to be useful for system reorganization, redesign, enhancement or further development.

The application model is not an end in itself; it constitutes a precise model of the application which is the beginning of the formal system building process. Furthermore, for a non-trivial application, it would be foolish to believe that a complete and correct application model can be built before prototyping has been completed satisfactorily. In practice, it is realistic to assume that an application model for a complex application will never be totally complete, or totally correct.

During the early stages of knowledge acquisition, the aim of the knowledge acquisition technique should be to extract in an orderly fashion as many relevant facts and as few irrelevant facts as possible from the domain expert. We will also see that, during knowledge acquisition, the analyst pays particular attention to the correct analysis of the data in the application. The analyst should attempt to extract facts in a form which may be easily represented in the language of the application model. Thus, during knowledge acquisition, the knowledge analyst is confronted with a complex problem of eliciting facts from the domain expert, while knowing that some of these facts may be used, and that those that will be used will eventually become either data, information, knowledge or constraints, but not knowing which of the four it will be, and, at the same time, trying to ensure that the gathered facts satisfy the requirements of the data, information, knowledge and constraint representations! In other words, the analyst must keep one eye on the business of constructing a good model quickly while the other eye is checking that the

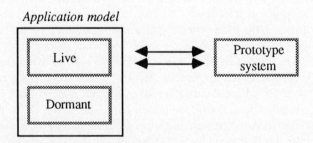

Figure 6.1 The "live" and "dormant" models

gathered facts are in a form suitable for representation. If these two goals are not pursued at the same time, then this will inevitably lead to many frustrating, repeated interviews with the domain expert.

6.3 THE LANGUAGE OF THE APPLICATION MODEL

The language that we have chosen for the application model is "stylized natural language". Most domain experts will communicate with the knowledge analyst in written or spoken natural language, formulae, charts, diagrams, graphs and other domain-specific media. We feel that it is both counterproductive and unnecessary to insist that the domain expert master some new formalism or become fluent in some formal language, just for the purpose of communicating with the analyst. We will not attempt to give a complete definition of the language of the application model because it may need to include some domain specific features, and so, in practice, a little improvisation may be necessary. We will, however, discuss enough of the flavor of the language to clearly set the tone for such improvisation.

The language of the application model contains much of the spirit of the first-order predicate calculus with equality. In particular, a clear distinction is drawn between things which are individual objects and things which are sets of objects. This distinction can pose problems unless it is made in some context. For example, the phrase "savings accounts" could be an individual object in a set of objects called "account types", or it could be a set of individual objects, each of which is a particular savings account. In our development the context for drawing the distinction between things and objects is provided by a type hierarchy which is developed as the application model is developed. During the knowledge acquisition phase, the application model and the type hierarchy are prevented from developing inconsistencies, such as the dual interpretation of "savings accounts" discussed above. This is achieved by insisting that all individual facts gathered satisfy the "uniqueness requirement" which is described shortly.

The basic construct of the language of the application model is the "simple statement". Important components of "simple statements" are "individual objects" and "structural variables". Individual objects are references to particular things in the application. Structural variables are references to things, but no particular thing, in the application. A *simple statement* in the language of the application model will assert that either:

- an individual object, or structural variable, exists and belongs to a particular set of objects; or
- two or more individual objects, or structural variables, belong to a relationship between two or more sets of individual objects.

In addition, each <simple statement> may be the subject of a single *modal operator* such as:

> **it is likely that** [. . .]
> **it is unlikely that** [. . .]
> **it is possible that** [. . .]
> **it is certain that** [. . .]
> **it is uncertain that** [. . .]
> **with probability x** [. . .]
> **with certainty x** [. . .]
> **with degree of belief x** [. . .]

where the values of 'x' will be in some appropriate range. Presumably for probabilities this range is [0, 1].

A "statement" in the language of the application model may be a "construct" of simple statements in which any structural variables are quantified with "for all values of" or " for at least one value of". The following are permitted "constructs":

> <construct>   ::=   **if** <construct> **then** <construct> |
> <construct> **and** <construct> |
> **not** <construct> |
> <simple statement> |
> **for all values of x** <construct>$_x$ |
> **for at least one value of x** <construct>$_x$

where | means "or", and <construct>$_x$ denotes that x is a structural variable in the construct <construct> that is not the subject of a quantifier, that is, there is no "for all values of" or "for at least one value of", for that variable within the construct <construct>. Parentheses should be used if necessary to avoid structural ambiguities. A *statement* either:

- establishes the existence of a set of individual objects;
- establishes the existence of a relationship between two or more set of individual objects;
- establishes the existence of an association between two or more relationships and/or sets of individual objects; or
- is a construct in which all structural variables are "bound" by quantifiers.

Note that the use of **or** is discouraged. For example, the form:

> **if** A **or** B **then** C

should be written as:

> **if** A **then** C
> **if** B **then** C

Also, for example, the form:

> **if** A **then** B **or** C

should be rejected, and clarification should be sought from the domain expert as to when A leads to B and when A leads to C. This discussion may lead to the development of two new statements of the form:

> **if** (A **and** E) **then** B
> **if** (A **and** F) **then** C

or, perhaps, two new statements of the form:

> **if** A **then** **with probability x** [B]
> **if** A **then** **with probability y** [C]

A *compound statement* is a construct which is not a simple statement in which all structural variables are "bound" by quantifiers. In the representation of <simple statements> the use of vague verbs such as "is" or "are" is discouraged. For example, our example "the interest rate on savings accounts is likely to be 5 percent" is not acceptable but the following is acceptable:

> "the value of the interest-rate on savings accounts is likely to equal 5 percent".

The following are acceptable compound statements but are not simple statements:

> "**if** an account belongs to the class of savings accounts, **then** **it is likely that** [the interest rate on that account equals 5 percent]".
> "**if** 'account-type' has value 'savings', **then** **it is likely that** ['account-interest-rate' has value '5 percent']".

Note that in the description of the language of the application model given above we have restricted the modal operators to apply to simple sentences only. In other words, we have specifically excluded, for example, statements of the form:

> **it is likely that** [**if** A **then** B]
> **with probability x** [**it is certain that** [A]]

However, modal operators can be the subjects of logical operators. For example, consider:

> **not** **with probability x** [A]

It is important to realize that the last example given above is *not* equivalent to:

> **with probability (1 - x)** [A]

The language of the application model lies beyond the power of Horn clause logic in two important respects. First, the use of modal operators is permitted, and second, the logical structure may contain "nots" or "ors" which often prevent logical expressions from being represented directly as a Horn clause. We can accommodate the first of these differences by permitting modal operators to be applied to predicates; for example:

> **it is likely that** [invoice/status(x, 'Error')] ←
> invoice/total(x, y:$), y > 10000:$

> **it is likely that** [invoice/status(x, 'OK')] ←
> invoice/total(x, y:$), y < 300:$

which represents the rule "invoices for over $10,000 are likely to be in error, and invoices for less than $300 are likely to be OK". We refer to (Horn) clauses in which one or more of the predicates have been permitted to be the subject of modal operators as *modal clauses*. If a group of clauses contain one or more modal clauses, then the group is called a *modal group*. Concerning the second way in which the language of the application model lies beyond the power of pure Horn clause logic, that is, by inclusion of "nots" or "ors", this can be accommodated by using (non-Horn) clauses of the form

$$(A \lor B \lor ... \lor D) \leftarrow (E \land F \land ... \land H)$$

However, examples which require non-Horn clause logic are not common and are seen to lie beyond the scope of this discussion. (*See* Bundy, 1983, or any good book on computational logic, for a discussion of computation with non-Horn clauses.)

The rationale that lies behind our language of the application model is that by phrasing facts in this language, the analyst is forced to acknowledge both the logical and the modal structure of each fact; other features of the fact can be expressed in natural language and will be the subject of detailed analysis at a later stage. In other words, the important point is that the modal structure and logical structure must be made explicit.

6.4 OBJECT RECLASSIFICATION

When constructing the application model, the analyst's task is to gather facts in a form that will facilitate representation as either data, information, knowledge or constraints. As we have already noted, each gathered fact will be required to satisfy our "individual requirements" which have yet to be described. We will see that, in the satisfaction of the "individual requirements", the analyst must bear in mind the way in which a gathered fact *may* eventually be represented, and should ensure that the fact is in a form which is suitable for representation. Setting constraints aside for the moment, the alternatives for representing a fact are shown in Figure 6.2. One might hope that if a certain gathered fact had the property that it could be represented correctly in any of these three forms, then it should be possible to convert any one of these representations to the other two. We now indicate, in the context of a simple example, how this might be achieved.

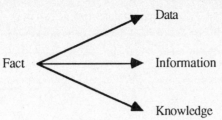

Figure 6.2 Alternative representations of a fact

Let us consider again the sample fact "The interest rate on savings accounts is likely to be 5 percent". As a starting point let us subject this fact to a "B-R-like" analysis (*see* Nijssen and Halpin, 1989 or Verheijen and Van Bekkum, 1982). We might well construct the B-R diagram shown in Figure 6.3 where we have extended the notation to include the particular labels "savings" and "5 percent" in rectangular boxes at the bottom of the diagram. The heavy arrow indicates functionality of "likelihood" in the logical sense of "if savings then is likely 5 percent". We could interpret this diagram by isolating the "5 percent" box, interpreting the rest of the diagram as defining the name-population "the likely interest rate on savings accounts" whose *only* label is named "5 percent". Alternatively we could have isolated the "savings" box, and interpreted the rest of the diagram as defining the name-population "account types whose interest rates are likely to equal 5 percent" *one of whose* labels is named "savings".

Suppose now that the analyst decides to introduce a relation "account-type/interest-rate". Then this could be represented as the diagram shown in

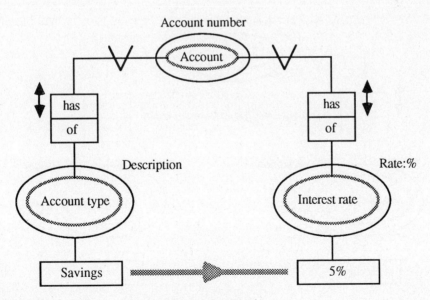

Figure 6.3 First diagram for "interest rate" example

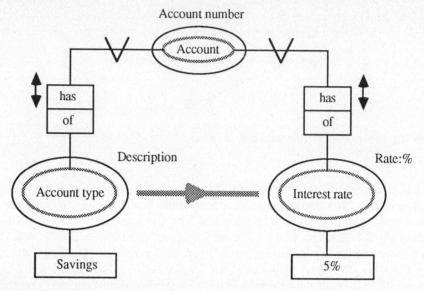

Figure 6.4 Second diagram for "interest rate" example

Figure 6.4 which can be interpreted as defining a relation into which tuples such as (savings, 5%) may be placed. In which case, we may assert that:

<u>it is likely that</u> [account-type/interest-rate('savings', 5:%)]

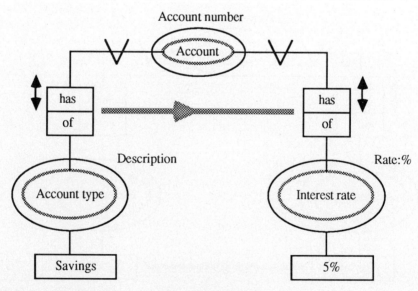

Figure 6.5 Third diagram for "interest rate" example

Alternatively, because account is a total role in, and is the primary key of, the two relations with which it is connected on the diagram shown in Figure 6.4, we can draw the arrow between these two relations which indicates that the sample fact is to be interpreted as a functional association between two relations; this is shown in Figure 6.5. In other words, it is knowledge. It could be expressed in logic as a group. One member of this group would be the clause for savings accounts. That clause could be expressed in logic as:

it is likely that [account/interest-rate(x , 5:%)] ←
            account/account-type(x , 'savings')

This discussion provides a framework in which we can give an interesting definition of the particular functional association from "savings accounts" to "5 percent"; this functional association is precisely that which is in common with Figures 6.3, 6.4 and 6.5.

What is emerging here is a calculus of B-R diagrams which allows us to move freely between the data, information and knowledge representations of a fact. The principle that we have "discovered" may be stated as follows. Consider a diagram of the form shown in Figure 6.6 for which the fact, "if the value of A is 'a' then the corresponding value of B is 'b'" is true, then this fact may be represented:

- as data *either* by establishing a name-population derived from the whole diagram excluding 'b', and a unique, single label named 'b', *or* by similarly excluding 'a' to establish a name-population one of whose labels is named 'a';
- as information by storing the tuple (a,b) in an A/B relation;
- as knowledge by the clause:

    C/B(x , b) ← C/A(x, a)

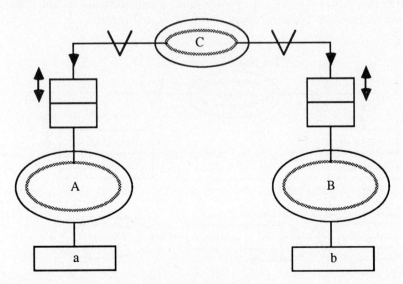

Figure 6.6 Generalization of "interest rate" example

We have just seen how a B-R diagram for a fact can be interpreted in three different ways thereby classifying the fact as data, information and knowledge respectively. It is interesting to see that this classification can be pre-empted by considering three different representations of a sample fact in the language of the application model. These are respectively:

it is likely that [['account-interest-rate' **such that** (the account has
('account-type' = 'savings'))] = '5%']
if 'account-type' = 'savings' **then**
it is likely that ['account-interest-rate' = '5%']
if an account has ('account-type' = 'savings') **then**
it is likely that [that account has ('account-interest-rate' = '5%')]

It is not difficult to see that we have found an example of a rule for manipulating statements in the language of the application model. This rule will convert a statement which pre-empts one of the three different classifications (i.e., data, information and knowledge) to a statement which pre-empts another classification. We will not pursue this here, although this clearly poses the interesting problem of finding an abstraction of the language of the application model which is invariant under the action of such manipulation rules.

As another example, consider the sample fact, "workers are supervised by the manager of the department in which they work". The information in this fact could be represented as the diagram shown in Figure 6.7. Note that this diagram is of the general form just described. Thus, suppose the second sample fact, "The Hardware Department is managed by Jones" is true. Then this second fact may be represented:

•   as data *either* by establishing a name-population "The Hardware Department Manager" whose only label is "Jones", *or* by establishing a name-population "The Departments which are managed by Jones" one of whose labels is "Hardware".

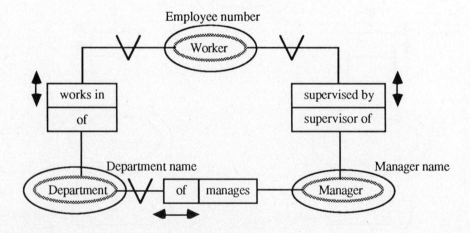

Figure 6.7 Information in "supervision" example

- as information by inserting the tuple ('hardware', 'Jones') in a relation:

  Department/Manager(. . . , . . .)

- as knowledge by the clause:

  Employee/Supervisor(x, 'Jones') ← Employee/Department(x, 'Hardware')

The sample fact "workers are supervised by the managers of the department in which they work" also contains some knowledge. This knowledge may be represented on the diagram shown in Figure 6.7 by noting that the diagram is "commutative". A *commutative diagram* is one in which if there are two "information dependency" paths from one node to another, then following either path for any particular initial object leads to the same object at the end of the path. In this example, if we follow the dependencies from worker to manager by the two different routes we arrive at the *same* particular manager for any particular worker. The commutativity of this diagram may be represented by the following "if and only if" statement:

$$\text{Employee/Supervisor}(x, y) \leftrightarrow \text{Employee/Department}(x, z),$$
$$\text{Department/Manager}(z, y)$$

The "if" part of this statement could be represented by the heavy arrows on the diagram shown in Figure 6.8.

6.5 THE INDIVIDUAL REQUIREMENTS

Any individual fact that is gathered will be phrased in the language of the application model, but is also required to satisfy the "individual requirements". The *individual*

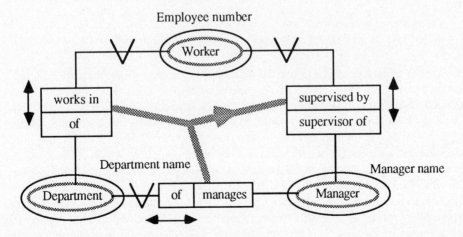

Figure 6.8 Knowledge in "supervision" example

requirements are the "uniqueness requirement", the "type identification requirement" and the "atomic requirement". The individual requirements apply equally to statements which are destined to become either data, information or knowledge. The uniqueness requirement is concerned with the clarification of the *wording* of a fact. The type identification requirement is concerned with the clarification of the *structure* of the data in a fact. The atomic requirement is concerned with the scope of the *meaning* of a fact.

The *uniqueness requirement* is concerned with the standardization of jargon. This requirement insists that the words, phrases and technical jargon used should be correct and that there should be no "duplication of reference". By "duplication of reference", we mean that each word and phrase in the application model should refer to, at most, one thing of interest in the application, and each thing of interest in the application should be referred to by, at most, one phrase. This applies both to words, phrases and technical jargon used to describe objects in the application and to words, phrases and technical jargon used to describe processes in the application. Thus, the uniqueness requirement essentially insists that the normal form principle D.1 is observed. For example, if the new fact "the Managing Director is the owner of the company" is presented, the analyst should first confirm that this statement asserts that the "Managing Director" and the "owner" are one and the same person. If it does, then the analyst should enquire as to whether this fact was going to be true for the foreseeable future. In other words, the analyst will enquire whether this fact is a *general rule* that should hold "for all time". If it is, then the analyst should enquire whether it is necessary to refer to both the "Managing Director" and the "owner" in the discourse with the domain expert; perhaps some elided form such as "MD/owner" might be acceptable. As another example, we have already discussed the ambiguity in "savings accounts" which could refer to an individual object in a set of objects called "account types", or it could refer to the "set of all accounts which are savings accounts". We avoid this ambiguity by rejecting the phrase "savings accounts" and using instead the predicate "is-a[savings-account](...)" which is satisfied by the set of all numbers which are the numbers of savings accounts, and "savings-account-type" which represents the object. Note that these two forms may be linked by the if and only if statement:

$$\text{is-a[savings-account]}(x) \leftrightarrow$$
$$\text{account/account-type}(x , \text{`savings-account-type'})$$

An example of jargon used to describe a process is the use of the phrases "crate up", "prepare for dispatch" and "parcel" to describe what happens to goods after they have been delivered to the Dispatch Department and before they have actually been dispatched.

Part of the uniqueness requirement, as stated above, insists that the words, phrases and technical jargon used should be *correct*. One common situation in which the words used can often be incorrect occurs when dealing with populations which contain just one label. For example, suppose that there is a name-population "managing-director-name" with which the single label "Mr Boss" is associated. Suppose the expert enunciates that "Mr Boss is responsible for organizing the Christmas party". Is this correct? Does the responsibility for organizing the Christmas party lie with "Mr Boss" or with "the person who is managing director"? If it is the latter, then the fact should be rephrased as, "the managing director is responsible for organizing the Christmas party". The analyst should be ever vigilant to watch out for facts which contain a label which is the only label in a single-label population.

The *type identification requirement* is concerned with the development of the data dictionary including a type hierarchy. This requirement insists that all phrases referring to fundamental, indivisible objects in the application should be identified as such, and should be recorded as either a population or a label in a data dictionary which supports a type hierarchy. Each new label will be attached to any name-population of which it is a member. For each new thing-population the identifying name-population will be recorded, and any sub-type or super-type relationships between it and other thing-populations will be recorded in the type hierarchy. The type identification requirement insists that the data in the application should be accurately identified; the analyst will classify each fundamental, indivisible object as either a population name, a label name or both. If a fundamental, indivisible object can be classified as both a population name and a label name, then to satisfy the uniqueness requirement, that object will be given two separate names, one for the population name and one for the label name.

In a sense, the type identification requirement forces the knowledge analyst to take a "top down" approach to the analysis of data during knowledge acquisition. That is, the analyst should be persistently checking the extent to which each real concept in the presented facts should be decomposed. It is important that the analyst should not try to impose preconceived ideas on the extent of this decomposition. For example, the phrase, "the interest rate on bank savings accounts" might refer to a fundamental, indivisible, real object in the mind of a domain expert who works as the financial controller in a building society. One of the market variables that this financial controller observes could well be, "the interest rate on bank savings accounts". On the other hand, this same phrase extracted from the mind of a banker whose bank issues savings accounts, as well as other forms of accounts, could be decomposed into two indivisible objects, namely "interest rate" and "savings account". The strategy that we prescribe is for the analyst *to decompose concepts as much as is necessary and no more*. Where by "necessary" we mean that the decomposition should prove, in the context of the application, to be sufficient for the foreseeable future. As another example, suppose that the thing-population "employee" with identifying population "employee name" has already been introduced. Suppose a new fact refers to the "Managing Director" who happens to be called Mr Boss. Then the analyst might enquire whether "Mr Boss, M.D." counts as an employee, and, if so, the label "Mr Boss, M.D." should be noted as a *member* of the population of employee names. Developing the same example, suppose that another new fact establishes the existence of the thing-population "engineers" with identifying population "engineers' names". Then the analyst might enquire whether the engineers' names referred to are all employee names, and, if so, the population engineers should be noted as a subtype of the population employees. We will discuss a strategy for directing the analyst's question sequence in the next section.

The *atomic requirement* insists that the fact is "atomic". An *atomic fact* is one which contains at most a single functional association and can be expressed as a statement in the language of the application model. Alternatively, we could define an atomic fact as one which *can be interpreted* as having one of the following forms:

1. The definition of a new population:

E.g. "We are interested in part numbers" or "The day of the week is of fundamental importance."

2. The specification of a constraint on a known name-population:
   E.g. "Part numbers all lie between 100 and 999."

3. The identification of a label for a known name-population:
   E.g. "456 is a valid part number" or "Today's date is August 8, 1988."

4. The definition of a relation for two or more populations:
   E.g. "The cost of a spare part may be determined by knowing its spare part number."

5. The specification of a constraint on a known relation:
   E.g. "The cost of any spare part is greater than $1 and less than $100." or "The cost of any spare part will never change by more than 20 percent."

6. The identification of a tuple for a known relation:
   E.g. "The cost of spare part number 456 is $23."

7. The definition of a group (which may be modal) for two or more populations and/or relations:
   E.g. "The selling price for a spare part item is determined by the cost price of that item, the customer discount rate and, if appropriate, a factor for slow moving stock", *or* "The likelihood of rain can be deduced from the extent of the cloud cover and the previous day's rainfall."

8. The specification of a constraint on a known group:
   E.g. "The selling price of a spare parts item will always depend on the cost price of that item."

9. The identification of a clause (which may be modal) for a known group:

   E.g. "The selling price for fast moving spare part items is the cost price of that item plus 35 percent, and then less the customer discount rate", or "Rain is likely if cloud cover is greater than 70 percent and yesterday's rainfall was greater than 0.5 cm."

In the alternative longer definition of an atomic fact which has just been quoted, we have used the adjective "known", for example in "known population". By "known" we mean that the population, or whatever, has already been defined; in particular, a "known population" will have been recorded in the data dictionary and, if it is a thing-population, entered in the type hierarchy. Note that the examples given in the above definition are examples of facts that *could be interpreted* as having the form that they illustrate. In addition, many of these examples could, in fact, illustrate more than one of the nine forms quoted. Note that the description of a sub-type relationship between two known thing-populations is not an atomic fact. In a sense, sub-type relationships are knowledge. For example, suppose that two thing-populations "employees" and "engineers" have been defined, and that the statement is made that "all engineers are employees", then this establishes a sub-type relationship between the two thing-populations "employees" and "engineers". This sub-type relationship could be expressed as the clause:

   is-a[employee](x) ← is-a[engineer](x)

and hence thought of as an explicit functional association; in other words, it is knowledge.

Note that the definition of an atomic fact excludes facts which contain explicit functional associations and which cannot be represented in the language of the application model as a statement with the basic Horn clause structure. For example, statements containing "nots" or "ors" may well be excluded. As we have already noted, we consider statements which cannot be expressed as either Horn clauses or modal clauses as lying beyond the scope of this discussion. Also note that the satisfaction of the atomic requirement requires both that the sample fact be expressible as a statement in the language of the application model and that the fact be classifiable as a member of one of the nine categories listed. The second requirement may appear to be more strict than the first but it is important to realize that these two requirements are both necessary. To see this, note that constraints (see categories 2, 5 and 8) are only required to be expressible in the language of the application model. The first requirement draws the analyst's attention to the logical and modal structure of the fact. The second requirement draws the analyst's attention to the functional associations, if any, and hence to the suitability of the fact for representation. The reason that we have stated these two requirements separately is that the first requirement is quite independent of the choice of formalism for representing the facts, whereas the second requirement is intentionally concerned with ensuring that each fact may be phrased naturally in either our chosen data, information or knowledge language. If other languages are to be used then the nine conditions in the definition of the atomic requirement should be rephrased accordingly.

In contrast with an atomic fact, a *divisible fact* is one that contains two or more atomic facts. Recall that all facts will have satisfied both the uniqueness requirement and the type identification requirement, and thus the data (i.e. the populations and labels) will have been identified. This greatly simplifies the business of checking that the atomic requirement is satisfied. For example, consider the given fact, "#234 is a spare part number; these are the part numbers which lie between #100 and #999". Suppose that in the satisfaction of the uniqueness and type identification requirements for this and previously presented facts, the following decisions have been made:

- "parts" is a thing-population;
- "part number" is the identifying population of the population "parts";
- "spare parts" is a thing-population;
- "spare part number" is the identifying population for the population "spare parts";
- #234 is a label which belongs to the population "part number".

The given fact is required to satisfy the atomic requirement, so we now identify the following functional association and the two following constraints as three atomic facts:

- #234 belongs to the population "spare part number";
- all spare part numbers are greater than or equal to 100;
- all spare part numbers are less than or equal to 999.

Thus, we see that the given fact is a divisible fact comprising three atomic facts; in addition, the given fact establishes the sub-type relation between the populations "spare parts" and "parts".

During knowledge acquisition newly gathered facts are yet to be classified as knowledge, information or data so the atomic requirement may seem premature. On the contrary, the atomic requirement attempts to detect divisible facts before the classification stage because if this can be achieved, then it will greatly assist in the satisfaction of the principle of "each real object being represented in one place and in one place only". The essence of the atomic requirement is that a fact should contain at most one functional association. In addition, satisfaction of the atomic requirement can help to reduce the amount of reinterviewing of the domain expert and so it should help to reduce the amount of work on subsequent visits to the knowledge acquisition phase.

Satisfaction of the atomic requirement entails that either the sample fact be a constraint or that the sample fact both be expressible as a statement in the language of the application model and contain precisely one functional association. In our experience, these requirements do not constitute any real restriction. Consider the requirement which insists that the sample fact be representable as a statement in the language of the application model. A statement in the language of the application model will either be a simple statement or a compound statement. If the sample fact can be represented as a simple statement, then this is equivalent to satisfying requirements 1, 3, 4 or 6 in the definition of an atomic fact. If the sample fact can be represented as a compound statement, then this will restrict the syntax in which statements of forms 2, 5, 7, 8 and 9, in the definition of an atomic fact, can be expressed. In the alternative form of the definition of an atomic fact, note the wording ". . . that *can* be interpreted . . .". As we shall see, this preliminary classification is of great assistance in guiding the knowledge elicitation process. We stress that this preliminary classification should not in any way influence the final classification of objects; this takes place during the following phase, namely, knowledge analysis.

The definition of an atomic fact refers to facts which "can be interpreted" as "the specification of a constraint". In practice, when facts are presented it is often not possible to decide whether they will be classified eventually as constraints or as knowledge. We will see later that this decision is often made in the fourth phase, namely "knowledge implementation". Thus, as far as knowledge acquisition is concerned, it is simpler not to refer to constraints explicitly, and to tentatively view any fact, which could be seen as a potential constraint, as knowledge.

The satisfaction of the individual requirements, in particular the type identification requirement, will have identified labels and populations and thus will have identified those facts which are destined to become data. It is, however, premature to conclude that the remaining facts will have been classified as information or knowledge. It is also undesirable for the analyst to even contemplate this as, during knowledge acquisition, the analyst should concentrate on the data and on getting the data correct. However, one useful division of facts can be made. Some facts will have the property that they can be interpreted as having form 1, 4 or 7 in the definition of an atomic fact; such a fact is called a *general fact* or *GEF*. Other facts will not have this property, such a fact is called a *particular fact* or *PAF*. It is interesting to note that, if the uniqueness requirement and the type identification requirement have not been satisfied, then a real fact can give rise to both a GEF and a PAF. For example, in the fact "this bank has savings accounts" the phrase "savings accounts" could be interpreted as a thing-population with identifying population "account number" whose labels would be identifiers for each savings account. Alternatively, "savings account" could be a label name belonging to the name-population of "account types". It will be the analyst's job to distinguish between these interpretations and to remove any ambiguity in the context of the application, and to ensure that the data dictionary reflects unambiguously these different interpretations. Examples of GEFs could be "The number of shopping days to Christmas is important", "Mark-up rate for an item is determined solely by whether the item type is classified slow, medium or fast moving stock" and "The selling price for an item is determined by knowing the mark-up rate for that item, the customer discount rate and the tax rate applicable to that item". Examples of PAFs could be "Today's date is 8-8-88", "Mark-up rate for hardware items is 20 percent." and "Workers are supervised by the managers of the departments in which they work".

The analyst will attempt to gather facts which satisfy the three individual requirements described above. It is important to realize that the satisfaction of these three requirements should result in "useful pre-processing" of the facts. The satisfaction of the individual requirements is not absolutely essential to the final generation of a good system, but it should make the process of system generation more efficient. In particular, if the data has not been identified correctly, as required by the type identification requirement during knowledge acquisition, then this can lead to extensive and expensive reanalysis later on.

6.6 KNOWLEDGE ELICITATION

Thus far we have discussed the acquisition and representation of single facts in the language of the application model. During this operation, the analyst should have meticulously dissected the components of each fact when identifying the data in that fact. We have not yet addressed the issue of how the analyst should systematically lead the domain expert to enunciate atomic facts and then to develop these facts in an orderly and directed sequence. The technique for doing this is called *knowledge elicitation*.

Knowledge acquisition in general which includes knowledge elicitation in particular, is a procedure that is performed by the analyst "on the fly". Knowledge acquisition should make efficient use of the domain expert's time. The procedure that we describe for knowledge elicitation is simple and directed. The procedure gives the analyst some simple tools that enable knowledge to be gathered in a uniform way so this procedure is suitable for team work. In our view, knowledge elicitation should proceed at a reasonable pace to prevent the expert (and the analyst) from becoming bored and losing concentration. Thus, knowledge elicitation is not a procedure which permits a thorough analysis of what is going on; the domain expert's time is usually too precious for that. Our strategy is to gather as much knowledge as we can in a sufficiently ordered way for it to form useful "blocks", in the time available.

Suppose that the domain expert has just enunciated the sample fact "the interest rate on savings accounts is likely to be 5 percent"; what should the analyst do next? There are many choices as this fact has established directly, or by implication, a number of concepts including: accounts, account-type, savings, interest, interest-rate and the value 5 percent. Having ascertained that this fact satisfied the individual requirements, the analyst could ask any of the following questions:

• what other things are there of interest beside accounts?

- what other things are associated with accounts beside "account type" and "interest rate"?
- what other sorts of accounts are there beside "savings accounts"?
- what other interest rates apply beside 5 percent?
- are the concepts "account type" or "interest rate" associated with any other things beside accounts?
- is "savings" associated with anything other than an account, as in a "savings account"?
- is 5 percent associated with anything other than the interest rate on savings accounts?

It is easy to see that any of these questions could lead the discussion well away from the context of the fact under consideration. Our approach to knowledge elicitation determines a specific sequence of questions which the analyst should ask. It is interesting to note that this sequence is quite independent of whether the fact will eventually be classified as data, information or knowledge. It is also interesting to note that this sequence of questions should prevent the discussion from moving away from the fact under consideration until the whole context surrounding that fact has been gleaned.

When checking that a sample fact satisfies the atomic requirement, the analyst may form a tentative, or subconscious, view as to how that fact could be classified. No matter whether this view classifies the sample fact as data, information or knowledge, the fact, "the interest rate on savings accounts is likely to be 5 percent" is basically about a functional association between "an account of type savings" and "an interest rate of value 5 percent". This is shown in Figure 6.9. The analyst should first confirm that this functional association is well defined by asking "Do you mean that for *all* savings accounts the interest rate is likely to be 5 percent?". Assuming that the answer is affirmative, the analyst now knows that all accounts of type savings are likely to have an interest rate of 5 percent; in other words, the functional association recorded is "well defined".

In the next step, the analyst decides whether the fact is a GEF or a PAF. Note that it cannot be interpreted as both because such ambiguities have been removed in the satisfaction of the individual requirements by the identification of the populations and the establishment of the data dictionary.

If the analyst regards a fact as a GEF, then the fact is recorded. In particular, if the GEF is the definition of a new thing-population, then the analyst should immediately inquire what the identifying name-population is. No matter what the GEF states, the analyst should then attempt to identify sufficient PAFs to fully define that GEF. We might describe this process as *particularization*. When the analyst is advised that sufficient PAFs have been presented to specify the given GEF fully, then the GEF is called a *complete GEF*.

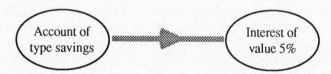

Figure 6.9 A functional association

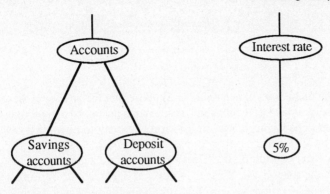

Figure 6.10 Segments of type hierarchy

If the analyst regards a fact as a PAF, then the fact is recorded and the analyst will then attempt to "generalize" the PAF as we now describe. The *generalization* of a PAF is a particular GEF to which the given PAF belongs. To illustrate "generalization" we consider the business of generalizing the fact, "The interest rate on savings accounts is likely to be 5 percent". Suppose that "savings accounts" is interpreted as a label and that the fact is seen as being of class 6 in the definition of an atomic fact; that is, the fact is a PAF. As we have seen, a crude analysis of this fact is as a premise "account of type savings" and a likely conclusion "interest of value 5 percent". To generalize this PAF we generalize these two items; to do this we need to know what is "particular" about these items as they are. In this example, it seems reasonable to suspect that what is particular about the premise is that the account is a *savings* account, and what is particular about the conclusion is that the interest rate is *5 percent*. However, some of this information may already be recorded in the type hierarchy. Suppose that segments of the type hierarchy are as shown in Figure 6.10.

Then, to generalize the given functional association between "savings accounts" and "5 percent", the analyst will look for associations, first, between all associated concepts and second, between the immediately superior concepts in the type hierarchy. Thus, the next two questions should be, "Do all deposit accounts have a certain interest rate?" and

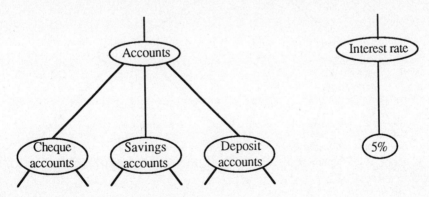

Figure 6.11 Segments of type hierarchy

Figure 6.12 Example of a GEF

"Are there any other sorts of accounts?". Suppose that the answer to these questions are, "Yes, it is likely to be 4 percent" and "Yes, cheque accounts", respectively. The analyst will then enter "cheque accounts" in the type hierarchy to obtain the diagram shown in Figure 6.11.

Next the analyst should ask, "Do all cheque accounts have a certain interest rate?". Suppose that the answer is, "Yes, it is fixed at 3 percent". The analyst should now confirm these observations by checking the immediately superior concept in the type hierarchy; the analyst should ask, "So all accounts have an interest rate of some value associated with them?". Suppose that the answer is "Yes", then the GEF shown in Figure 6.12 is the generalization of the original PAF because it is "just superior" to the original PAF in the type hierarchy.

The analyst may consider it prudent to develop this generalization process further. To do this, the analyst should focus on the "conclusion" of this newly found GEF and should ask, "Are there any other objects which have an interest rate?". Suppose that the answer is, "Yes, fixed bonds attract 7 percent interest.". Once again the analyst should inspect the type hierarchy, it is as shown in Figure 6.13.

The next two questions should be, "Do all variable bonds have an interest rate?" and "Are there any other objects which have an interest rate?". Suppose that the answer to these questions is, "Yes, 6 percent." and "No, that is all.". By now, the analyst has identified two more GEFs making three in total; these are shown in Figure 6.14. The analyst should confirm that these are correct. This completes the description of our technique for generalizing a PAF to its natural GEF. Having constructed this GEF, the analyst should then check that it is complete in the sense described earlier.

By this stage in the knowledge elicitation process we have theoretically obtained a

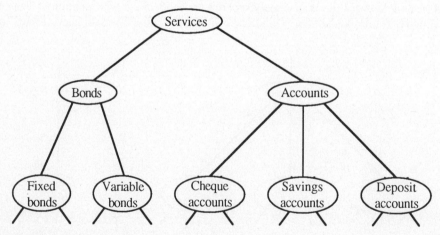

Figure 6.13 Segment of type hierarchy

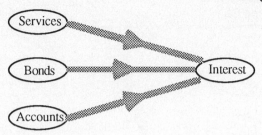

Figure 6.14 The three GEFs identified

complete GEF. In practice, the GEF may well be incomplete. This hopefully complete GEF has either been constructed by completing a given GEF or by generalizing and completing a given PAF. Also note that the construction of a GEF by the process of generalization depends on the state of the type hierarchy. If the type hierarchy contains omissions, then the GEF constructed may be "too high up" the type hierarchy; this should not be a matter of great concern.

Suppose that we have a GEF, the general idea is now to try to extract any knowledge from the domain expert that would enable us to calculate, or deduce, the PAFs in this GEF *from* other facts. For example, suppose that we have the complete GEF referred to above, "The type of an account determines the interest rate on that account". Associated with this GEF, we have the three PAFs, "account of type savings is likely to have an interest rate of 5 percent", "account of type cheque has an interest rate of 3 percent" and "account of type deposit is likely to have an interest rate of 4 percent". It is quite reasonable to think of this GEF as information, that is, this GEF could be represented by a relation in which the three PAFs could then be represented. The next question for this example should be, "Can the interest rate on the various account types be deduced from anything else?". If the analyst is told that, "No, the interest rates are set by the chief manager each morning and sometimes fluctuate from day to day with the chief manager's mood", then this line of questioning can be abandoned, unless it is considered relevant to investigate the chief manager's moods. However, if the analyst is told that, "The interest rate for each account type can be derived from a formula based on the security factor of the account type and the base interest rate", then the analyst has discovered two new objects "base interest rate" and "security factor" as well as a new functional association between "base interest rate", "security factor" and "interest rate". The analyst has also discovered a new GEF linking these together. It may be represented by the heavy arrow on the diagram as shown in Figure 6.15. This new functional association must be subjected to the basic test to determine whether it is well defined. Thus, the analyst should ask, "Do you mean that the interest rate associated with *all* account types can be deduced from the security factor associated with the account and the base interest rate?". If the answer is affirmative, the analyst will either abandon this line of questioning, or seek other ways in which the relation account-type/interest-rate could be deduced from the contents of other relations. Note that once again our strategy is to seek more facts by working back from the conclusion of a given functional association. This strategy helps to prevent the question sequence from drifting aimlessly away from incomplete "bundles" of facts.

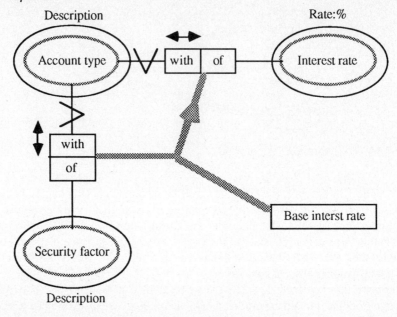

Figure 6.15 New GEF in "interest rate" example

Our method has brought us a long way from the original fact, "The interest rate on savings accounts is likely to be 5 percent". We summarize the method so far. Given a fact:

1. Confirm that it satisfies the individual requirements; if it fails to satisfy these requirements then it should be rejected and reconstructed.
2. Confirm that any functional association in the fact is well defined.
3. Note whether the fact is a PAF or a GEF.
4.1 If the fact is a GEF and, in particular, defines a new thing-population, then find the identifying name-population; then, no matter what form the GEF has, complete it.
4.2 If the fact is a PAF, then construct the natural GEF to which it belongs and complete this GEF. Note that all new facts introduced in this step or elsewhere must satisfy the individual requirements.
5. Then the analyst looks for knowledge which enables the PAFs in this GEF to be deduced from other facts.
6. The analyst attempts to associate the complete GEF just constructed by looking for other GEFs which have the same "conclusion" as the given GEF.

In short, this procedure has led us from a single fact to a set of statements; this set of statements is called a *bundle* generated by the original fact. Note the conservative, introverted nature of the strategy which continues to seek facts which lead "into" and not "away from" the initial fact. Thus, the strategy seeks to find out all it can about one thing before moving on to another. This should help to minimize unnecessary to-ing and fro-ing.

As a means of remembering this method, the following may be useful:

For any fact presented:

- *Check* that it satisfies the individual requirements.
- *Confirm* that any functional association in the fact is well defined.
- *Classify* it as a PAF or a GEF.

Given a GEF:

- *Identify* the name-population of a new thing-population.
- *Complete* that GEF.

Given a PAF:

- *Explore* other similar PAFs.
- *Generalize* to a complete GEF.

Given a complete GEF, note its "premise" and "conclusion":

- *Deduce* the PAFs in this GEF from knowledge involving other GEFs.
- *Associate* this given GEF with other GEFs whose "conclusions" are either the "premise" or the "conclusion" of this given GEF.

Having constructed a (hopefully) complete bundle by following the above method, what should the analyst do next? This will depend on the purpose of the inquiry. After all, the analyst may be pursuing a long chain of reasoning to unravel the way in which the domain expert comes to some complex conclusion. In which case, the analyst will be guided to a great extent by an understanding of the logical structure which supports this complex conclusion. On the other hand, the analyst may simply be "fishing for facts" and attempting to build up a picture of the domain expert's world. In which case, the analyst should then focus on any new functional associations discovered during the "deduce" and "associate" steps in the above method and should explore associations between them and other functional associations, and so on, and so on. One major concern of any approach to knowledge elicitation is that the same fact may be gathered, recorded and represented in the system more than once. This can be dangerous if one of the representations of such a fact is changed later. However, note that the chances of this happening should be substantially reduced by the development and maintenance of the data dictionary and the type hierarchy. When a new fact is presented, the data in it will be compared with, and checked against, the data in the data dictionary. If duplications are not recognized at this stage, then they should be detected when an attempt is made to enter the data in the type hierarchy. Once duplications in the data have been correctly identified, duplications in any information or knowledge built with that data should be easy to determine.

The description of our approach to knowledge elicitation may seem simple; it is intended to be. In our view the knowledge elicitation procedure should restrict the style of the analyst as little as possible, while trying to satisfy the goals of being a procedure which:

- gathers knowledge in a uniform way that is suitable for team work;
- gathers knowledge quickly and without fuss, thus respecting the domain expert's time;
- groups the gathered knowledge into small blocks which will be useful in the system building process;
- gathers knowledge in such a way that the gathered knowledge can realistically be described as "complete";
- gathers knowledge in a way that is quite comprehensible to the the domain expert;
- may be performed "on the fly" and will not intrude unnecessarily on the interview.

6.6.1 Worked example

We now illustrate our approach to knowledge elicitation by considering a worked example. In this worked example we assume that our analyst has been sent to an organization called Egs P/L to investigate the organizational structure and the salary structure of this business. This worked example will also be used in the four following chapters to illustrate the following four phases of our approach; these are, knowledge analysis, knowledge base engineering, knowledge base implementation and knowledge base maintenance. In this chapter the worked example is used to illustrate knowledge acquisition. When the knowledge acquisition phase is complete, the application model has been developed and is ready for knowledge analysis which is discussed in the next chapter.

It is suggested that the reader should maintain a piece of notepaper on which the present state of the data dictionary and type hierarchy should be developed as this section is read. Remember that the analyst should be continually referring to these two structures. We have tried to keep our approach independent of any particular approach to information analysis. However, if the reader is proficient in some information analysis technique, then the reader may wish to develop a rough information model using that technique while reading this section. When working through the following case study, the important thing to note is that the question sequence follows a rigidly defined pattern which systematically extracts the facts from the domain expert.

In what follows we will adopt the convention that, in the satisfaction of the atomic requirement, objects that are interpreted as populations will be written entirely in lower case characters, and objects that are interpreted as labels will have a name beginning with an upper case character.

Before any interviews begin, we presume that the analyst has decided that:

1.1 There are businesses (1).
1.2 Businesses are identified by a business-name (1).
1.3 "Egs P/L" is the name of a business (3).

where we have annotated each fact with the number of the form, written in parentheses, that it has been interpreted as having in the satisfaction of the atomic requirement. Thus, the analyst attempts to complete the GEF in 1.1 and 1.2, and asks, "As far as this investigation is concerned, are there any other businesses that are to be considered in addition to Egs P/L?". The answer is "No".

1.4   Egs P/L is the only business name (2).

Thus, the analyst now identifies the above statements as bundle [1]. There is no "premise" or "conclusion" in this GEF, so the analyst adds "business", "business-name" and "Egs P/L" to the data dictionary and moves on.

The analyst then moves towards the task at hand which clearly involves people. (Note: from here on we identify the analyst's questions with a "[Q]" and the replies with an "[A]".) [Q] "Would it be appropriate to refer to all people who work at Egs P/L as 'persons'?", [A] "Yes".

2.1   There are persons (1).

[Q] "How are persons identified?", [A] "By their unique name. If we have two people with the same real name, we add something to one of the names so that it is unique."

2.2   Each person is identified by a unique person-name (1).

The analyst now tries to complete this GEF, [Q] "Where can I find a complete list of person names?", [A] "In the file marked 'personnel file'."

2.3   The "personnel file" contains all person-names (3).

Once again there is no premise or conclusion in this GEF, the analyst adds "persons", "person-name" and the persons listed in the personnel file to the data dictionary and moves on. Each new thing-population, name-population and the corresponding labels are always entered into the data dictionary; thus, for brevity, we will not mention the details of these entries from here on.

3.1   Persons work at businesses (4).
3.2   All persons work at the business named Egs P/L (5).

As this GEF refers to all persons and to one business, Egs P/L, there is really nothing to complete.

The analyst now moves towards the first subject of the investigation, namely "organizational structure". [Q] "How are persons at Egs P/L organized?", [A] "Into three classes. Mr Boss, the General Manager, is said to have class 1, Tom Jones, Mary Smith, Peter Clark and Mary Hughes all have class 2 and the rest have class 3". A lot of information is contained here. For want of a better strategy, the analyst focuses on the first new concept in this fact namely "class". [Q] "The classes are identified by a class-number?", [A] "Yes", [Q] "How many class numbers are there?", [A] "Just 1, 2 and 3".

4.1   There are classes (1).
4.2   Classes are identified by a class-number (1).
4.3   1, 2 and 3 are the only class numbers (3).
5.1   Persons have a class (4).
5.2   Each person has exactly one class (5).

[Q] "How can I find a complete list of the class for each person?", [A] "From the personnel file".

5.3   The personnel file contains the class number for each person (6).

[Q] "Is there any way that I can deduce a person's class from other information?", [A] "No". (Note that this is an error; in fact, as we will see, a person's class can be deduced from the name of the job that the person has. This error will be corrected during information analysis; it has been deliberately included here to show that the knowledge acquisition process can tolerate errors without jeopardizing the quality of the final system.) Next, the analyst takes up the PAF, "there is a General Manager" and tries to generalize it, [Q] "There is a General-Manager, are there other jobs and, if so, what are the job-names?", [A] "General Manager, Department Manager and Worker".

6.1   There are jobs (1).
6.2   Jobs are identified by a job-name (1).
6.3   "General-Manager", "Department-Manager" and "Worker" are the only job names (3).

Next, the analyst takes up the PAF "Mr Boss is the General-Manager" and tries to generalize it, [Q] "At Egs P/L all persons have just one job?", [A] "Yes, each person holds just one job."

7.1   Persons have jobs (4).
7.2   Each person has exactly one job (5).

[Q] "How can I find out which job each person has?", [A] "In the personnel file".

7.3   The personnel file contains the job-name for each person (6).

This GEF has premise "person" and conclusion "job"; thus, the analyst proceeds, [Q] "Given a person, is there any other information that would enable me to work out which job that person has?", [A] "At present you could work out a person's job if you knew their salary." (Note: As we will see later, this answer is incomplete as the job-name can always be deduced from the class-number. In fact, this is another deliberate error which has been included for the same reason as the error referred to above.) [Q] "Will that always be true?", [A] "Not necessarily". Thus, the analyst ignores any possible functional association between "salary" and "job".

The analyst has just investigated the organization of the persons at Egs P/L, and now decides to investigate the organization of Egs P/L itself. [Q] "How is Egs P/L itself organized?", [A] "All employees are assigned to a unique department." [Q] "Do you mean, all *persons* are assigned to a unique department?", [A] "No, Mr Boss the General Manager is not assigned to a department." [Q] "Are all persons other than the General Manager referred to as employees?", [A] "Yes". (Note that the analyst has been careful to check that the truth of this fact is not related to the particular label "Mr Boss", but instead to the population "General Manager" to which this single label belongs.) This has introduced a new sub-population "employees".

8.1   There are employees (1).

8.2   The employees are the persons listed in the personnel file excluding the particular person whose job is General-Manager (3).

8.3   All employees are persons (7).

This GEF establishes that employees are a sub-type of persons. The conclusion of this GEF is "persons" which consists of everybody in the application, thus the analyst decides not to pursue this conclusion, but asks [Q] "How can I deduce if somebody is an employee?", [A] "If they are class 2 or 3", which adds nothing and this line of questioning is abandoned. Now, the analyst is in a position to pursue the organizational structure of Egs P/L as introduced above.

9.1   There are departments (1).

[Q] "How are the departments identified?", [A] "Each of the four departments has a unique department name", [Q] "What are the names of the departments?", [A] "They are shown on the organization chart."

9.2   Each department is identified by a unique department-name (1).

9.3   The organization chart contains all the department names (3).

9.4   There are four department-names (2).

10.1   Employees are assigned to departments (4).

[Q] "Is each employee assigned to one particular department?", [A] "Yes".

10.2   Each employee is assigned to one particular department (5).

[Q] "How can I find out which department each employee is assigned to?", [A] "From the organization chart".

10.3   The organization chart shows a department for each employee (6).

[Q] "Is there any way I can deduce which department an employee is assigned to?", [A] "Yes, by knowing the employee's "supervisor", but we haven't talked about supervisors yet", [Q] "We'll come back to supervisors later; how are the departments organized?", [A] "Each department has a unique department manager."

11.1   Departments have department-managers (4).

11.2   Each department has a unique department-manager (5).

[Q] "How can I find out the name of the department manager for each department?", [A] "From the organization chart".

11.3   The organization chart contains the name of the department-manager for each department (6).

[Q] "Is there any other way that I can deduce the name of the department manager in a given department?" [A] "The department manager will be the supervisor of the workers in that department; also, the department manager is the only class 2 person in a department". Before dealing with this new concept of "supervisor" the analyst should note that sentence 11.1 has been interpreted as type (4) in the satisfaction of the atomic requirement; this sentence represents a functional association between "departments", which is in the data dictionary (see 9.1), and "department-managers", which is not in the data dictionary. Note that atomic requirement 4 requires that the populations involved be "known". Thus, the analyst now notes that:

12.1   There are department-managers (1).
12.2   Department-managers are employees (7).
12.3   The department-managers are the class 2 persons listed in the personnel file (3).

Before analysing the "supervise" association we interrupt the interview and display the contents of the data dictionary and type hierarchy developed so far. The present state of the type hierarchy is, of course, in front of the analyst during the whole knowledge acquisition process. We hope that the reader has developed a version of the type hierarchy while reading this section and that the reader's version is essentially the same as ours! Our type hierarchy is as shown in Figure 6.16, where:

- "bus" are the businesses (1.1).
- "pers" are the persons (2.1).
- "emp" are the employees (8.1).
- "mngr" are the department managers (12.1).
- "class" are the employee classes (4.1).
- "dept" are the departments (9.1).
- "job" are the jobs (6.1).

The numbers in parentheses are the numbers of the corresponding statements in the application model.

Having reviewed the present state of the type hierarchy we now return to the interview. The analyst now takes up the business of "supervisors". [Q] "So there are supervisors?", [A] "Yes, the General Manager and the Department Managers are the supervisors."

13.1   There are supervisors (1).

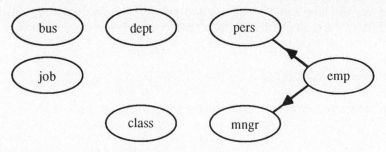

Figure 6.16 State of the type hierarchy

13.2 Supervisors are persons (7).
13.3 The supervisors are the class 1 and class 2 persons in the personnel file (3).
13.4 Department managers are supervisors (7).

[Q] "You mentioned that employees are supervised. Are all employees supervised?", [A] "Yes". [Q] "Is the General Manager supervised?", [A] "No". [Q] "Does each employee have a unique supervisor?", [A] "Yes".

14.1 Employees are supervised by supervisors (4).
14.2 Each employee has a unique supervisor (5).

[Q] "How can I find the supervisor of each employee", [A] "From the organization chart".

14.3 The organization chart contains the name of the supervisor for each employee (6).

[Q] "Is there any way that I can deduce the supervisor of an employee?", [A] "Yes, the department manager supervises the workers in that department". [Q] "So workers are supervised by the managers of the departments in which they work?", [A] "Yes". The analyst now looks for other similar PAFs. [Q] "Who supervises the other employees?", [A] "The department managers are supervised by Mr Boss". [Q] "Do you mean that the department managers are supervised by the *General Manager*?", [A] "Yes".

15.1 The supervisor of an employee may be deduced from that employee's job and that employee's department (7).
15.2 **if** an employee's job is a worker **and** if that employee works in a certain department, **then** that employee is supervised by the Department Manager of that department (9).
15.3 **if** an employee's job is a Department Manager, **then** that employee is supervised by the General Manager (9).

[Q] "Is there any other way of deducing the supervisor of a given employee", [A] "Not that I can think of". [Q] "Are there any other aspects of the organization of Egs P/L, or the persons within Egs P/L, that we have not discussed?", [A] "Not that I can think of".

The analyst now turns to the second part of the investigation, which is an investigation of the salary structure. [Q] "Is it correct to use the term "salary"?", [A] "Yes".

16.1   There are salaries (1).

[Q] "How are salaries described, in dollars per week, month or year?", [A] "In dollars per year".

16.2   Salaries are identified by a salary-rate expressed in dollars per annum (1).

[Q] "Is there a wide variety of different salaries?", [A] "No, at present there are just three salary rates $50,000, $40,000 and $30,000."

16.3 $50,000, $40,000 and $30,000 are the only salary rates (3).

[Q] "Who is paid a salary?", [A] "All persons at Egs P/L receive just one salary."

17.1   Persons receive salaries (4).
17.2   Each person receives a single salary (5).

[Q] "Where can I find the salary of each person?", [A] "In the personnel file".

17.3   The personnel file contains the salary for each person (6).

[Q] "Is there any other way that I can deduce a person's salary?", [A] "Yes, Class 1 persons receive $50,000, Class 2 persons receive $40,000 and Class 3 persons receive $30,000". [Q] "So each person's salary is determined by the person's class?", [A] "Yes". [Q] "Is the general principle of a person's salary being determined by the class of that person going to remain for the foreseeable future?", [A] "Yes".

18.1   A person's salary may be deduced from that person's class (7).
18.2   **if** a person has class 1, **then** that person receives a salary of $50,000, **and if** a person has class 2, **then** that person receives a salary of $40,000, **and if** a person has class 3, **then** that person receives a salary of $30,000 (9).
16.4   There are, at most, three different salary-rates (2).

Note that the statement 16.4 above belongs to bundle 16. [Q] "So class is clearly associated with salary?", [A] "Yes". [Q] "To each class there corresponds a unique salary?", [A] "Yes".

19.1   Class is associated with salary (4).
19.2   Each class is associated with a unique salary (5).
19.3   Class 1 is associated with $50,000, class 2 is associated with $40,000 and class 3 is associated with $30,000 (6).

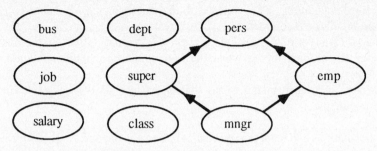

Figure 6.17 Final state of the type hierarchy

[Q] "Is there any other way that salaries could be determined other than by class?" [A] "No". (Note: as we will see later on, this is incorrect as the salary can be deduced from the job name. The important point is that this error does not jeopardize the knowledge acquisition process.) This completes the interview.

The complete type hierarchy is now as shown in Figure 6.17, where in addition to the population descriptions previously quoted we now have:

*   "super" are the supervisors (13.1).
*   "salary" are the salaries (16.1).

6.7   BUILDING THE DATA MODEL

The data dictionary and type hierarchy are developed concurrently with the business of performing knowledge acquisition. Thus, it seems logical to consider the business of building the data model as being part of the knowledge acquisition phase. The *data model* consists of:

1.   a representation of each thing-population in the application model;
2.   a representation of the identifying name-population for each thing-population in the application model;
3.   a representation of each name-population in the application model;
4.   a representation of all type-hierarchy relationships between thing-populations in the application model;
5.   a representation of all labels associated with each name-population in the application model;
6.   the specification of any population constraints for each population in the application model;
7.   the specification of any label constraints for the labels associated with each name-population in the application model;
8.   the specification of which of the labels, associated with each name-population, are to be considered "fixed" (the notion of a label being "fixed" is discussed below);
9.   the identification of any query types or update types which are directly associated with

each thing population. This is added to the data model when the knowledge base engineering phase is complete;

10. the classification of thing populations as "real", "virtual", "live" or "dormant". This is added to the data model when the knowledge base implementation phase is complete;

11. a statement of what it means to say that a certain label is associated with a given name-population;

where all populations and labels are normal as defined in Chapter 5. In 10 above we refer to "real", "virtual", "live" and "dormant" populations. Recall that populations may play a role in clause groups; for example, "tomorrow's date may be derived from today's date":

$$\text{is-the[tomorrow's-date]}(x) \leftarrow \text{is-the[today's-date]}(y), \quad x = y + 1$$

also a group may refer to the labels in any population using the "is-a" or "is-the" predicates:

$$\text{is-the[general-manager]}(x)$$

Also note that each group and each relation will either be selected to form part of the final system or they will not. If a population is in the body of one or more selected groups but is not the head of a selected group, it is called a *real population*. If a population is the head of a selected group, it is called a *virtual population*. If a population is neither real nor virtual but is a domain in a selected relation, then it is called a *live population*. If a population is not real, virtual or live it is called a *dormant population*. In other words, real populations must be physically stored in the final system, virtual populations are calculated in the final system, live populations are referred to by relations in the final system, and dormant populations have nothing to do with the final system.

The normal form principle K.1.1 distinguished between two types of label. This distinction is based on whether or not the "possibility of having to subsequently replace that particular label with another label" is "inconceivable". This distinction is important to the representation of knowledge using clauses; if a label is never going to be replaced with another, then it may be used in a clause without restriction. For example, consider the attempt to represent the knowledge "the Department Managers are those persons who are supervised by Mr Boss the General Manager":

$$\text{pers/job}(x, \text{'Department-Manager'}) \leftarrow \text{emp/super}(x, \text{'Mr-Boss'})$$

This clause contains two labels "Department-Manager" and "Mr-Boss". The first of these would only change if the title given to those who manage departments were to change or if the basic structure of the business were to change. The second label, "Mr-Boss", would change if the General Manager were to change. Thus, it might be reasonable to decide that the label "Department-Manager" was not likely to change during the life of the system, but that the label "Mr Boss", as the occupant of the position General Manager, could easily change. It is useful to formalize this distinction by nominating some labels as "fixed". A *fixed label* is a label which the analyst has decided is not likely to change during the life of the system. Thus, a fixed label may be used explicitly in clauses in the expression of knowledge, but if it should need to be replaced, then such an operation must be performed with great care. On the other hand, if a label is not nominated as fixed, then it should not occur explicitly in the expression of knowledge and can therefore be replaced as a routine matter. Thus, designating labels as "fixed" or "not fixed" is really a data constraint. However, as this distinction is often made by the analyst rather than extracted from the application model, we choose to acknowledge this distinction separately from the data constraints.

It is important to realize that, although the data model is constructed during the knowledge acquisition phase, it will usually be modified during the next, knowledge analysis, phase. In particular, the data model is frequently modified while the information model is being constructed. One way in which this can happen is when duplicate populations are identified in, and then are removed from, the information model. Thus, it is incorrect to regard the data, information and knowledge models as being fixed and independent of one another. These three models interact with each other, and are often subjected to modifications both during the initial design of the knowledge system and during the subsequent maintenance of the system throughout its operational life.

6.7.1 Worked example

For the worked example developed in the previous section, the data model would be as shown in Figure 6.18, where:

* business-name(x) means "x is the name of a business, at present Egs P/L is the only business name";
* person-name(x) means "x is the name of a person";
* class-number(x) means "x is the number of a class, at present the class numbers are 1,2 and 3";
* dept-name(x) means "x is the name of a department";
* job-name(x) means "x is the name of a job";
* salary-rate(x) means "x is a salary rate expressed in dollars per annum".

The labels and populations noted above all satisfy the normal forms for data with the possible exception of the person and department names which may contravene principle D.2. However, this should not effect the validity of the design. Note in the data model that the analyst has nominated all the labels in the populations "dept" and "job" as being fixed.

Thing-population	Bundle	Sub-type of	Name-population	Labels	Population constraints	Label constraints	Fixed labels
bus	1		business-name	Egs P/L	one label only		
pers	2		person-name	(see 2.3)	each label unique		
class	4		class-number	1,2,3	3 unique labels	= 1, 2 or 3	
super	13	pers			= class 1,2 pers		
emp	8	pers			= class 2,3 pers		
mngr	12	emp, super			= class 2 pers		
dept	9		dept-name	(see 9.3)	4 unique labels		all
job	6		job-name	(see 6.3)	3 unique labels	= GM,DM Workr	all
salary	16		salary-rate	(see 16.3)	3 labels or less	positive integer	

Figure 6.18 The data model

6.8 SUMMARY

We have seen that the application model plays a key role in the design and maintenance of a knowledge system. A stylized form of natural English has been proposed as a suitable language for the application model. We have explored the reclassification of objects once they have been represented. The three individual requirements may be thought of as a powerful filter which ensures that the facts as initially represented are in an acceptable form. We have seen how a rigorous technique for knowledge elicitation can be phrased which ensures conformity of approach to the extent that the method can be used successfully by a team of analysts.

Knowledge analysis

7.1 INTRODUCTION

In this chapter we discuss the phase of the design process that requires the most technical work by hand. The following two phases are also technical in nature but should be substantially automated; in fact, algorithms for the following two phases are quoted in their respective chapters. Application of the work in the present chapter can benefit from the assistance of a "knowledge analyst's assistant" which principally looks after the "housekeeping" during this phase; we have constructed and used a prototype "knowledge analyst's assistant" and found it to provide very valuable support in practice. A "Knowledge Analyst's Assistant" which has been designed for professional use is presently being constructed; details of this software are given in Section 10.8 of Chapter 10. Most of the work reported in this chapter is central to our argument and the reader is urged to study it carefully, the only exception being Section 7.7 which can be omitted on the first reading.

The knowledge systems design problem is concerned with the construction of a good knowledge system for a given application. Our solution to the knowledge systems design problem attempts to achieve the goal of representing each "individual thing of interest" in the application in one place and in one place only in the knowledge system. A key feature of our solution is the construction of a formal model of the application. This model is quite independent of the particular language or expert system shell that may be chosen to implement the knowledge system.

In Chapter 6 we discussed the first phase of the design process, namely "knowledge acquisition". The product of knowledge acquisition is the application model and a developed data dictionary including a type hierarchy; this is the starting point for knowledge analysis. In this chapter we discuss the second phase, namely "knowledge analysis". The knowledge analysis phase is concerned with building the information model and the knowledge model which are two separate formal models; one is of the information and the other is of the knowledge in the application. A key feature of these models is that at this stage they do not attempt to represent the tasks that the implemented system will be expected to perform. The inclusion of these tasks takes place in phase three of our procedure and will be discussed in Chapter 8. Thus, the objective of this chapter is simply to present an approach to modeling and normalizing knowledge. Our approach attempts to be compatible with established techniques for modeling information.

As we have indicated previously, the information model should be constructed before the knowledge model. We first discuss the relationship between the traditional approach to information analysis and our approach to knowledge analysis. The different ways in which a real object may be classified are discussed, and unacceptable ways are identified; this leads to a discussion of our approach to object classification. Next, the information model is constructed. Then we introduce our approach to the construction and normalization of the knowledge model; this approach assumes that the data dictionary, the type hierarchy and the information model have all been constructed. And last, an analysis of inverse associations is presented.

7.2 INFORMATION ANALYSIS AND KNOWLEDGE ANALYSIS

There is nothing new about knowledge processing as such. In rough terms, the business of programming is substantially concerned with the implementation of knowledge. In a typical database application where the "rules" are implemented in some procedural host language; these rules are precisely what we now refer to as knowledge. What is new is the approach that we take to knowledge. No longer do we view a piece of "raw knowledge" as the specification for a program or a set of programs. We now treat single chunks of knowledge as individual artifacts which can be represented and implemented directly, and, hopefully, modified simply. We also treat a collection of chunks of knowledge as a collection of artifacts whose inter-relationships are of paramount importance. It should be clear that if a single chunk of essentially declarative knowledge is represented and implemented as a *set* of imperative programs, then the relationships between this single chunk and other chunks of knowledge will be difficult to comprehend.

It is important to remember the difference between "database", "deductive database" and "knowledge base". This has been discussed in Section 3.5. One difference is the range of queries that they are directly capable of servicing, another is the way in which the distinction between "updates" and "maintenance" is made. Most databases are designed on the assumption that day-to-day update modifications will be to the stored contents of the update relations; modifications to the definition of the relations or to the rules are generally not seen as a day-to-day event and are classed as a substantial maintenance task. In other words, updates to tuples may be performed as a routine matter by people unfamiliar with both information analysis and the design of the database in question; updates to the specification of relations, clauses or groups should be performed only by a skilled analyst. Knowledge bases, on the other hand, should be designed on the assumption that day-to-day modifications can be to the values of the data labels, the contents of the update relations, the contents of existing groups and the specification of existing constraints; modifications involving alterations to the definition of populations, relations or groups will continue to be seen as a maintenance operation requiring skilled attention, as will the introduction of new populations, relations, groups and, possibly, constraints. Day-to-day modifications to the contents of groups will only be made to those groups which have been designed for modification; that is, groups which have been identified as "update groups" and have been carefully constrained.

As we have foreshadowed, facts in the application model are represented in the knowledge system in one of three components:- the data base, the information base and the knowledge base. We have deliberately preserved the separate identity of the concepts "data base" and "information base"; this separation is not usual in the presentation of "database" technology. Furthermore, our approach to knowledge base design does not depend intentionally on any particular approach to modeling the data and the information. There are many fundamentally different approaches to modeling information in general use today. To have based our approach on one of them would have restricted the application of our approach. To have proposed a new approach to modeling information would have introduced yet another competitor for the business of information analysis; this, we feel, would have been both undesirable and unnecessary. Instead, we have designed our approach to be compatible with many of the information modeling techniques in current use; this has been achieved by treating the "data" and the "information" separately from the "knowledge". We assume that the knowledge analyst is also proficient in information analysis, and perhaps uses one of the many approaches based on either the E-R or the B-R philosophies. The one thing that we do assume about the technique is that whatever technique is employed for information analysis, the product of the application of that technique may be readily interpreted as a set of relations.

We could summarize in a diagram the business of conventional information analysis as shown in Figure 7.1. In our approach we advocate the construction of an "application model" which is a rigorous description of the application expressed in restricted, stylized natural language. In constructing the application model, the analyst will have paid close attention to the analysis of the data in the application so the knowledge acquisition phase contains the business of "data analysis" as a component. The construction of this application model is the task of the previous phase, namely *knowledge acquisition*. Once it has been constructed, the application model is then subjected to conventional information analysis. Those features of the application model which are not captured by the information model are then subjected to knowledge analysis. It is important to realize that, for each bundle of facts in the application model, knowledge analysis is performed *after* information analysis because knowledge is explicit functional associations between items of information and/or data. Thus, data analysis and information analysis identify the objects in terms of which the knowledge will be expressed; in simple terms, the data analysis identifies the populations and the information analysis identifies the relations in terms of which the knowledge will be expressed as clause groups. Thus, our approach may be represented in a diagram as shown in Figure 7.2.

The problem of *object classification* is the business of deciding whether a fact in the application will be classified as data, information or knowledge. In our approach, object

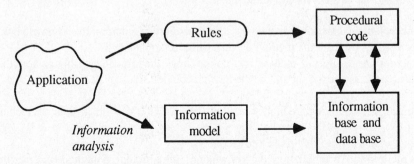

Figure 7.1 Conventional information analysis

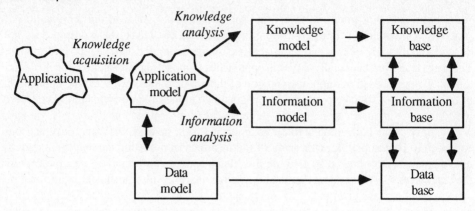

Figure 7.2 Our approach to knowledge analysis

classification is partially resolved by the identification of the data during the knowledge acquisition phase, and partially by the identification of the information during the application of a conventional information analysis technique. In an ideal example, when all the preceding steps have been performed correctly, once the populations are determined, the information may be phrased naturally in terms of them, and once the relations are determined, the knowledge may be phrased naturally in terms of them and, perhaps, populations. In practice, object classification can be rather more complex than this.

The business of object classification is greatly complicated if the uniqueness requirement has not been satisfied for all facts gathered, and if the data dictionary and type hierarchy have not been developed accurately. The first task of knowledge analysis is to analyse the complete application model. Components of this model may have been constructed by different analysts working as a team. It is essential to confirm that a real concept which one analyst has left as a single unit (e.g. "the interest rate on savings accounts") has not been subdivided by another analyst. Before the design process can proceed, homogeneity of both jargon and the depth of analysis performed on the concepts is essential. Once this has been achieved, the data in the application should have been identified correctly. This leaves the problem of deciding whether the remaining facts will be classified as information or knowledge.

A knowledge analysis technique must:

- incorporate a consistent method for distinguishing information from knowledge;
- be compatible with the method used for information analysis;
- incorporate a rigorous method for "completing" the knowledge; that is, a method for systematically acquiring all knowledge that could reasonably be regarded as relevant.

In addition, the following are highly desirable features of a knowledge analysis technique:

- a method for simplifying the knowledge;
- a method for "normalizing" the knowledge; in particular, a method for ensuring that individual chunks of knowledge do not "overlap". If two chunks of knowledge

"overlap", then the knowledge base could become inconsistent if one of the chunks was changed;

• a method for establishing the (internal) consistency of the model (Miyachi et al., 1984).

7.3   CLASSIFICATION   OPTIONS

For some facts, an intuitive understanding of the context may not be sufficient to classify those facts with any level of certainty.   Consider again "the interest rate on savings accounts equals 5 percent".   Four possible classifications are shown in the diagram in Figure 7.3.   Classification [A] corresponds to Analysis 1 in Section 3.3. Likewise, [B] corresponds to Analysis 2, and [D] corresponds to Analysis 3. Classification [C] denotes any (clause) group which has the relation:

account-type/interest-rate

as head.

In choosing between these four possible classifications, we must decide whether a functional association of form [A] might not be better grouped with others in form [B]; whether a functional association of form [B] could be deduced more efficiently from a clause group [C], and whether a functional association of form [D] is more appropriate than forms [B] and [C].   On what basis are we to choose between these four alternatives? The choice between data, [A], and information, [B], will have been determined by the

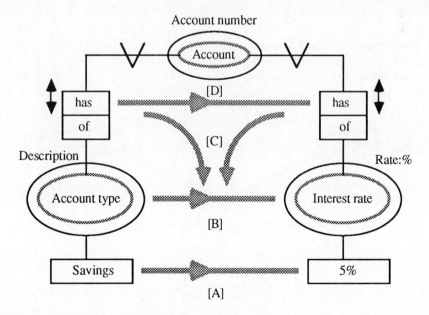

Figure 7.3 Classification of the interest rate example

analysts during knowledge acquisition; this fact will not be acceptable as data if any of the analysts have identified other "account types" which are associated with "interest rate". As we will now show, the choice between information, [B], and knowledge, [C], is not an issue for knowledge analysis. Form [B] indicates that the relation:

    account-type/interest-rate

exists independently, at least conceptually, as an object; form [C] indicates that this object is to be deduced from other objects. The choice between these two options will be made during our fourth phase "knowledge implementation". The criterion used to make this choice will be related to the business of generating an "optimal" system. In general, the choice of whether a relation should be "real", that is, the relation is actually stored, or "virtual", that is, the tuples in the relation are deduced, is the business of "knowledge base implementation" and not knowledge analysis. For the time being, we simply note that both choices are available.

The choice between [B] and [C], and [D] depends in part on the nature of the functional association, in particular whether it is fundamentally implicit or fundamentally explicit. For example, there may be some smart rule that enables the interest rate of all account types to be deduced from the label describing the account type *only* (which would be most unlikely); if this were so, then form [D] could be more appropriate than forms [B] and [C].

In Section 3.3 six options were considered for the fact "the interest rate on savings accounts equals 5 percent"; the first three of these are shown on the diagram shown in Figure 7.3 and have been discussed. We now discuss the fourth, fifth and sixth options of Section 3.3.

In the fourth of those six options three relations were identified:

    account/account-type(# , description)
    account/mean-balance(# , balance in $s)
    account/interest(# , interest in $s)

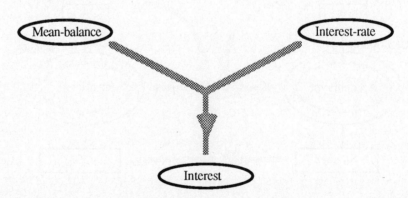

Figure 7.4 A functional association

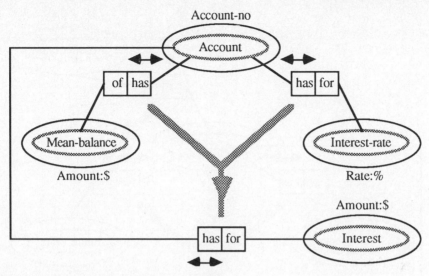

Figure 7.5 The population "account" is added

and the fact was represented in terms of them as:

$$\text{account/interest}(x , y) \leftarrow \text{account/account-type}(x , \text{'savings'}),$$
$$\text{account/mean-balance}(x , z), \ y = z \times (1 + 5/100)$$

To see how this option relates to the three just described, note that this representation is, in fact, a distortion of the original fact because the concept "interest rate" does not appear explicitly; the fourth option is based on the rule "interest payable equals mean balance multiplied by interest rate percent". This rule is a functional association between three populations as shown in Figure 7.4.

The fourth option is derived in three steps from this rule. First, the identifying name-population "account-no." is associated with each of these three populations as the primary key. The result of this operation is shown in Figure 7.5.

Second, we note that account/interest-rate may be deduced from account/account-type, for savings accounts at least. Adding this piece of knowledge to the diagram shown in Figure 7.5, we obtain the diagram as shown in Figure 7.6.

Third, we combine the two pieces of knowledge in the diagram shown in Figure 7.6 to obtain a representation of the fourth option as shown on the diagram in Figure 7.7.

Thus, we now see that the fourth option really contains two pieces of knowledge. These are, first, "the interest on an account may be deduced from the mean balance of that account and the interest rate of that account", and second, "the interest rate on an account is determined by the account type of that account if the account type is 'savings' ". Thus, it contravenes normal form principle K.1.3, and it is not acceptable.

In the fifth option, the same three relations were identified as in option four. However, these relations are then used to represent the fact directly for every savings account in the application. Thus, option five suffers from the shortcomings of option four. In addition, it has three other undesirable features. First, it includes the fact that

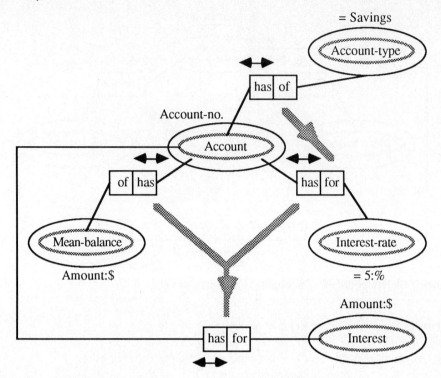

Figure 7.6 Knowledge is added

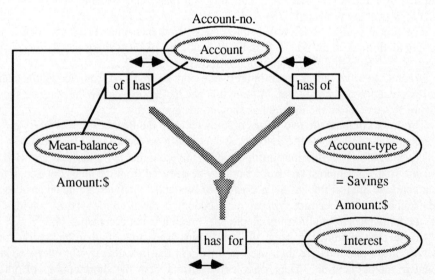

Figure 7.7 Final analysis

account number 1234 is a savings account. Second, the fact ceases to be represented at all if, for a while, there happen to be no savings accounts in the application. Third, if the interest rate for savings accounts should change, this could result in a substantial update exercise for the system.

In the sixth option, one relation has been identified:

account/interest-rate($\underline{\#}$, rate:%)

As in option five, this relation is used to represent the fact directly for every savings account in the application. It suffers from the same three undesirable features referred to above for option five.

In conclusion, the first three analyses are acceptable and the choice between them can only be made in the context of the analysis of the complete application; on the other hand, the remaining three analyses are not acceptable under any circumstances.

7.4 OBJECT CLASSIFICATION

The business of object classification is to take a raw statement of the application model and to identify the information, and possibly the knowledge within it. Thus, object classification is not so much concerned with, "Here is a statement, is it information or knowledge?" as with, "Here is a statement, what 'information' does it contain, and what 'knowledge' does it contain?". After all, recall that knowledge is functional associations between items of data and/or information so any statement containing knowledge must also contain data and/or information. Consider the example, "the interest payable on an account may be deduced from the mean balance of that account and the interest rate of that account"; when interpreted in this way, this statement may be seen to contain both information and knowledge, as we have already discussed above. Object classification is concerned with simply recognizing this and not with deciding whether either the information or the knowledge or both will form part of the final system. It is important to remember that object classification is part of the knowledge analysis phase; that is, it is part of the "knowledge model building" phase. Thus, it is not the role of object classification to decide *how* a statement is to be actually represented in the final implementation. For example, the functional association between "account" and "interest-payable" might well be classified as information; and, as a separate matter, another functional association, which specifies how the PAFs in this association might be deduced from other facts, might be classified as knowledge and expressed as an explicit rule. This second functional association would be classified as knowledge.

We do not deny that for handling a large number of statements which have been classified as information that a relational database may well be a suitable medium to use. However, the work reported here is concerned with modeling, and although it is directed at the KPM architecture, it is thus still relevant even if the knowledge system is not to be implemented on a computer at all; and, if it is to be implemented on a computer, then it is still relevant no matter what sort of architecture that computer might have or what sort of computer languages might be available. Our approach is just as vital and as valid for those systems destined for implementation on some new knowledge processing machine as for those systems which are to be implemented in a simple programming language such as BASIC on some traditional architecture.

We divide the problem of classifying objects into two sub-problems. First, we will extract the information. Second, we extract the knowledge. Remember that the input to this classification process is the application model. The application model consists of bundles of statements together with a developed data dictionary which incorporates a type hierarchy.

To extract the information we apply an information analysis technique to the statements in the application model. In fact, the only thing that is new here is that the statements in the application model have been developed by our knowledge elicitation procedure and grouped in bundles; this procedure, we believe, gives a more satisfactory starting point for the application of information analysis than an undirected interview. Thus, during information analysis we are identifying "potential relations" as information. By "potential relations" we mean structures which *could* be stored as relations if the subsequent knowledge implementation phase so requires.

In general, each bundle will contain some knowledge. Once again, the knowledge identified will be "potential groups". By "potential groups" we mean groups which *could* be employed if the subsequent knowledge implementation step so requires. In general, groups *may* be required to be part of the knowledge base. Alternatively, they may be required to be constraints, or, perhaps, some of them will not be required at all. Thus, we see that knowledge classification is not a matter of considering a fact and deciding whether it is information or knowledge. It is a matter of looking at a fact and identifying the information and knowledge within it. Some, but probably not all, of this identified information and knowledge will be employed in the final system.

For illustration we refer back to the example considered at the beginning of Section 7.3 "the interest rate on savings accounts equals 5 percent". The identification of the data, that is the three populations "account", "account-type" and "interest-rate", will take place during knowledge acquisition. The identification of the existence of functional associations between these populations will take place during information analysis. It is reasonable to assume that the three binary associations between these three populations could all be stored as relations. Thus, information analysis establishes the existence of associations which could, if required, be represented as relations. The identification of any explicit rules, or knowledge, which enable any of the data or information to be deduced from other data or information items will take place during knowledge analysis. Thus, referring back to the diagram shown at the beginning of Section 7.3, form [B] is seen as information which establishes the *existence* of the functional association between account-type and interest-rate; whereas form [C] is seen as knowledge which shows how this functional association might be *deduced*. Thus, forms [B] and [C] are seen as presenting different aspects of the original fact.

7.5 BUILDING THE INFORMATION MODEL

In our discussion, the rules of a knowledge base will be represented using logic, where possible, as Horn clauses. These clauses will be expressed in terms of populations and predicates which are often relations. These relations may be thought of as containing information, represented as tuples, in their domains. Thus, in a sense, the populations and predicates constitute the vocabulary in terms of which the knowledge is to be expressed. Thus, before the knowledge itself can be expressed, this vocabulary must be determined. This may be achieved by conventional information analysis. We use a version of Binary Relationship modeling to analyse and represent those features in the application which cannot be represented in Horn clause logic, (*see* Nijssen and Halpin, 1989 *and* Verheijen and Van Bekkum, 1982). Our approach to knowledge base design does not depend on the use of Binary Relationship modeling; any reputable information analysis method for identifying relations may be employed (Tsichritzis and Lochovsky, 1982).

It is important to note that we do not employ the full expressive power of B-R modeling. In particular, facts that can be expressed in logic are omitted from the information model. For example, subset and equality constraints as used in B-R modeling are expressed using clauses. After all, if the set of tuples which satisfy the relation P(x, y) are noted as being a subset of the set of tuples which satisfy the relation Q(x, y) then this can be represented in logic as:

$$Q(\,x, y\,) \leftarrow P(\,x, y\,)$$

Likewise, the B-R equality constraint are represented using clauses.

Satisfaction of the uniqueness requirement during knowledge acquisition should have identified populations which are essentially equivalent but some equivalences will not have been detected at that stage. We have already discussed the additional cost caused by having two populations which essentially mean the same thing so we now try to detect equivalences which might have escaped detection during knowledge acquisition. The information model is useful for this. The analyst should check that the diagram developed during information analysis contains all valid information dependencies. Having done this, the analyst should then check to see if two populations are in a one-to-one relationship; this will be denoted on a B-R diagram by a double arrow attached to each part of the rectangular box which represents that relationship. If two populations are in a one-to-one relationship, then the analyst should enquire whether one of them may be omitted altogether and replaced by reference to the other. If this is possible, then the application should be adjusted to reflect this change.

The *information model* consists of:

1. a representation of each item of information in the application model (recall that "information" is implicit functional associations between items of data);
2. a representation of the domains involved in an implicit functional association;
3. an identification of the key domain(s), if any, in an implicit functional association;
4. the specification of any relation constraints for each relation identified. (One important relation constraint is to note whether or not its domains are "total". A *total domain* has the property that *all* of its labels occur in the tuples of the relation.);
5. the specification of any tuple constraints for the tuples associated with each relation identified;
6. the identification of any query types or update types which are directly associated with each item of information; (this is added to the information model when the knowledge base engineering phase is complete);

7. the classification of relations as "real", "virtual query", "virtual update" or "dormant"; (this is added to the information model when the knowledge base implementation phase is complete);
8. a statement of what it means to say that the members of a certain tuple satisfy the given implicit functional association,

where all data, relations and tuples are normal as defined in Chapter 5. In 7 above we refer to "real", "virtual" and "dormant" relations. Each group and relation will either be selected to form part of the final system or they will not. If a relation is selected to form part of the final system and is actually stored, it is called a *real relation*. If a relation is selected to form part of the final system and is not actually stored, it is called a *virtual relation*. We distinguish between virtual relations which are part of the query mechanism, the *virtual query relations*, and virtual relations which are part of the update mechanism, the *virtual update relations*. If a relation is not selected to form part of the final system, it is called a *dormant relation*.

7.5.1 Worked example

The information in the application can be extracted from the application model and represented in relations. The structure of these relations can be displayed using a B-R diagram as shown in Figure 7.8.

The diagram shown in Figure 7.8 provides a convenient means of confirming the information structure with the domain expert. The relations displayed in it are:

- pers/class($\underline{x}$, y) means "x is the name of a person whose class number is y" (5.1).
- emp/dept($\underline{x}$, y) means "x is the name of an employee who works in the department named y" (10.1).
- emp/super($\underline{x}$, y) means "x is the name of an employee whose supervisor is the person named is y" (14.1).
- dept/mngr($\underline{x}$, y) means "x is the name of a department whose manager's name is y" (11.1).
- pers/salary($\underline{x}$, y) means "x is the name of a person whose salary is \$y per annum" (17.1).
- pers/job($\underline{x}$, y) means "x is the name of a person whose job description is y" (7.1).
- class/salary($\underline{x}$, y) means "class number x is associated with a salary of \$y per annum" (19.1).
- pers/bus(x , y) means "person named x works for business named y" (NB. Strictly speaking there is no key because one person can work for more than one business. However, in this example, the only label for the population "bus" is 'Egs P/L'.) (3.1).

The numbers in parentheses are the numbers of the corresponding statements in the application model. This diagram also shows four sub-type relationships. These sub-type relationships, together with the numbers of the corresponding statements in the application model are:

- "emp" is a sub-type of "pers" (8.3).
- "mngr" is a sub-type of "emp" (12.2).

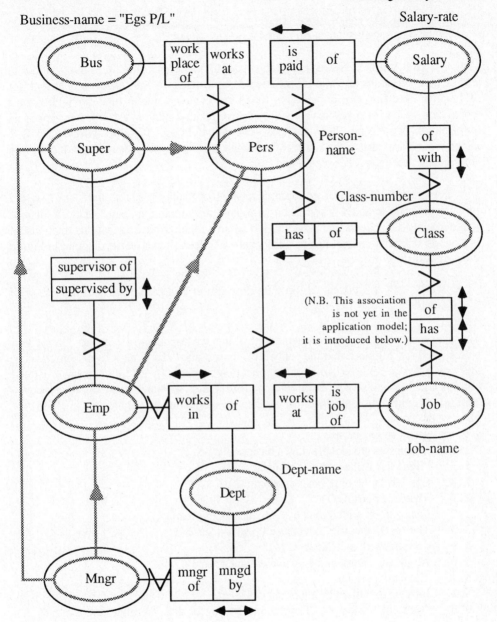

Business-name = "Egs P/L"

Salary-rate

Person-name

Class-number

(N.B. This association is not yet in the application model; it is introduced below.)

Dept-name

Job-name

Figure 7.8 B-R diagram for the information

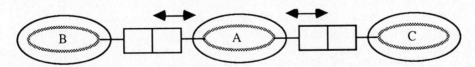

Figure 7.9 Two populations sharing a third

- "super" is a sub-type of "pers" (13.2).
- "mngr" is a sub-type of "super" (13.4).

As we have mentioned above, the analyst should now check the information model to ensure that it contains all valid information dependencies. A fruitful scenario to look for in practice is to find two populations which are in two different relations with a third population which is the key for both of those two relations, and to ask whether there is an information dependency between these two populations. In other words, in a B-R diagram, for any structure of the form shown in Figure 7.9, ask whether there is an information dependency between B and C.

For example, in our worked example any two of "salary", "class" and "job" have the property referred to above when taken with the third population "pers". Let us suppose that our analyst discovers that class and job are in a relationship and that this relationship is a one-to-one relationship; this has in fact already been shown on the diagram in Figure 7.8.

job/class($\underline{x}$, y) means "a job with description x is associated with a class with number y".

The analyst should then inquire whether one of the two populations "class" or "job" could be disposed of. Suppose that the analyst is advised that "class" may be dispensed with, and then class is removed from the application model. To do this, we have deleted bundles 4 and 5, and have replaced references to "class" with corresponding references to "job" in the remaining sentences. The application model now reads:

1.1   There are businesses (1).
1.2   Businesses are identified by a business-name (1).
1.3   "Egs P/L" is the name of a business (3).
1.4   Egs P/L is the only business name (2).
2.1   There are persons (1).
2.2   Each person is identified by a unique person-name (1).
2.3   The "personnel file" contains all person-names (3).
3.1   Persons work at businesses (4).
3.2   All persons work at the business named Egs P/L (5).
6.1   There are jobs (1).
6.2   Jobs are identified by a job-name (1).
6.3   "General-Manager", "Department-Manager" and "Worker" are the only job names (3).
7.1   Persons have jobs (4).
7.2   Each person has exactly one job (5).
7.3   The personnel file contains the job-name for each person (6).
8.1   There are employees (1).
8.2   The employees are the persons listed in the personnel file excluding the particular person whose job is General-Manager (3).
8.3   All employees are persons (7).

9.1	There are departments (1).
9.2	Each department is identified by a unique department-name (1).
9.3	The organization chart contains all the department names (3).
9.4	There are four department-names (2).
10.1	Employees are assigned to departments (4).
10.2	Each employee is assigned to one particular department (5).
10.3	The organization chart shows a department for each employee (6).
11.1	Departments have department-managers (4).
11.2	Each department has a unique department-manager (5).
11.3	The organization chart contains the name of the department-manager for each department (6).
12.1	There are department-managers (1).
12.2	Department-managers are employees (7).
12.3	The department-managers are listed in the personnel file (3).
13.1	There are supervisors (1).
13.2	Supervisors are persons (7).
13.3	The supervisors are listed in the personnel file (3).
13.4	Department managers are supervisors (7).
14.1	Employees are supervised by supervisors (4).
14.2	Each employee has a unique supervisor (5).
14.3	The organization chart contains the name of the supervisor for each employee (6).
15.1	The supervisor of an employee may be deduced from that employee's job and that employee's department (7).
15.2	**if** an employee's job is a worker **and** if that employee works in a certain department, **then** that employee is supervised by the Department Manager of that department (9).
15.3	**if** an employee's job is a Department Manager, **then** that employee is supervised by the General Manager (9).
16.1	There are salaries (1).
16.2	Salaries are identified by a salary-rate expressed in dollars per annum (1).
16.3	$50,000, $40,000 and $30,000 are the only salary rates (3).
16.4	There are at most three different salary-rates (2).
17.1	Persons receive salaries (4).
17.2	Each person receives a single salary (5).
17.3	The personnel file contains the salary for each person (6).
18.1	A person's salary may be deduced from that person's job (7).
18.2	**if** a person has job "General Manager", **then** that person receives a salary of $50,000 **and if** a person has job "Department Manager", **then** that person receives a salary of $40,000 **and if** a person has job "Worker", **then** that person receives a salary of $30,000 (9).
19.1	Job is associated with salary (4).
19.2	Each job-name is associated with a unique salary-rate (5).
19.3	Managing-Director is associated with $50,000, Department-Manager is associated with $40,000 and Worker is associated with $30,000 (6).

All duplications have now been removed. This should be the final form of the application model unless it is necessary to modify it during the construction of the knowledge model. The data model now becomes as shown in Figure 7.10, where:

- business-name(x) means "x is the name of a business, at present Egs P/L is the only business name".
- person-name(x) means "x is the name of a person".
- dept-name(x) means "x is the name of a department".
- job-name(x) means "x is the name of a job".
- salary-rate(x) means "x is a salary expressed in dollars per annum".

The "information structure" of the application model may be displayed on a B-R diagram as shown in Figure 7.11.

Recall that the role of relations is to represent information as *associations* between domains. We will see in the next section that the role of clause groups is to represent knowledge as *associations* between relations and domains. The information model is shown in Figure 7.12.

Thing-population	Bundle	Sub-type of	Name-population	Labels	Population constraints	Label constraints	Fixed labels
bus	1		business-name	Egs P/L	one label only		
pers	2		person-name	(see 2.3)	each label unique		
super	13	pers			= job GM and DM		
emp	8	pers			= job DM and Workr		
mngr	12	emp, super			= job DM		
dept	9		dept-name	(see 9.3)	4 unique labels		all
job	6		job-name	(see 6.3)	3 unique labels	= GM,DM Workr	all
salary	16		salary-rate	(see 16.3)	3 labels or less	positive integer	

Figure 7.10 The data model

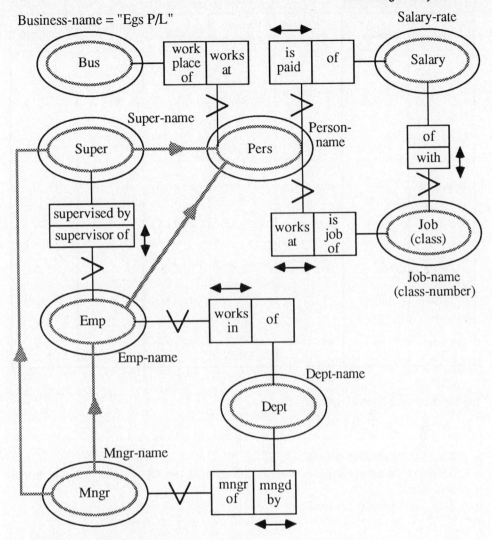

Business-name = "Egs P/L"

Salary-rate

Figure 7.11 B-R diagram for the information

In Figure 7.12 the constraints are:

- IC1.1 is "domain-2 is total".
- IC2.1 is "domain-1 is total".
- IC3.1 is "domain-1 is total".
- IC3.2 is "no employee can be in a department for which there is no manager".
- IC4.1 is "domain-2 is total".
- IC4.2 is "managers must work in the department which they manage".
- IC5.1 is "domain-1 is total".
- IC5.2 is "no employee can supervise themselves".

Relation	Bundle	Key domain	Other domains	Tuples	Relation constraints	Tuple constraints
bus/pers	3		business-name	(see 3.2)	IC1.1	
			person-name			
pers/job	7	person-name	job-name	(see 7.3)	IC2.1	
emp/dept	10	emp-name	dept-name	(see 10.3)	IC3.1	IC3.2
dept/mngr	11	dept-name	mngr-name	(see 11.3)	IC4.1	IC4.2
emp/super	14	emp-name	super-name	(see 14.3)	IC5.1	IC5.2
pers/salary	17	person-name	salary-rate	(see 17.3)	IC6.1	IC6.2
job/salary	19	job-name	salary-rate	(see 19.3)	IC7.1	IC7.2

Figure 7.12 Information model

- IC6.1 is "domain-1 is total".
- IC6.2 is "a person's salary must be the same as the salary of the job which that person has".
- IC7.1 is "domain-1 is total".
- IC7.2 is "(salary of GM) > (salary of DMs) > (salary of Workers)".

and the relations are:

- bus/pers(x, y) means "x is the name of a business and y is the name of a person who works at that business".
- pers/job(x, y) means "x is the name of a person and y is the name of the unique job that that person has".
- emp/dept(x, y) means "x is the name of an employee and y is the name of the unique department in which that employee works".
- dept/mngr(x , y) means "x is the name of a department and y is the name of the unique manager of that department".
- emp/super(x, y) means "x is the name of an employee and y is the name of the unique supervisor of that employee".

- pers/salary(x, y) means "x is the name of a person and y is the unique salary of that person in dollars per annum".
- job/salary(x, y) means "x is the name of a job and y is the unique salary in dollars per annum associated with that job".

7.6 BUILDING THE KNOWLEDGE MODEL

We derive three "system" models from the application model in the design of a knowledge system; these are: the data model, the information model and the knowledge model. The data model was discussed in the previous chapter, and the information model was discussed in the previous section. These three models are interdependent. The information in the information model is phrased in terms of the data in the data model. The knowledge in the knowledge model is phrased in terms of both the information in the information model and the data in the data model. Thus, the information model will place demands on the data model, and the knowledge model will place demands on both the information model and the data model. The construction of the information model will often lead to changes in the data model. Likewise, the construction of the knowledge model will often lead to changes in the information model and the data model. Subsequent modifications to any of the three models will usually lead to changes in the other two. In this section we discuss the construction of the knowledge model.

We have already noted the cost in having two populations in the data model which essentially refer to the same thing. In fact, satisfaction of the uniqueness requirement should prevent such equivalences from being recorded in the first place. It is not uncommon, however, for equivalences of this form to escape detection during knowledge acquisition. Should this occur then, as we have described, these duplications should be detected during information analysis as one-to-one relationships between populations; this was discussed in 7.5. As it is important to ensure that these equivalences are removed completely, we now show how the one-to-one relationship between the populations "class" and "job" could have been recognized during an analysis of the knowledge if it had not been recognized during knowledge acquisition or information analysis. This particular equivalence might have been hidden within the knowledge that "the class of a person may be deduced from the job that that person holds"; the clauses for this group might be:

pers/class(x , 1) ← pers/job(x , 'General Manager')
pers/class(x , 2) ← pers/job(x , 'Department Manager')
pers/class(x , 3) ← pers/job(x , 'Worker')   [1.1]

These clauses essentially assert that "the information in pers/class may be deduced from the information in pers/job". The dependency diagram for this group is shown in Figure 7.13. Note that we have indicated that this group is both categorical and unique.

pers/class   [1.1]   pers/job

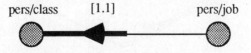

Figure 7.13 Dependency diagram for group [1.1]

The analyst would now attempt to complete the cluster to which this group belongs, and would enquire whether the reverse dependency is true. It would be no surprise to find that it were and that it was established by:

pers/job(x , 'General Manager') ← pers/class(x , 1)
pers/job(x , 'Department Manager') ← pers/class(x , 2)
pers/job(x , 'Worker') ← pers/class(x , 3)   [1.2]

defining pers/job in terms of pers/class. The dependency diagram for these two groups is shown in Figure 7.14.

Recall that in dependency diagrams, each arrow corresponds to a group of logic clauses, each group fully defines the head relation in terms of the other body relations. In this particular diagram, we see that pers/class and pers/job are, in a very real sense, equivalent. Groups [1.1] and [1.2] together form a complete cluster. As the population "pers" is the key of both of these relations it should be clear that this cluster asserts that the populations "class" and "job" are in a one-to-one relationship. If such an equivalence is not discovered until this late stage, then it should still be dealt with by recording this fact in the application model and removing any unnecessary duplications that have proliferated throughout the information model and, if development of the knowledge model has begun, in the knowledge model itself. In fact, in our worked example, the duplication between "class" and "job" was discovered during information analysis and has already been removed from application model which is as shown at the end of Section 7.5.1.

We have distinguished between categorical and non-categorical groups, and between unique and non-unique groups. Recall that a group is called a *categorical group* if it contains sufficient knowledge to enable *all* the information in the head predicate to be deduced from the body predicates. A non-categorical group does not have this property and, unless it is augmented, is only likely be of use in the design of integrity checks. An example of a non-categorical group is:

item/cost-price:$(f(y), y) ← y < 1000, y ≥ 1

which represents the rule: "For every dollar amount between $1 and $999 there is an item which costs that amount". A group is called a *unique group* if, when used in conjunction with the find-all mechanism of logic, it calculates each tuple which satisfies its head predicate once and only once.

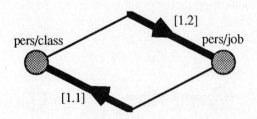

Figure 7.14 Dependency diagram for groups [1.1] and [1.2]

The knowledge model contains representations of groups. These groups are gathered into clusters. To construct each cluster:

1. Select a bundle which contains knowledge from the application model.
2. Represent the knowledge in that bundle as a group.
3. Complete the cluster for this group.
4. Normalize the groups that comprise the cluster.
5. Demonstrate that the cluster is (information model) consistent.

The next bundle to be selected is chosen by picking a bundle whose knowledge functional association leads *into* one of the predicates in one of the clusters developed so far. If there are no bundles with this property, then a bundle is chosen whose knowledge functional dependency leads *out of* one of the predicates of the clusters developed so far. If there are no bundles with this property, then the knowledge in the application model is not "connected", and the analyst should either solicit additional knowledge so that the application model is "connected" or choose a bundle at random.

As we will see, the business of completing a cluster usually involves the elicitation of additional knowledge from the domain expert. Thus, strictly speaking, completing a cluster will usually entail revisiting the knowledge acquisition phase. As this additional knowledge is gathered, it will be recorded in the application model within the same bundle as the other knowledge in the cluster. Furthermore, the business of normalizing a cluster often involves rephrasing the statements in the application model. Thus, we see that the application model will in general undergo substantial change during the knowledge analysis phase.

The *knowledge model* consists of:

1. a representation of each cluster;
2. a representation as a group of each item of knowledge in the cluster (recall that "knowledge" is explicit functional associations between items of information or data)
3. a representation of the head predicate, or population, of each group;
4. a representation of the body predicates, or populations, of each group;
5. the specification of any cluster constraints for each cluster identified;
6. the specification of any group constraints for each group identified;
7. the identification of any query types or update types which are directly associated with each group (this is added to the knowledge model when the knowledge base engineering phase is complete);
8. the classification of groups as "update", "query", "integrity check" or "dormant" (this is added to the knowledge model when the knowledge base implementation phase is complete);

where all clauses and groups are normal as defined in Chapter 5. In 8 above we refer to "update", "query", "integrity check" and "dormant" groups. The meaning of these terms will be clarified in Chapter 9.

7.6.1   Worked example

Within the aim of this discussion, our worked example is intentionally simple. The information in it has been expressed in relations without any difficulty. The knowledge in it can be expressed directly in Horn clauses, and the queries, which are introduced in the next chapter, do not require complex techniques to navigate the data base; (*see* Neves, et al., 1983 *and* Debenham and McGrath, 1983). The representation of the knowledge in the worked example does not involve modal operators. The groups representing the knowledge in the worked example are entirely categorical. The design and incorporation of integrity checks has been dealt with informally. The worked example is framed as a snapshot; that is, the time dimension is not present in the statement of the problem. It is important to realize that a real application would be unlikely to exhibit many of these simplifying characteristics. Debenham and McGrath, 1982, contains comments on broader issues, including knowledge base maintenance, which are illustrated with a similar example.

Having used knowledge acquisition and information analysis to complete the vocabulary in terms of which the knowledge is to be represented, we now commence the general business of analysing the knowledge and building the knowledge component of the knowledge base. Some of the text in the application model for the worked example has already been used during knowledge acquisition to identify the populations, labels and type hierarchic associations; in addition, much of the remaining text has been used by information analysis to identify the relations and to identify the key domains within those relations. We will now see that two remaining bundles in the application model contain knowledge which may be represented in Horn clause logic.

Sentences 15.2 and 15.3 in the application model imply that:

$$emp/super(\ x\ ,\ y\ )\ \leftarrow\ pers/job(\ x\ ,\ \text{`Worker'}\ ),$$
$$emp/dept(\ x\ ,\ z\ ),\ dept/mngr(\ z\ ,\ y\ )$$
$$emp/super(\ x\ ,\text{`Mr Boss'})\ \leftarrow\ pers/job(\ x\ ,\text{`Department Manager'})\qquad\qquad [2.1]$$

These clauses essentially assert that "the information in emp/super may be deduced from the information in pers/job, emp/dept and dept/mngr". The corresponding dependency diagram is shown in Figure 7.15. Note that the analyst has asserted that this group is both categorical and unique.

The analyst now attempts to construct other knowledge dependencies in the cluster to which this group belongs. Suppose that the analyst first investigates whether pers/job is dependent on any of the other relations in the diagram. After consultation with the domain expert, the following knowledge is added to the application model:

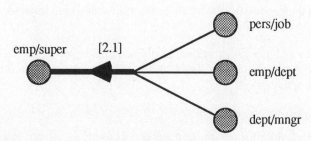

Figure 7.15 Dependency diagram for group [2.1]

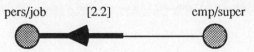

Figure 7.16 Dependency diagram for group [2.2]

15.4.1 The job of an employee may be deduced from knowing that employee's supervisor.

15.4.2 **if** an employee is supervised by the General Manager, **then** that employee's job is Department Manager.

15.4.3 **if** an employee's supervisor is in turn supervised by the General Manager, **then** that employee's job is Worker.

This knowledge enables us to construct a categorical group with the pers/job relation as head:

> pers/job('Mr Boss' , 'General Manager') ←
> pers/job(x ,'Department Manager') ← emp/super (x ,'Mr Boss')
> pers/job(x , 'Worker') ← emp/super(x , y), emp/super(y , 'Mr Boss')   [2.2]

The dependency diagram for these clauses is shown in Figure 7.16. Once again, the analyst has asserted that this group is both categorical and unique.

Next, the analyst investigates whether the information in emp/dept may be defined in terms of the information in the other three relations. After consultation with the domain expert, the following knowledge is added to the application model:

15.5.1 The department in which an employee works may be deduced from knowing that employee's supervisor and the managers of each department.

15.5.2 **if** a person is manager of a department, **then** that person is said to work in that department.

15.5.3 **if** a person has a supervisor who is manager of a department, **then** that person works in that same department.

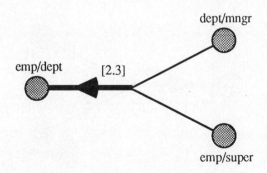

Figure 7.17 Dependency diagram for group [2.3]

This knowledge enables us to construct a categorical group with the emp/dept relation as head:

emp/dept(x , y) ← dept/mngr(y , x)
emp/dept(x , y) ← emp/super(x , z), dept/mngr(y , z)   [2.3]

and the dependency diagram is shown in Figure 7.17.

Next the analyst investigates whether the information in dept/mngr may be defined in terms of the other relations in the cluster. After consultation with the domain expert the following knowledge is added to the application model:

15.6.1 The manager of a department may be deduced from knowing the employees in that department and the supervisors of the employees in that department.
15.6.2 **if** an employee is supervised by the General Manager **and** that employee works in some particular department, **then** that employee is manager of that department.

This knowledge enables us to construct a categorical group with the dept/mngr relation as head:

dept/mngr(x , y) ← emp/super(y , 'Mr Boss'), emp/dept(y , x)   [2.4]

and the corresponding dependency diagram is shown in Figure 7.18.

Groups [2.1], [2.2], [2.3] and [2.4] together form a complete cluster. This cluster may not be normal. We will consider normalization shortly. Note that each chunk of knowledge in bundle 15 in the application model corresponds directly to a clause in one of these four groups. This is a good example of knowledge that has no inherent knowledge dependency. In other words, the domain expert's knowledge on this matter encompasses all four groups which make up this cluster. Recall that the domain expert's original pronouncements were, "The department manager supervises the workers in that department" and "The department managers are supervised by Mr Boss". Neither of these

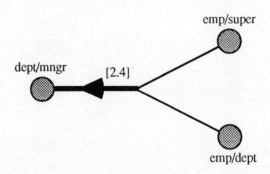

Figure 7.18 Dependency diagram for group [2.4]

two statements contain a particular knowledge dependency; they are both simple statements of fact. The important point is that any one of these four groups could represent the particular knowledge dependency that will be required to play a part in performing some task. At the knowledge analysis stage, there is often no way of telling which one of the dependencies will actually be required. Thus, for the time being, we retain all four of them. Knowledge is quite unlike information in this respect. The intended information dependencies in information tend to be fairly easy to identify. For knowledge, this is often not so. The identification of which knowledge dependencies are intended by the domain expert usually requires careful analysis. Once the intended knowledge dependencies have been determined, the matter of which of them are going to be useful is usually something that neither the analyst nor the domain expert know instinctively even when small quantities of knowledge are being gathered.

We now look for a bundle whose knowledge functional dependency leads into one of the predicates in cluster [2]. There is none, but the functional dependency in sentence 18.2 leads out of pers/job. This sentence could be represented as:

$$\text{pers/salary}(x , y) \leftarrow \text{pers/job}(x , z), \text{job/salary}(z , y) \tag{3.1}$$

and the dependency diagram for this group is shown in Figure 7.19. Once again, we have asserted that the group is both categorical and unique.

The analyst now attempts to construct the other knowledge dependencies in the cluster to which this group belongs. The analyst would now enquire whether pers/job could be defined in terms of one or both of pers/salary and job/salary. Let us suppose that the response is, "At present, pers/job could be defined in terms of pers/salary and job/salary, but it would not be correct to quote this as a general rule, because one day there may be fewer than three different pay rates", in which case, the analyst would not record this dependency. Next, the analyst would enquire whether "job/salary" could be defined in terms of "pers/job" and/or "pers/salary". Conceivably this could be achieved by:

$$\text{job/salary}(x , y) \leftarrow \text{pers/job}(z , x), \text{pers/salary}(z , y)$$

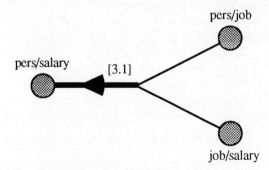

Figure 7.19 Dependency diagram for group [3.1]

This definition of job/salary might be rejected on the grounds that its validity depends on there being at least one person in each job category; in which case, this dependency would not be recorded either.

The knowledge in the worked example has now been represented and completed. The next step is to normalize this knowledge.

Groups [2.1], [2.2] and [2.4] contravene principle K.1.1 because of the presence of the label "Mr Boss". To satisfy K.1.1, the explicit reference to this label should be replaced by implicit references. Note that the corresponding statements in bundle 15 in the application model do not refer to Mr Boss explicitly. Thus, these three groups are really not good representations of bundle 15 anyway, and, in satisfying K.1.1, there is no need to adjust the statements in bundle 15 in the application model. In this particular example we could remove all explicit references to "Mr Boss" by employing:

    pers/job(x, 'General Manager')

but as this approach would not be generally applicable to the removal of all labels; we choose instead to deal with this matter in a way that does have general application. To achieve this, we introduce a new population "gen-man" which is a sub-type of supervisor and is associated with all labels of persons who are General Managers. This new population will be entered into the data model and is established by the new bundle:

20.1   There are general managers (1).
20.2   General managers are supervisors (7).
20.3   There is only one general manager (2).
20.4   "Mr Boss" is a general manager (3).

As the new population "gen-man" is subject to the constraint that it will be associated with one label, this label may be referred to implicitly using the predicate:

    is-the[gen-man](x)

Using this predicate, we replace groups [2.1], [2.2] and [2.4] so that they comply with principle K.1.1:

$$emp/super(\ x, y\ ) \leftarrow pers/job(\ x,\ 'Worker'\ ),$$
$$emp/dept(\ x, z\ ),\ dept/mngr(\ z, y\ )$$
$$emp/super(\ x, y\ ) \leftarrow pers/job(\ x,\ 'Department\text{-}Manager'\ ),$$
$$is\text{-}the[gen\text{-}man](\ y\ ) \tag*{[2.1']}$$

$$pers/job(\ x,\ 'General\text{-}Manager'\ ) \leftarrow is\text{-}the[gen\text{-}man](\ x\ )$$
$$pers/job(\ x,\ 'Department\text{-}Manager'\ ) \leftarrow emp/super(\ x, y\ ),$$
$$is\text{-}the[gen\text{-}man](\ y\ )$$
$$pers/job(\ x,\ 'Worker'\ ) \leftarrow emp/super(\ x, y\ ),\ emp/super(\ y, z\ ),$$
$$is\text{-}the[gen\text{-}man](\ z\ ) \tag*{[2.2']}$$

$$dept/mngr(\ x, y\ ) \leftarrow emp/super(\ y, z\ ),\ emp/dept(\ y, x\ ),$$
$$is\text{-}the[gen\text{-}man](\ z\ ) \tag*{[2.4']}$$

the dependency diagrams for these new groups are the same as the diagrams for the groups from which they were derived. In other words, we do not show this "is-the" predicate on the dependency diagram. After all, this predicate just provides an indirect reference to the single label 'Mr Boss', and 'Mr Boss' was not shown on the preceding dependency diagram. It is interesting to note that it is possible to remove all labels in this way. For example, [2.1'] could be written as:

$$\text{emp/super}(x, y) \leftarrow \text{is-a[worker]}(x), \text{emp/dept}(x, z),$$
$$\text{dept/mngr}(z, y)$$
$$\text{emp/super}(x, y) \leftarrow \text{is-the[gen-man]}(y), \text{is-a[mngr]}(x)$$

where "worker" is a new population to which all labels for persons with job name "Worker" will be attached. Note that in this new form of [2.1'] all the label names have been exchanged for population names. Although this form has a certain attractive purity, we can see little benefit in it. After all, the labels that have been removed are "fixed" in the data model.

Using the principle K.1.3 noted in Chapter 5, the only candidates for normalizing are the use of [2.2'] to normalize [2.3] and [2.4']. [2.3] cannot be normalized but [2.4'] becomes:

$$\text{dept/mngr}(x, y) \leftarrow \text{pers/job}(y, \text{‘Department-Manager’}),$$
$$\text{emp/dept}(y, x)$$ [2.4"]

and the dependency diagram is now shown in Figure 7.20. Note that [2.4] contains a reference to the particular occupant of a job and as a consequence contravenes normal form K.1.1, and [2.4"] does not. The analyst also adjusts the corresponding statements in bundle 15 in the application model. These statements now reads:

15.6.1 The manager of a department may be deduced from knowing the employees in that department and the jobs of the employees in that department.
15.6.2 **if** an employee has the job of department manager **and** that employee works in some particular department, **then** that employee is manager of that department.

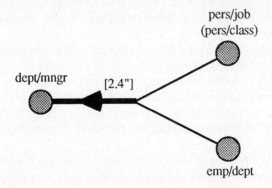

pers/job
(pers/class)

dept/mngr   [2.4"]

emp/dept

Figure 7.20 Dependency diagram for group [2.4"]

The analyst then notes that [2.4"] is a candidate for normalizing [2.1'], but this is not possible. In a sense, the normalization of a group by using principle K.1.3 is the reverse of resolution. For example, if [2.4"] is resolved with the second clause in [2.2'] then the result is [2.4']; in other words, the resolvant of two normal clauses can be non-normal.

The first clause in [2.1'] contravenes principle K.1.4; it could be simplified by introducing a predicate emp/mngr(x, y) which means that "x is the name of an employee and y is the name of the manager of the department in which x works". Using this predicate, the first clause in [2.1'] could be split into two clauses:

emp/super(x, y) ← pers/job(x, 'Worker'), emp/mngr(x, y)
emp/mngr(x, y) ← emp/dept(x, z), dept/mngr(z, y)

However, we consider that this does not really amount to much of an improvement, if any. Thus, we choose to ignore this breach of K.1.4. The knowledge is thus considered to be normal.

During the knowledge analysis phase substantial changes have been made to bundle 15. This bundle now contains:

15.1   The supervisor of an employee may be deduced from that employee's job and that employee's department.

15.2   **if** an employee's job is a worker **and** if that employee works in a certain department, **then** that employee is supervised by the Department Manager of that department.

15.3   **if** an employee's job is a Department Manager, **then** that employee is supervised by the General Manager.

15.4.1 The job of an employee may be deduced from knowing that employee's supervisor.

15.4.2 **if** an employee is supervised by the General Manager, **then** that employee's job is Department Manager.

15.4.3 **if** an employee's supervisor is in turn supervised by the General Manager, **then** that employee's job is Worker.

15.5.1 The department in which an employee works may be deduced from knowing that employee's supervisor and the managers of each department.

15.5.2 **if** a person is manager of a department, **then** that person is said to work in that department.

15.5.3 **if** a person has a supervisor who is manager of a department, **then** that person works in that same department.

15.6.1 The manager of a department may be deduced from knowing the employees in that department and the jobs of the employees in that department.

15.6.2 **if** an employee has the job of department manager **and** that employee works in some particular department, **then** that employee is manager of that department.

In the next step the analyst combines the diagrams to obtain a complete picture of the knowledge; this composite diagram is shown in Figure 7.21. This diagram is called the *combined group diagram*. This picture makes no reference to how the knowledge is to be

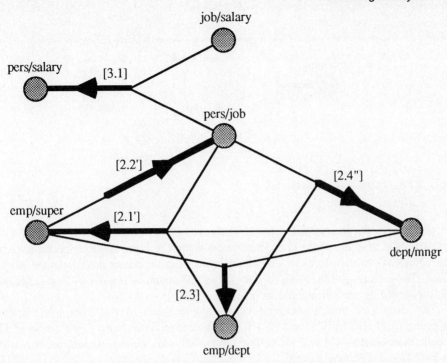

Figure 7.21 The combined group diagram

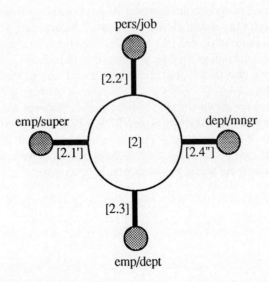

Figure 7.22 Diagram for cluster [2]

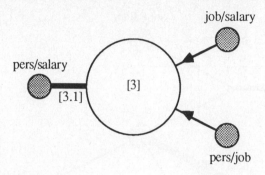

Figure 7.23 Diagram for cluster [3]

used. It is important to note that it is *not* just a step in the design process. This picture summarizes the structure of the knowledge in the application; in addition, it comprises an index to the individual pieces of knowledge which are represented as groups of logic clauses. The picture, and the associated logic, will be maintained and will be regarded as the kernel of the system throughout its operational life.

The simplified and normalized knowledge consists of one complete cluster, comprising [2.1'], [2.2'], [2.3] and [2.4"], and one incomplete cluster, comprising [3.1]. We call these clusters [2] and [3] respectively; they may be represented as shown in Figures 7.22 and 7.23 respectively.

The next step is to show that these clusters are consistent. As we have already discussed, this can be difficult in general. We will show, with a simple example, how we might set about demonstrating that the above two clusters are "information model consistent". To do this, we construct a complete model of the information; that is, we specify values for the tuples in every relation. These might be as shown in Figure 7.24. Then we use each group to deduce the tuples of its head predicate from the tuples for the body predicates given in the model shown in Figure 7.24; and last we check that these deduced tuples match those in the model. Note that once the information model has been set up, the rest of the calculation may be performed automatically. Note also that this does not actually prove consistency, but it can be a useful way of testing the validity of the logic in the groups.

We now represent these two clusters together on the *combined cluster diagram*. The combined cluster diagram is shown in Figure 7.25. This picture gives an "executive view" of the structure of the knowledge. The clusters represented in the diagram may be "plugged onto" other clusters with which they have one or more relation in common. Thus, the cluster diagrams are useful in visually building systems.

bus/pers	
business-name	person-name
Egs P/L	Fred
Egs P/L	Joe
Egs P/L	Mary
Egs P/L	Jane
Egs P/L	Bill
Egs P/L	Susan
Egs P/L	Jenny
Egs P/L	Peter
Egs P/L	Jean

pers/job	
person-name	job-name
Fred	GM
Joe	DM
Mary	DM
Jane	DM
Bill	DM
Susan	Worker
Jenny	Worker
Peter	Worker
Jean	Worker

pers/salary	
person-name	salary-rate
Fred	50,000
Joe	40,000
Mary	40,000
Jane	40,000
Bill	40,000
Susan	30,000
Jenny	30,000
Peter	30,000
Jean	30,000

emp/dept	
person-name	dept-name
Joe	Maint
Mary	Office
Jane	Store
Bill	Shop
Susan	Maint
Jenny	Office
Peter	Store
Jean	Shop

emp/super	
person-name	person-name
Joe	Fred
Mary	Fred
Jane	Fred
Bill	Fred
Susan	Joe
Jenny	Mary
Peter	Jane
Jean	Bill

job/salary	
job-name	salary-rate
GM	50,000
DM	40,000
Worker	30,000

dept/mngr	
dept-name	person-name
Maint	Joe
Office	Mary
Store	Jane
Shop	Bill

Figure 7.24 Sample information model

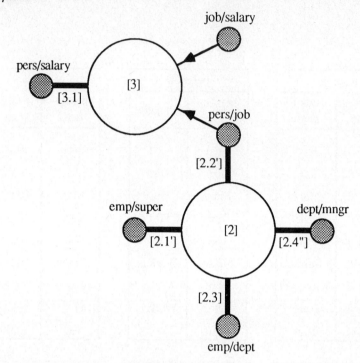

Figure 7.25 Combined cluster diagram

It is important to note that the technique for knowledge analysis illustrated above is principally concerned with the pragmatic issues in knowledge base design, and reflects the structure of Horn clause groups. The notation is designed to model this structure; it has no pretence of being a general purpose, abstract framework for knowledge representation (Schefe, 1982).

This completes the knowledge analysis phase. The product of this phase is three models, the data model, the information model and the knowledge model. For convenience, we give these models in Figures 7.26, 7.27 and 7.28.

Thing-population	Bundle	Sub-type of	Name-population	Labels	Population constraints	Label constraints	Fixed labels
bus	1		business-name	Egs P/L	one label only		
pers	2		person-name	(see 2.3)	each label unique		
super	13	pers			= job GM and DM		
emp	8	pers			= job DM and Workr		
mngr	12	emp, super			= job DM		
dept	9		dept-name	(see 9.3)	4 unique labels		all
job	6		job-name	(see 6.3)	3 unique labels	= GM,DM Workr	all
salary	16		salary-rate	(see 16.3)	3 labels or less	positive integer	
gen-man	20	super		Mr Boss	one label only		

Figure 7.26 The data model

In Figure 7.26:

- business-name(x) means "x is the name of a business, at present Egs P/L is the only business name";
- person-name(x) means "x is the name of a person";
- dept-name(x) means "x is the name of a department";
- job-name(x) means "x is the name of a job";
- salary-rate(x) means "x is a salary expressed in dollars per annum".

Note that the population "gen-man" has been included in the data model in Figure 7.26. This population was introduced during knowledge analysis.

Relation	Bundle	Key domain	Other domains	Tuples	Relation constraints	Tuple constraints
bus/pers	3		business-name person-name	(see 3.2)	IC1.1	
pers/job	7	person-name	job-name	(see 7.3)	IC2.1	
emp/dept	10	emp-name	dept-name	(see 10.3)	IC3.1	IC3.2
dept/mngr	11	dept-name	mngr-name	(see 11.3)	IC4.1	IC4.2
emp/super	14	emp-name	super-name	(see 14.3)	IC5.1	IC5.2
pers/salary	17	person-name	salary-rate	(see 17.3)	IC6.1	IC6.2
job/salary	19	job-name	salary-rate	(see 19.3)	IC7.1	IC7.2

Figure 7.27 The information model

In Figure 7.27:

- bus/pers(x, y) means "x is the name of a business and y is the name of a person who works at that business";
- pers/job(x, y) means "x is the name of a person and y is the name of the unique job that that person has";
- emp/dept(x, y) means "x is the name of an employee and y is the name of the unique department in which that employee works";
- dept/mngr(x , y) means "x is the name of a department and y is the name of the unique manager of that department";
- emp/super(x, y) means "x is the name of an employee and y is the name of the unique supervisor of that employee";
- pers/salary(x, y) means "x is the name of a person and y is the unique salary of that person in dollars per annum";
- job/salary(x, y) means "x is the name of a job and y is the unique salary in dollars per annum associated with that job".

Cluster	Bundle	Group	Head	Body	Cluster constraints	Group constraints
[2]	15				complete	
	15.1	[2.1']	emp/super	pers/job emp/dept dept/mngr		categ. & unique
	15.4.1	[2.2']	pers/job	emp/super		categ. & unique
	15.5.1	[2.3]	emp/dept	emp/super dept/mngr		categ. & unique
	15.6.1	[2.4"]	dept/mngr	pers/job emp/dept		categ. & unique
[3]	18				pers/salary only	
	18.1	[3.1]	pers/salary	job/salary pers/job		categ. & unique

Figure 7.28 The knowledge model

7.7 ANALYSING INVERSE ASSOCIATIONS

In the next chapter we will introduce the query types and update types into the system and will derive a functional model of the application. It is not uncommon for the initial collection of knowledge to be inadequate to interact with the query and update types. If this is so, then the knowledge analysis phase is revisited and the deficiencies in the knowledge are rectified. One common instance of the knowledge being inadequate is when a query type is naturally associated with an inverse predicate. For example, the query type, "to find all employees supervised by a given person" is naturally associated with the "inverse predicate" of emp/super:

super/emp-list(<u><supervisor></u> , <list of employees>)

which could be implemented by searching the second domain of emp/super if it were actually stored or by a for-all logic search if it were not. This is an example of an *inverse predicate*. Recall that one way of defining an inverse predicate is in terms of its "original" predicate and the tuple/find-all-list predicate. For example, the above inverse predicate can be defined by:

super/emp-list(x, y) ← emp/super(z, x), tuple/find-all-list((z), y)

super/emp-list   emp/super

Figure 7.29 Dependency diagram for clause with "for all" predicate

Recall the notation for a dependency diagram of a clause which contains the tuple/find-all-list predicate. In this case, the dependency diagram does not show a node for the predicate tuple/find-all-list but instead shows a wedge on the arc to emp/super. This is shown in Figure 7.29.

Note the "wedge" across the line in Figure 7.29 at the emp/super end; this is intended to draw attention to the fact that emp/super is required to be available in a form which is compatible with the find-all mechanism. Note also that the notion of an inverse predicate is not *necessary* to support this query type; after all, this inverse predicate may be defined in terms of the relation emp/super and the predicate tuple/find-all-list using a conventional logic program. We have specifically drawn attention to inverse predicates purely to provide the facility for acknowledging that there is a requirement to search a non-key domain in the satisfaction of a major query type; in the interests of efficiency, the system designer may choose to incorporate this requirement in the design. It is important to realize that an inverse predicate may only operate efficiently when used in an information-goal-dependent way. In other words, it is designed to "receive input" through its primary key domain(s), and to "return output" through the other domain(s). Thus, in general, inverse predicates should be used with great care in general logic programming. Their efficient use is restricted to particular tasks for which the information flow is known and fixed. Their significance is purely one of efficiency.

An important property of an inverse predicate is that it is required to find *all* of the labels in the secondary domain(s) corresponding to a given set of labels for the primary domain(s). Thus, in the above example, super/emp-list is required to find *all* employees supervised by a given supervisor. Hence, if super/emp-list is defined in terms of other predicates, then it is essential that those other predicates are established in such a way as to ensure that *all* employees will be found. In particular, if the definition of an inverse predicate involves the use of the find-all mechanism, then all body predicates in that definition must be compatible with the find-all mechanism; that is, all groups employed by the definition must be "unique" groups.

As we have remarked in Chapter 2, an inverse predicate may be defined in terms of its "original" predicate and the find-all mechanism, or it may be defined in terms of other predicates in the system, some of which may have to be inverted. Suppose that a given group has head predicate P and body predicates {B}; if it is required to derive a group for an inverse of P then this can often be achieved using as body predicates the set of predicates {B} some of which may have to be inverted themselves. For example, we have noted above that super/emp-list may be defined in terms of its "original" predicate emp/super, and recall that emp/super can be defined in terms of pers/job, dept/mngr and emp/dept. We will shortly see that super/emp-list may be defined efficiently in terms of job/pers-list and dept/emp-list. Thus the system designer will have the choice of whether to define an inverse predicate in terms of its original predicate and the find-all mechanism, or whether to define the inverse predicate in terms of other (possibly inverse) predicates, thus percolating the inverses across the combined cluster diagram. The system designer will choose between these two options on the grounds of efficiency. This decision will also be influenced by the availability of clusters which are composed of unique groups; this is denoted by the absence of "bars" on the arcs of the cluster diagrams. As we will see, the system designer may well choose to define an inverse predicate in terms of other (possibly inverse) predicates when there are a number of query types that could benefit from an efficient mechanization of such inverse predicates.

At present we are in the knowledge analysis phase and our concern is modeling. If it transpires during the next knowledge engineering phase that inverse predicates are required and that their importance is significant, then the analyst will revisit the knowledge analysis phase and will model the inverse predicates.

7.7.1   Worked example

We now extend the worked example by "inverting" the knowledge analyzed so far as represented by clusters [2] and [3].

First, consider the group [2.1'] which has emp/super as head predicate. The inverse of this predicate is super/emp-list. This inverse predicate may be defined by:

super/emp-list(x, y) ← is-the[gen-man](x),
        job/pers-list('Department Manager', y)
super/emp-list(x, w) ← pers-job(x, 'Department Manager'),
        emp/dept(x, y), dept/emp-list(y, z),
        pers-list/worker-list(z, w)
pers-list/worker-list($\emptyset$, $\emptyset$) ←
pers-list/worker-list(x.y, x.z) ← pers-list/worker-list(y, z),
        pers/job(x, 'Worker')
pers-list/worker-list(x.y, z) ← pers-list/worker-list(y, z),
        is-the[gen-man](x)
pers-list/worker-list(x.y, z) ← pers-list/worker-list(y, z),
        pers/job(x, 'Department Manager') $[2.1']^{-1}$

where the predicate pers-list/worker-list is of computational significance only and is considered to be an "internal predicate" in this group. An *internal predicate* is a subsidiary head predicate in a group which is of purely computational significance, an internal predicate is not recognized as a head predicate or a body predicate of that group. Note that the reason that we had to introduce pers-list/worker-list in the above example was purely in response to the limited power of Horn clause logic; this new predicate has no identified significance in the general context of the application. That is, as far as the management of this group is concerned, pers-list/worker-list is neither a head predicate nor a body predicate of the group. The predicate pers-list/worker-list(x, y) means "that x is a list of persons and y is a list of those workers in list x". The "-1" in the number of this group, $[2.1']^{-1}$, should be read as "the inverse of [2.1']". The dependency diagram for this inverse association is shown in Figure 7.30. Note that the inverse predicates are shown as square nodes on the diagram, while the "ordinary" predicates are shown as conventional, circular nodes. Note also that each inverse predicate is linked to its corresponding,

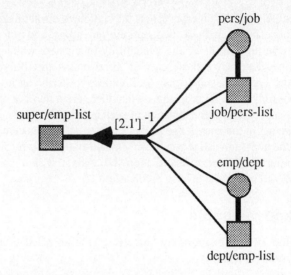

Figure 7.30 Dependency diagram for group [2.1']$^{-1}$

original predicate with a heavy line; this denotes that each inverse predicate may be defined in terms of its original predicate using the find-all mechanism. As all inverse predicates have this property, and as the clause groups that establish this all have the same form, we do not bother to quote these clause groups. Strictly speaking, the heavy line from the circular node to its corresponding square node should be marked with an arrow in this direction but, as they would all be so marked, we do not choose to complicate the diagram unnecessarily.

Next consider the group [2.2] which has pers/job as head predicate. The inverse of this predicate is job/pers-list. This inverse predicate may be defined by:

job/pers-list('General Manager', x.∅) ← is-the[gen-man](x)
job/pers-list('Department Manager', x) ← is-the[gen-man](y),
          super/emp-list(y, x)
job/pers-list('Worker', x) ← is-the[gen-man](w),
          super/emp-list(w, y), super-list/pers-list(y, z)
super-list/pers-list(∅, ∅) ←
super-list/pers-list(x.y, z) ← super-list/pers-list(y, w),
          super/emp-list(x, u), append(w, u, z)
append(∅, x, x) ←
append(x.y, z, x.w) ← append(y, z, w)   [2.2']$^{-1}$

in this group, the predicates "super-list/pers-list" and "append" have purely computational significance and are considered to be internal predicates in the group. The predicate append(w, u, z) means "list z is a concatenation of list w and list u". These two predicates are required solely because of the inability of logic programming to handle lists of lists in a natural way. The predicate super-list/pers-list(x, y) means "y is the

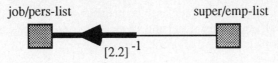

job/pers-list   super/emp-list

$$[2.2]^{-1}$$

Figure 7.31 Dependency diagram for group $[2.2]^{-1}$

list of persons supervised by the list of supervisors x". The dependency diagram for this group is shown in Figure 7.31. Note that this diagram does not have any circular nodes; this means that the group does not refer to any "ordinary" predicates.

Next consider the group [2.3] which has emp/dept as head predicate. The inverse of this predicate is dept/emp-list. This inverse predicate may be defined by:

dept/emp-list(x, y.z) ← dept/mngr(x, y), super/emp-list(y, z) $[2.3]^{-1}$

Note that the body of this group contains one ordinary predicate, dept/mngr, and one inverse predicate, super/emp-list. Its dependency diagram is shown in Figure 7.32.

As an amusing diversion, it is interesting to note that the inverse group $[2.3]^{-1}$ can be derived directly from the corresponding original group [2.3]. First, dept/emp-list can be defined in terms of emp/dept and the find-all mechanism by:

dept/emp-list(x, y) ← emp-dept(z, x), tuple/find-all-list((z), y)

Second, note that [2.3] enables *all* the information in emp-dept to be deduced from the information in dept/mngr and emp/super. Thus, all the information in dept/emp-list can be deduced by substituting [2.3] in the above clause:

dept/emp-list(x, y) ← dept/mngr(x, z), tuple/find-all-list((z), y)
dept/emp-list(x, y) ← emp/super(z, w), dept/mngr(x, w),
        tuple/find-all-list((z), y)

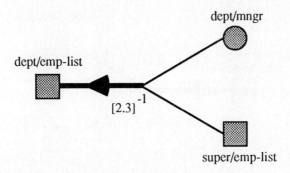

dept/mngr

dept/emp-list

$$[2.3]^{-1}$$

super/emp-list

Figure 7.32 Dependency diagram for group $[2.3]^{-1}$

Third, note that the body of the first clause contains an expression for mngr/dept-list in terms of the find-all mechanism and the second clause contains an expression for super/emp-list in terms of the find-all mechanism. Thus:

dept/emp-list(x, y) ← dept/mngr-list(x, y)
dept/emp-list(x, y) ← dept/mngr(x, w), super/emp-list(w, y)

Fourth, note that as there is only one manager for each department, the first of these two clauses may be rewritten using "w.∅" for list y:

dept/emp-list(x, w.∅) ← dept/mngr(x , w)

Fifth, note that this version of the first clause calculates single element emp-lists and may, in fact, be combined with the second clause to give:

dept/emp-list(x, w.y) ← dept/mngr(x, w), super/emp-list(w, y)

which is just $[2.3]^{-1}$. This completes our derivation of $[2.3]^{-1}$.

Next, consider the group [2.4"]: the head of this group is dept/mngr. As each department has only one manager, there is little to be gained in constructing the inverse predicate "mngr/dept".

Next, consider the group [3.1] which has pers/salary as head predicate. The inverse of this predicate is salary/pers-list. This inverse predicate may be defined by:

salary/pers-list(x, y) ← salary/job-list(x, z), job-list/pers-list(z , y)
job-list/pers-list(∅ , ∅) ←
job-list/pers-list(x.v, w) ← job-list/pers-list(v, u),
                    job/pers-list(x, z), append(u, z, w)
append(∅, x, x) ←
append(x.y, z, x.w) ← append(y, z, w) $[3.1]^{-1}$

In this group, the predicates job-list/pers-list and append only have computational significance and are internal predicates. The dependency diagram for the group $[3.1]^{-1}$ is shown in Figure 7.33.

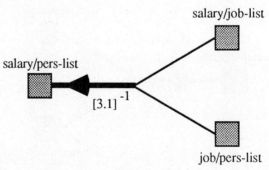

salary/job-list

salary/pers-list

$[3.1]^{-1}$

job/pers-list

Figure 7.33 Dependency diagram for group $[3.1]^{-1}$

This completes the construction of the inverse predicates for the knowledge represented in the combined cluster diagram. We now draw a combined diagram consisting of the dependencies identified for the inverse predicates; this diagram is called the *inverse group diagram*. This diagram is shown in Figure 7.34. The predicates, clauses and groups shown in the inverse group diagram all satisfy the normal form principles for predicates, clauses and groups with the exception of the first clause in $[2.1']^{-1}$ which contravenes principle K.1.4. We regard this transgression as being of little significance. The (information model) consistency of the groups in the inverse group diagram may be demonstrated automatically using the same information model as was employed in the previous Section 7.6.1.

It is also useful to construct the "inverse cluster diagram". The *inverse cluster diagram* is drawn just as the combined cluster diagram except that if a predicate and its inverse are in the inverse group diagram, then only the inverse (i.e. a "square box") is shown on the inverse cluster diagram. Recall that the cluster diagram is intended to give an "executive view" of the application; if there is an inverse predicate then surely there will be a corresponding ordinary predicate, thus it seems unnecessary to show both in an "executive view". The inverse cluster diagram for the above example is shown in Figure 7.35.

There is little to be gained in drawing the combined group or cluster diagram together with the inverse group or cluster diagram. The inverse diagrams are only of use in designing the computational support for query types that are directly supported by inverse predicates.

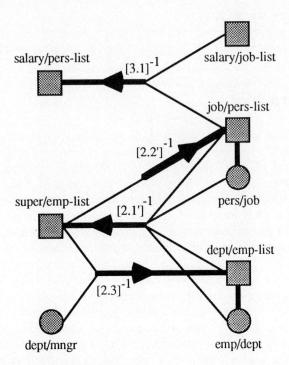

Figure 7.34 Inverse group diagram

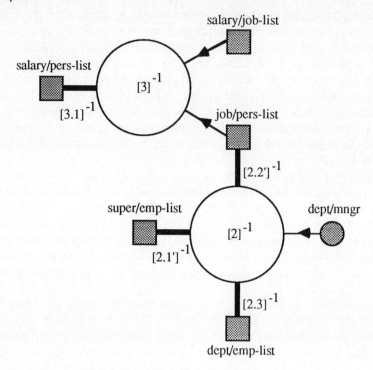

Figure 7.35 Inverse cluster diagram

7.8 SUMMARY

We have discussed the activities involved in the model building process, and have seen how these activities relate to the traditional approaches to building information systems. The classification of objects has been analysed and those classifications which are unacceptable have been identified. We have seen that the business of object classification is concerned more with identifying the information and knowledge in a fact than it is with actually classifying the fact itself as information or knowledge. The process of building the knowledge model pre-supposes the successful completion of the knowledge acquisition phase. When the knowledge acquisition phase is complete, a model of the data will have been constructed. Then, information analysis is performed before knowledge analysis. In knowledge analysis we have given a systematic way of developing the knowledge, and have shown how to normalize the knowledge and how to show that it is consistent. We have employed cluster diagrams as a convenient notation for describing the way in which the knowledge "fits together". The actual design of a knowledge system has been presented in three components, the data model, the information model and the knowledge model. Finally, the analysis of inverse associations has been presented; inverse associations can be of assistance in supporting complex query types efficiently.

⑧ Knowledge base engineering

8.1 INTRODUCTION

In this chapter we address the apparently simple problem of selecting the "least complex" items of knowledge identified during knowledge analysis to perform the required tasks. It turns out that this problem is, in fact, surprisingly hard. In practice the work described in this chapter is mechanized so if the reader's interests are primarily with modeling knowledge, then the reader may choose not to study this chapter in great detail. In particular, Section 8.4, in which the complexity of the knowledge base engineering problem is proved, will appeal only to the mathematically minded reader. In any case, the reader is advised to study Section 8.3 carefully.

Knowledge base engineering is the third phase in the design of a knowledge system. In simple terms, knowledge base engineering is concerned with taking the product of the previous phase, namely knowledge analysis, adding in the functional requirements and deriving a functional system which will perform the required tasks and has, in some sense, the least complexity. Thus, the input to the knowledge base engineering phase is the gathered knowledge as represented on the combined group diagram and as summarized on the combined cluster diagram. The output of the knowledge base engineering phase is a functional system; this functional system will be represented on a "combined functional diagram".

In this chapter we first discuss the specification of the functional requirements of a knowledge system. The "knowledge base engineering problem" is introduced as the problem of deriving a functional system; the complexity of this problem is investigated. To enable us to state that one solution to the knowledge base engineering problem is "better than" another, we introduce complexity measures for groups. We then discuss two Algorithms which enable a reasonable solution to the knowledge base engineering problem to be derived quickly. And last the worked example discussed in the previous chapter is extended into the knowledge base engineering phase.

This chapter contains algorithms and techniques which give rise to fairly extensive calculations. These calculations are illustrated in worked examples. We wish to stress that in practice these calculations are not performed by hand.

8.2 THE FUNCTIONAL REQUIREMENTS

As we have discussed in Section 3.5, knowledge systems are systems in which the knowledge is encoded in a knowledge language, which employ a database management system for information and data storage. The form of the system query types is knowledge, information and data, and the scope of the system update types is knowledge, information and data. Thus, the specification of the functional requirements for a knowledge system will include the specification of functional requirements for both query and update types which are related directly to the data, information and knowledge components of the knowledge system.

The update types for a knowledge system will include update types for data, information and knowledge. An example of a data update type might be "the specification of today's date"; a particular label "8-8-1988" could be attached to a population called "today's-date". An example of an information update type might be, "the cost in dollars of a particular spare part"; a particular tuple (1234, 12:$) could be attached to a relation:

    spare-part/cost:$

An example of a knowledge update type might be, "the rule for calculating the pre-tax selling price of particular spare parts". A particular clause for tractor spare parts could be:

    spare-part/pre-tax-selling-price:$(x, y) ← spare-part/cost:$(x, z),
                 spare-part/spare-part-type(x, 'tractor'),
                 spare-part-type/mark-up-factor('tractor', w),
                 $y = (z \times w) + 12$

This clause states that the pre-tax selling price of tractor spare parts carries a fixed charge of \$12 above the amount calculated by the standard mark-up procedure. This clause could be attached to a group with head predicate:

    spare-part/pre-tax-selling-price

Thus, unlike conventional database systems, we include in the update types for a knowledge system the possibility of particular bits of the knowledge base being identified as being directly associated with update types. In other words, in general, knowledge systems are designed to receive regular update transactions which are directly associated with the data, information *and* knowledge. It is vital to the maintenance of the integrity of a knowledge system that each update type be carefully constrained. Thus, in addition to the conventional constraints for data and information, a knowledge system will contain constraints for the knowledge update types. For example, the clause quoted above might be subjected to the following constraint: the clause must contain at least:

    spare-part/cost
    spare-part/spare-part-type
    spare-part-type/mark-up-factor

as body predicates.

The query types for a knowledge system will include query types for data, information and knowledge. An example of a data query type might be "What is today's date?". An example of an information query type might be "What is the cost of spare part number 1234?". An example of a knowledge query type is "How was the selling price of spare part number 1234 calculated?". In our opinion, the ability to explain succinctly and meaningfully how any calculation has been performed is an essential hallmark of a good knowledge system. Another example of a knowledge query type might be "Can all the tuples which satisfy the predicate:

> spare-part/pre-tax-selling-price:$

be deduced from the tuples which satisfy the predicates:

> spare-part/cost:$
> spare-part/spare-part-type
> spare-part-type/mark-up-factor

and if so, how?".

In summary, the specification of the functional requirements for a knowledge system will include:

- the identification of the system query types for data, information and knowledge;
- the identification of the system update types for data, information and knowledge;
- the identification of the system integrity checks for data, information and knowledge.

As we have noted above, the ability of a knowledge system to explain how it has performed an operation is, by default, assumed to be one of the query types. Each query type and update type will be directly associated with one or more items of data information or knowledge. Once they have been identified, the query types and update types are added to the application model, and the items of data, information and knowledge associated with each query and update type are identified in the data, information and knowledge models.

8.3 THE KNOWLEDGE BASE ENGINEERING PROBLEM

The product of the previous phase, namely knowledge analysis, will be the information model and the knowledge model; these two models, together with the data model developed during knowledge acquisition, form a complete model of the application. A useful presentation of the structure of the knowledge model may be shown in the combined cluster diagram which presents a high level view of the knowledge. The combined cluster diagram provides an executive view of the combined group diagram which refers to collections of groups. Each group will consist of a collection of clauses. Each clause will refer to a collection of predicates. Each predicate will refer to a collection of domains. Each domain is permitted to refer to a particular collection of labels.

At this stage in our discussion we are not concerned with the decomposition of the product of knowledge analysis right down to labels as described above. In the knowledge base engineering phase we are concerned with clusters and groups only. However, we do assume that during knowledge analysis the groups, predicates and populations have all been normalized as described in Chapter 5. We also assume that, during knowledge analysis, the analyst has tried where possible to construct complete clusters, and has shown each cluster to be consistent at least within the limited meaning of "information model consistent". As the analyst has tried to construct complete clusters we would expect the combined cluster diagram to contain "circuits". A *circuit* is a sequence of predicates $\{ A^1 ,..., A^{n+1} \}$ where, for each pair (A^i , A^{i+1}) for $i = 1,...,n$, there is a clause group with A^i as its head and with A^{i+1} in its body, $A^1 = A^{n+1}$, and $n > 1$. If the combined cluster diagram does not contain a circuit then, intuitively, it has a very simple structure in that the represented knowledge contains a specific "direction".

Given a combined cluster diagram, a prerequisite to the derivation of a functional representation is the identification of those relations and populations which are associated in a natural way with the major query types, these relations and populations are called the *query relations* and *query populations*, and those relations and populations which are associated in a natural way with the major update types, these relations and populations are called the *update relations* and *update populations*. In other words, the query relations are those relations which contain sufficient information to satisfy each major query type directly. By "directly" we mean "without the use of additional knowledge". It is clear that a query type may be associated with more than one query relation. For example, the query type "to find the salary and job description for every employee in the business" might be associated in a natural way with the two following relations:

employee/salary
employee/job-description

In which case, these two relations would both be referred to as query relations. Likewise, the update relations are those relations which can represent the major update types directly. Once again, by "directly" we mean "without the use of additional knowledge". It is clear that an update type may be associated with more than one update relation. For example, the update type "an employee's time sheet shows, for each week for that person, the ordinary hours worked and the overtime hours worked" might be associated in a natural way with the two following relations:

person/week/ordinary-work:hours
person/week/overtime-work:hours

In which case, these two relations would be referred to as update relations. The first step in the derivation of a functional representation is to identify the update and the query relations and populations in the combined cluster diagram. If they are not already on that diagram, then additional knowledge may have to be acquired and included. This will involve revisiting the knowledge acquisition and knowledge analysis phases, but otherwise this first step does not give rise to much difficulty.

Once the query relations and populations and update relations and populations have been identified within, or added to the combined cluster diagram, we are in a position to choose a "selection" of groups that will enable the query relations and populations to be deduced from the update relations and populations. In general, if a set of clause groups enables the information (or data) in a set of predicates (or populations) X to be calculated from the information and data in a set of predicates and populations Y then that set of clause groups is said to *support* X on Y. A *selection* is a set of clause groups which supports the query relations on the update relations. We will restrict our discussion to selections which do not contain circuits. Thus, the groups will either be non-recursive or "primary recursive". In our experience, this does not impose a practical limitation on the ability of clauses to represent real knowledge. Denoting predicates by letters from the set {A,B,C,D,E}, a Horn clause of the form:

$$A \leftarrow A, B, C$$

that is, where a predicate name appears both as the head and within the body of the clause is called *primary recursive*. However, this restriction does mean that exotic forms of recursion such as:

$$A \leftarrow B, C, D$$
$$A \leftarrow B$$
$$C \leftarrow A, E, F$$
$$C \leftarrow E$$

where the group with head A has C in its body and vice versa, would be excluded.

The *complexity of a selection* is defined to be the sum of the complexities of the clause groups in that selection. (We will discuss measures for the complexity of clause groups later but for the time being we just assume that a clause group cannot have negative complexity.) This additive definition of complexity of clause groups in a selection is quite reasonable; to see this, note that any least complex selection will contain at most one clause group with any specified predicate or population as head. The *knowledge base engineering problem* is to find the selection of least complexity. In the next section, we will show that this problem is "NP-complete", and that it remains "NP-complete" even if the combined cluster diagram does not contain a circuit. To say that a problem is *NP-complete* means that it would appear that the execution time of any algorithm which completely solves that problem will grow exponentially with the size of the problem, (*see* Garey and Johnson, 1979). In other words, an NP-complete problem has no non-exponential solutions. Thus a practical algorithm for the general solution of an NP-complete problem must necessarily be sub-optimal.

A solution to the knowledge base engineering problem will be (hopefully) a selection of least complexity. This selection will be represented on a *combined functional diagram*. This diagram shows each group in the selection; the query and update relations and populations are identified and the diagram is customarily drawn with the functional associations going from right to left. An example of a combined functional diagram is given in the worked example at the end of this chapter.

A knowledge base engineering technique will be concerned with the solution of the knowledge base engineering problem. Thus, a knowledge base engineering technique must incorporate the following:

• A method for developing computational support for each query type based on the model constructed by knowledge analysis: this may be phrased in terms of some query language. This is essentially a "synthetic" component of the knowledge base engineering problem in that the answer to the query types have to be constructed from the available relations and populations.

- A method for developing computational support for the model of the knowledge in terms of the update types. This is essentially an "analytic" component of the knowledge base engineering problem in that the data and information in each update type has to be analysed to see which relations and populations are sufficient to represent that information.
- A method for extending the model where it is incomplete.
- A method for "arranging" the knowledge; that is, a method for extracting a sub-model which supports the query types and which may be completely maintained by the update types. This is the crucial step as this arrangement should be "sensible", in the sense that it should endeavour to be able to support minor changes such as the introduction of a new query type.

In addition, the following is a desirable feature of a knowledge base engineering technique:

- A method for automatically rearranging the knowledge in response to changes in the query or update types.

In summary, the knowledge base engineering phase introduces the query relations and populations and the update relations and populations into the combined cluster diagram which was developed during knowledge analysis, and derives a computationally feasible model of the application.

The complexity of the computations in knowledge analysis tends to vary as the number of rules in the system; but the complexity of the computations in knowledge base engineering and knowledge base implementation increase very rapidly with the size of the problem. Thus, in the small worked example developed first in Chapter 6 and considered again later in this chapter, the knowledge base engineering and implementation phases appear comparatively trivial; this is not the case for realistic, larger problems. For problems with ten or so initial clusters of knowledge, a manual solution would usually be very tedious if not unfeasible. Note that the worked example considered in the next section only contains two clusters of knowledge on completion of the knowledge analysis phase.

8.4 COMPLEXITY OF THE KNOWLEDGE BASE ENGINEERING PROBLEM

We now establish the complexity of the knowledge base engineering problem. We will show that this problem is NP-complete. In fact, our proof demonstrates that the knowledge base engineering problem is NP-complete even if we restrict the problem to circuitless sets of non-recursive, single-clause clause groups in which the predicates and populations do not contain any variables.

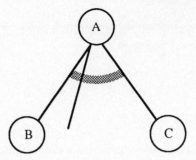

Figure 8.1 AND construct

RESULT
The knowledge base engineering problem is NP-complete.

Proof
By reduction to the "Optimum solution to AND/OR graphs" problem, (Sahni, 1974).

We show that an AND/OR graph can be transformed into a set of clause groups and that the problem of finding the optimum solution to the AND/OR graph is thus transformed into a restriction of the knowledge base engineering problem.

Given an AND/OR graph, proceed as follows:

Step 1
All AND constructs are replaced by a single-clause clause group; the AND construct shown in Figure 8.1 becomes:

$A \leftarrow B, .., C$

and the complexity of the clause group is the sum of the weights of the arcs flowing from the AND node.

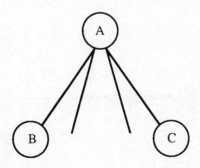

Figure 8.2 OR construct

Step 2

All OR constructs, with n arcs, are replaced with n single-clause clause groups; the OR construct shown in Figure 8.2 becomes:

$$A \leftarrow B$$
. . . .
$$A \leftarrow C$$

and the complexities of the n clause groups are the weights of the corresponding arcs flowing from the OR node.

(Note that the individual clause groups which have been constructed are non-recursive and consist of one clause each. Note that the clause groups constructed do not contain any variables. Also note that the set of clause groups which has been constructed does not contain a circuit.)

The (unique) predicate which is not in the body of another clause group is the (single) query relation and the set of predicates which are not the head of any clause group are the set of update relations. Thus, we have constructed a set of clause groups and the optimal solution to the original AND/OR graph will transform to the solution of the knowledge base engineering problem for this set of clause groups.

The proof of this result suggests the dependency diagram notation for clause groups. A clause group represents knowledge which defines one predicate (the head) in terms of others (the body). We have represented this with a "directed tree" called a dependency diagram as shown in Figure 8.3. The tree is labeled with a *cost* equal to the complexity of the clause group which it represents.

It is interesting to note from the proof of the result that the knowledge base engineering problem remains NP-complete for circuitless sets of non-recursive, single-clause clause groups. The difficulty with the knowledge base engineering problem is that if a structure of the kind shown in Figure 8.4 occurs, then if C is chosen to support A, it can also be used to support B at no extra cost. These are classic symptoms of a problem that will require "look ahead" and will admit only an exponential solution.

Head predicates which are also in the body of two or more clause groups are called *critical predicates*. Their corresponding nodes, which are the foot of more that one tree, are called *critical nodes*. Node x, in Figure 8.4, is an example of a critical node.

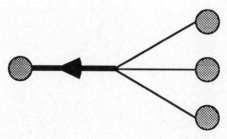

Figure 8.3 Dependency diagram

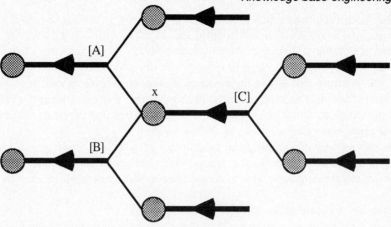

Figure 8.4 Symptoms of a problem requiring "look ahead"

8.5 COMPLEXITY MEASURES

Our measures of complexity are primarily intended to be measures of the complexity of the *representation* of the data, information and knowledge. They are not intended to be functional measures of complexity, that is, measures of the complexity in *using* the data, information and knowledge. Thus, notions such as the relative frequency of presentation of query types will not concern us here. The reason for this is that our complexity measures will be used to choose the least complex functional representation which should remain a good choice as demands on the system change.

The complexity measures noted below are fairly crude. Our intention is to define simple, meaningful measures which are effective in identifying the least complex clause groups. We make no pretence to presenting the last word in complexity measures for knowledge.

Examples of complexity measures for predicates include:

- The *trivial measure*, by which the complexity of any predicate is unity.
- The *domain measure*, by which the complexity of any predicate is its number of arguments.
- The *relation measure*, by which the complexity of any predicate is an estimate of the time to retrieve a tuple from that predicate if it were stored as a relation.

These simple measures make no attempt to capture the structure of the tuples within the predicates; for example, to distinguish between P(x, x) and P(x, a) for variable x and constant a.

A simple measure of the complexity of a clause is the sum of the complexities of the predicate occurrences in the body of it, where by "predicate occurrences" we mean that if the same predicate occurs more than once, then duplications are counted. The elementary wisdom behind this measure is that the complexity of the clause is the complexity of the operation of fully satisfying the clause; at the best, this will be achieved when each body predicate has been unified with a unit clause (a *unit clause* is a clause with no body), which will require just as many unifications as there are body predicate occurrences. Taking this idea one step further, we assume that the cost in fully satisfying a clause will be related to those predicates which are relations only. In other words, this measure will ignore the presence of internal predicates and "is-a" or "is-the" predicates. Thus, this measure takes no account of the "logical structure" of the clause, that is the extent to which the variables, constants, terms and predicates occur in more than one place in the clause.

A simple way of defining the complexity of a clause group is the sum of the complexities of the clauses in the group. This definition ignores the whole logical structure of the clause group and is too crude to be useful. Instead we proceed as follows:

1. Choose n, a non-negative integer constant.
2. Given a clause group, add to it all consequences that can be established by a sequence of no more than n resolutions involving recursive clauses only. That is, recursive clauses are resolved with themselves and with other recursive clauses up to resolution depth n.
3. Where possible, use non-recursive clauses, in all possible ways, to remove the recursive occurrences of head predicates in the bodies of clauses. Remove occurrences of internal predicates.
4. Delete any remaining recursive clauses.
5. The complexity of the clause group is defined to be the sum of the complexities of the remaining, distinct, individual clauses in this augmented group.

For example, consider the clause group:

item-list/price-list($\emptyset$, $\emptyset$) ←
item-list/price-list(x.y , u.v) ← item/cost(x , u), item-list/price-list(y , v)

where the predicate item-list/price-list(y , v) means "v is a list of prices corresponding to the list of item numbers y". Suppose that in step 1 the constant n is set to unity. Then in step 2 we add the clause:

item-list/price-list(x.y.z , u.v.w) ← item/cost(x , u),
        item/cost(y, v), item-list/price-list(z , w)

In step 3 we use the clause:

item-list/price-list($\emptyset$, $\emptyset$) ←

to remove recursive occurrences. The augmented group then contains:

item-list/price-list($\emptyset$, $\emptyset$) ←
item-list/price-list(x.$\emptyset$, u.$\emptyset$) ← item/cost(x , u)
item-list/price-list(x.y.$\emptyset$, u.v.$\emptyset$) ← item/cost(x, u), item/cost(u, v)

No recursive clauses remain and in step 5 we calculate the complexity of this group to be 3. For this measure to have a satisfactory interpretation, the constant n should be set to the mean expected number of applications of recursion for each group. However, recall that we are interested in complexity measures only as a tool for deciding whether one clause group is more complex than another; we are not interested here in obtaining measures of complexity that are meaningful in absolute terms. The calculations described above can be very tedious by hand, but it is clear that these calculations may be mechanized easily.

An example of a group containing an internal predicate is $[2.1']^{-1}$. Again choose $n = 1$. In step 2 we add:

pers-list/worker-list(x.y.z, x.y.w) ← pers-list/worker-list(z, w),
           pers/job(x, 'Worker'), pers/job(y, 'Worker')
pers-list/worker-list(x.y.z, y.v) ← pers-list/worker-list(z, v),
           is-the[gen-man](x), pers/job(y, 'Worker')
pers-list/worker-list(x.y.z, x.v) ← pers-list/worker-list(z, v),
           pers/job(x, 'Worker'), is-the[gen-man](y)
pers-list/worker-list(x.y.z, v) ← pers-list/worker-list(z, v),
           pers/job(x, 'Department Manager'), pers/job(y, 'Worker')
pers-list/worker-list(x.y.z, v) ← pers-list/worker-list(z, v),
           pers/job(x, 'Worker'), pers/job(y, 'Department Manager')
pers-list/worker-list(x.y.z, w) ← pers-list/worker-list(z, w),
           is-the[gen-man](x), is-the[gen-man](y)
pers-list/worker-list(x.y.z, w) ← pers-list/worker-list(z, w),
           is-the[gen-man](x), pers/job(y, 'Department Manager')
pers-list/worker-list(x.y.z, w) ← pers-list/worker-list(z, w),
           pers/job(x, 'Department Manager'), is-the[gen-man](y),
pers-list/worker-list(x.y.z, w) ← pers-list/worker-list(z, w),
           pers/job(x, 'Department Manager'),
           pers/job(y, 'Department Manager')

In step 3 we remove the recursive occurrences of the head predicate:

pers-list/worker-list(x.y.∅, x.y.∅) ← pers/job(x, 'Worker'),
           pers/job(y, 'Worker')
pers-list/worker-list(x.y.∅, y.∅) ← is-the[gen-man](x),
           pers/job(y, 'Worker')
pers-list/worker-list(x.y.∅, x.∅) ← pers/job(x, 'Worker'),
           is-the[gen-man](y)
pers-list/worker-list(x.y.∅, ∅) ← pers/job(x, 'Department Manager'),
           pers/job(y, 'Worker')
pers-list/worker-list(x.y.∅, ∅) ← pers/job(x, 'Worker'),
           pers/job(y, 'Department Manager')
pers-list/worker-list(x.y.∅, ∅) ← is-the[gen-man](x),
           is-the[gen-man](y)

pers-list/worker-list(x.y.$\emptyset$, $\emptyset$) ← is-the[gen-man](x),
         pers/job(y, 'Department Manager')
pers-list/worker-list(x.y.$\emptyset$, $\emptyset$) ← pers/job(x, 'Department Manager'),
         is-the[gen-man](y)
pers-list/worker-list(x.y.$\emptyset$, $\emptyset$) ← pers/job(x, 'Department Manager'),
         pers/job(y, 'Department Manager')

Next we remove the occurrences of internal predicates. The above clauses together with the clause:

per-list/worker-list($\emptyset$, $\emptyset$) ←

are now used to remove, in all possible ways, the predicate pers-list/worker-list from the second clause in $[2.1']^{-1}$. For reasons of space, we do not show the resulting set of clauses, but it is not hard to show that this resulting set has complexity 49.

In practice, quite reasonable results are obtained in this way with $n = 1$ in the above procedure and using the trivial measure for predicates. The elementary wisdom behind this measure is that the complexity of a group is the complexity in fully satisfying the clauses derivable from the group up to resolution depth n. In line with this approach we measure the complexity of groups which depend on the find-all mechanism as follows. Consider:

super/emp-list(x, y) ← emp/super(z, x), tuple/find-all-list((z), y)

Instead of constructing resolvants to resolution depth n we construct the equivalent clauses that would be required to represent the above clause restricted to n additional backtracks. For example, if $n = 1$, we construct:

super/emp-list(x, y.$\emptyset$) ← emp/super(y, x)
super/emp-list(x, y.z.$\emptyset$) ← emp/super(y, x), emp/super(z, x)

In which case, for $n = 1$ and with the trivial measure for predicates, this group has complexity 3. Recall from above that we will ignore the occurrence of internal predicates and "is-a" or "is-the" predicates. In the worked example in Section 8.7 we will use this measure with $n = 1$ and the trivial complexity measure for predicates.

8.6 SUB-OPTIMAL GROUP SELECTION

We have shown in Section 8.4 that the knowledge base engineering problem is NP-complete. The solution to this problem is the selection with least complexity. Recall from Section 8.3 that the complexity of a selection is defined to be the sum of the complexities of the groups in that selection. Thus, each clause group contributes its own complexity to the sum no matter how many times it is used by the other clause groups; we have seen that this is why the problem is NP-complete.

We now define an alternative notion of complexity. Consider the combined group diagram, for any particular clause group (or its dependency diagram) in a selection there will be a finite number of paths from its head to the query nodes. This number is the *dependency diagram weight* of that dependency diagram, or correspondingly the *clause group weight* of that group. The *tree complexity* of a selection of clause groups is defined to be the sum, over all the clause groups in that selection, of the products of the clause group complexities and clause group weights. The problem of finding the selection with least tree complexity is no longer the knowledge base engineering problem. It is the *tree cover problem* which may be solved in polynomial time. In general, in a combined graph, if Q is the set of identified query nodes and U is the set of identified update nodes, then we denote the selection which is the solution to the tree cover problem by T[Q , U].

The following Algorithm finds T[Q , U]. In it, all nodes are marked either "active" or "passive", and either "visited" or "unvisited". All groups, or their corresponding dependency diagrams, are marked either "chosen" or "not chosen". The Algorithm systematically marks each node x with a *least support cost*, this cost will be the tree complexity of the selection T[{x} , U].

The correctness of Algorithm A follows from the observation that *if* the active nodes are marked with their least support cost, *then* the cost marked on the head predicate of the group chosen in step 2 of the Algorithm must be the least support cost for that predicate. Also note that if it is possible to support the set Q on the set U then the Algorithm will terminate with each node in Q marked "visited". Note that Algorithm A systematically "builds across" from the update relations towards the query relations, but that it does not attempt to "look ahead" to identify any critical nodes which might offer a significant cost saving.

The complexity of Algorithm A depends on the amount of interconnectivity in the combined group diagram. For combined group diagrams in which each (critical) node is a body predicate in at most k groups, for some fixed constant k, the time complexity is a

---

ALGORITHM A.
1.   In the combined group diagram, mark all groups (or their corresponding dependency diagrams) "not chosen". Mark the set of nodes U "active" and "visited", and mark all other nodes "passive" and "unvisited", and mark the set of nodes U with zero cost.
2.   **while** there are nodes in Q marked "unvisited"

do for all groups with "active" body predicates and "unvisited" head predicates, calculate the sum of the group cost and all its body predicate costs, mark the group with the least such sum as being "chosen", mark the head predicate of that group with this sum, mark the head predicate of that group "active" and "visited", mark each body predicate of that group "passive" as long as that body predicate is not also a body predicate in another group whose head predicate is marked "unvisited".
   endwhile
3.   T[Q , U] will be the set of groups marked "chosen". The tree complexity of this selection, comp(T[Q , U]), will be the sum of the costs marked on the set of query nodes Q.

Figure 8.5 Algorithm A

ALGORITHM B.

1.   Initialize X to be the set, Q, of query nodes. Let U be the set of update nodes.
2.   **while** there is a critical point, c, in the combined graph, for which the expression
comp(T[X , U]) - comp(T[X , U ∪ {c}]) - comp(T[{c} , U])   is
positive
   do choose the critical point, c, for which the above expression is greatest **and** find
all nodes on direct paths from c to X in the calculation of T[X , U ∪ {c}] **and** add
these nodes to the set X
   endwhile
3.   The solution is T[X , U] when step (2) terminates;   the set X contains the
incorporated critical points.

Figure 8.6 Algorithm B

linear function of the number of groups in the combined graph. In general, it may be shown that the time complexity will be a quadratic function of the number of groups.

We now outline a method which finds reasonably intelligent solutions to the knowledge base engineering problem in polynomial time. The strategy is to start with the solution to the tree cover problem. Then to add critical points to it, in the order of the cost savings that they offer individually, provided that this cost saving is positive. The Algorithm quoted is in Figure 8.6. The interesting feature of our solution is that it can be phrased simply in terms of Algorithm A shown in Figure 8.5.

To see that Algorithm B, shown in Figure 8.6, implements the strategy described above, note that if the expression given in step 2 is positive, then at least two paths must go from {c} to the set X in the graph T[X , U ∪ {c}].

In Algorithm B, note that if c lies on T[X , U] then the expression quoted in step 2 will always be positive. In fact, the value of this expression will be a multiple of comp(T[{c} , U]). Thus, if all critical points lie on T[Q , U] then no new nodes will be added to the graph and the critical points will all be incorporated into the set X, one at a time, starting with those "nearest" the query nodes. On the other hand, if, at any stage, a critical point c is added which does not lie on T[X , U] then the result of applying one iteration of step 2 in the Algorithm will change the graph by adding node c and all nodes on all paths from c to U to the set X.

The complexity of Algorithm B depends on the proportion of nodes in the combined graph which are critical. It is quite realistic to assume that this will be bounded by a quadratic function of the number of trees in the combined graph, n. In which case, the time complexity of the Algorithm will be bounded by a cubic or quartic function of n, depending on the bound for the solution to the tree cover problem given in Algorithm A (*see* Figure 8.5). Note however, that if, in any iteration in Algorithm B, the critical node chosen in step 2 is already in the tree T[X , U] then the computation for that particular iteration is greatly reduced.

8.7   WORKED EXAMPLE

We now extend the simple worked example as developed in Chapter 7. Suppose that the query types are to:

Q1   find the supervisor of any given employee;
Q2   find the list of employees supervised by a given person;
Q3   find the manager of any given department;
Q4   calculate the total salary for any given department,

as well as to:

Q5   explain how the above four query types may be satisfied in general;
Q6   explain how any particular answer to one of the above four query types was derived.

The first query type is directly supported by the relation emp/super, and the third query type is directly supported by the relation dept/mngr. The second query type is supported by the "inverse predicate" of emp/super:

$\quad$ super/emp-list(<u>\<supervisor\></u> , \<list of employees\>)

which could be implemented by searching the second domain of emp/super if it were actually stored. If emp/super were not actually stored, this inverse predicate may either be calculated in terms of its "original" predicate and the tuple/find-all-list predicate:

$\quad$ super/emp-list(x, y) $\leftarrow$ emp/super(z, x), tuple/find-all-list((z), y)

or by using the group $[2.1']^{-1}$ discussed in the previous chapter. Group $[2.1']^{-1}$ defines super/emp-list in terms of other inverse predicates. The system designer will choose between these two options on the grounds of efficiency.

$\quad$ To service the fourth query type we introduce the new population "sal-bill", which is established by the following statements, which are added to the application model:

21.1   There are total-salary-bills.
21.2   Total-salary-bills are identified by a salary-bill-amount expressed in dollars per annum.
21.3   Salary-bill-amounts must be positive integers.

Then we introduce the new predicate:

$\quad$ dept/sal-bill(<u>x</u> , y) which means "x is the name of a department whose total salary bill is \$y per annum"

this is established by the following statement which is added to the application model:

22.1   Each department is associated with a total salary bill.

The knowledge required to deduce the tuples in the predicate dept/sal-bill is expressed in the following statements which are also added to the application model:

23.1   The total salary bill for a department may be deduced from the salary of the department manager and from the salaries of the employees who are supervised by that manager.

23.2   **if** a department has a manager **and** that manager supervises a collection of employees, **then** the total salary bill for that department is the sum of the salaries of the manager and the employees who are supervised by that manager.

then we define:

dept/sal-bill(x , y) ← dept/mngr(x , z), super/emp-list(z , w),
          pers-list/salary(z.w , y)
pers-list/salary(∅ , 0) ←
pers-list/salary(x.y , z) ← pers/salary(x , v), pers-list/salary(y , w),
          z = v + w   [4.1]

where pers-list/salary only has computational significance and is classified as an internal predicate in this group, pers-list/salary(x , y) means "x is a list of persons whose total salary bill is $y per annum". Note that pers-list/salary is *not* an inverse predicate. This predicate is an ordinary logic programming predicate; although note that if it is presented with "input" through its second argument, it could be expected to behave badly and possibly never terminate. Note also that pers-list/salary occurs on both sides of the third clause in [4.1], but, as it is an internal predicate in this clause, it is not shown on the dependency diagram. Recall that the dependency diagram should be interpreted as "all the information in the predicate dept/sal-bill may be calculated from the information in the predicates pers/salary, super/emp-list and dept/mngr": this is true, and is established by the (recursive) logic in [4.1]. Recall that "z.w" denotes a list with head element "z" and the list "w" as tail. Note that the body of the first clause in group [4.1] contains the predicate super/emp-list which will be activated with its first domain as the "input" as long as the head predicate of this clause is activated with its first domain as the "input"; note that this is precisely the requirement of Q4. The dependency diagram is shown in Figure 8.7. The system designer has the choice of defining super/emp-list either in terms of both emp/super and the predicate tuple/find-all-list or in terms of other predicates in the system, such as those in cluster [2]$^{-1}$ which were developed in the previous chapter, some of which may need to be inverted. If the system designer has decided that super/emp-list is to be defined in terms of emp/super and the find-all mechanism then the two dependency diagrams drawn together would be as shown in Figure 8.8. which, if this decision is made, may be drawn in the simpler form shown in Figure 8.9. In this worked example we will *not* draw the dependency diagrams in this simplified way.

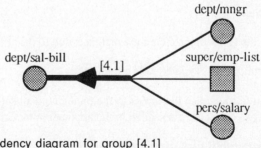

Figure 8.7 Dependency diagram for group [4.1]

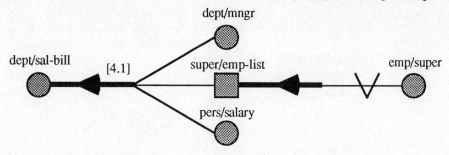

Figure 8.8 Dependency diagram for group [4.1] and super/emp-list group

As the knowledge represented above in [4.1] is specifically concerned with servicing the fourth query type, there is not likely to be much gained by investigating other dependencies in this diagram. In other words, there is not likely to be much point in completing this cluster.

We now attempt to simplify and normalize the knowledge expressed in [4.1]. The candidates for normalizing [4.1] are $[2.2']^{-1}$ and $[2.3]^{-1}$. $[2.2']^{-1}$ cannot be used but note the dependency in $[2.3]^{-1}$ shown in Figure 8.10 which is established by:

dept/emp-list(x , y.z) ← dept/mngr(x , y),
              super/emp-list(y , z) $[2.3]^{-1}$

This dependency may be used to normalize [4.1] to give:

dept/sal-bill(x , y) ← dept/emp-list(x , z), pers-list/salary(z , y)
pers-list/salary(∅ , 0) ←
pers-list/salary(x.y , z) ← pers/salary(x , v), pers-list/salary(y , w),
            z = v + w   [4.1']

The dependency diagram is shown in Figure 8.11. Thus, we now adjust the application model to reflect this change:

23.1   The total salary bill for a department may be deduced from the salaries of the employees who work in that department.

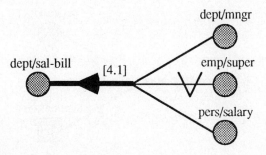

Figure 8.9 Alternative form for Figure 8.8

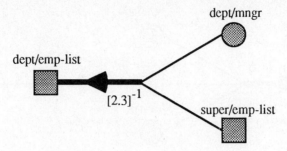

Figure 8.10 Dependency diagram for group $[2.3]^{-1}$

23.2   **if** a department has a collection of employees working in that department **and** the salary of each employee is known, **then** the total salary bill for that department is the sum of the salaries of the employees working in that department.

This completes our treatment of the query types. The query types are now added to the application model, and the items of data, information and knowledge which are associated with each query type are identified in the data, information and knowledge models.

Suppose that the natural update types are:

U 1   For any employee, the department, if any, in which that employee works.
U 2   For any employee, the title of the job which that employee holds.
U 3   For any job description, the salary rate for that job.

These three update types refer directly to the relations emp/dept, pers/job and job/salary respectively. Thus, these three relations can be nominated the "update relations" without further ado. Note that these update types do not contain knowledge update types. Knowledge update types will be considered in the case study. The update types are now added to the application model, and the items of data, information and knowledge which are associated with each update type are identified in the data, information and knowledge

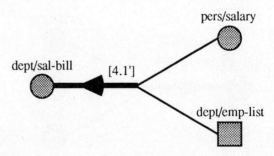

Figure 8.11 Dependency diagram for group [4.1']

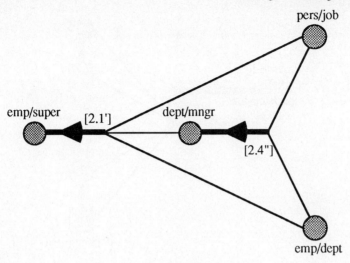

Figure 8.12 Diagram for first and third query types

models. The final application model, and data, information and knowledge models, for the worked example are given in the Section "Worked Example" in Chapter 10.

We now arrange the knowledge to obtain a picture of how the update relations will computationally support the query relations. The first and third query types can only be implemented in one way as shown in the combined diagram shown in Figure 8.12. In this diagram all arrows "point" from right to left. We have omitted to show any dependencies which flow out from the query relations or into the natural update relations; this is perfectly reasonable unless the values for one update (or, query) relation can be calculated in terms of other update (or, query) relations.

The second query type can be implemented in two different ways. First as, shown in Figure 8.13 which could be suitable if there were no efficient inverse predicates available. Alternatively, it can be implemented as shown in Figure 8.14. The decision between these two alternatives will be made shortly. For the present we simply note that there are two different ways of servicing the second query type.

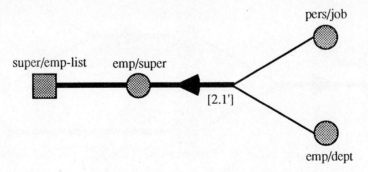

Figure 8.13 Diagram for second query type

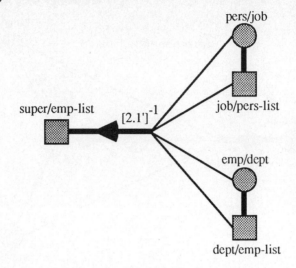

Figure 8.14 Alternative diagram for second query type

The fourth query type can only be implemented in one way as shown in Figure 8.15.

Combining the diagrams for the four query types we obtain the diagram shown in Figure 8.16.

We now illustrate the application of our two Algorithms, given in Figures 8.5 and 8.6, to the derivation of a (hopefully) optimal solution to the knowledge base engineering problem for this example. This example is, of course, very simple, the only decision that has to be made is whether to choose $[2.1']^{-1}$ for the super/emp-list query type or whether to derive this relation from emp/super using the find-all mechanism. We begin by calculating costs for each group. To do this we use our method discussed in Section 8.5 with $n = 1$ and the trivial measure for predicates. Recall the way in which we deal with

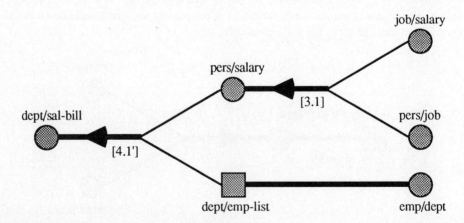

Figure 8.15 Diagram for fourth query type

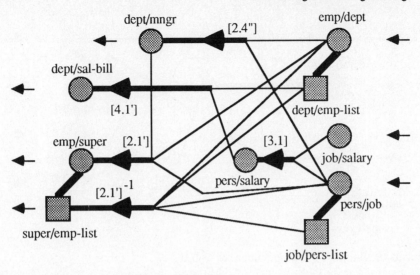

Figure 8.16 Diagram for the four query types

groups which contain the tuple/find-all-list predicate, and that internal predicates, "is-a" and "is-the" predicates are ignored in this calculation. The complexities of the groups referred to in the above diagram are:

comp([2.4"]) = 2
comp([4.1']) = 4
comp([2.1']) = 4

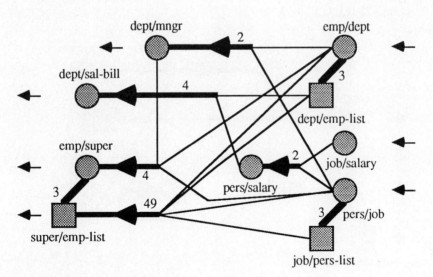

Figure 8.17 Diagram with complexities marked

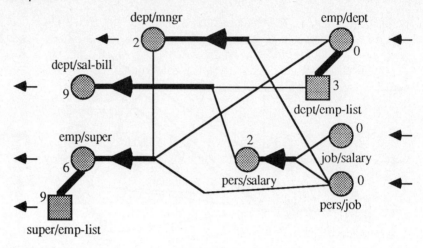

Figure 8.18 Diagram showing values for T[Q,U]

$$\text{comp}([2.1']^{-1}) = 49$$
$$\text{comp}([3.1]) = 2$$
$$\text{comp}(\text{ the three find-all groups }) = 3$$

Marking these amounts on the diagram we obtain the diagram shown in Figure 8.17. Using Algorithm A, we calculate T[Q, U] to be as shown in Figure 8.18. Next we look for critical points. There is only one; it is the node labeled dept/emp-list. Call this node c. Then we calculate T[Q, U ∪ {c}] which is as shown in Figure 8.19. Now it is clear that:

$$\text{comp}(\text{ T[\{c\}, U] }) = 3$$

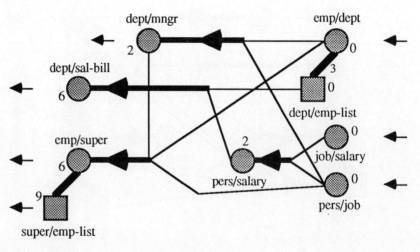

Figure 8.19 dept/emp-list is a critical point

Thus, the inclusion of this critical point will not reduce the cost of the original solution, and the final solution is thus to discard $[2.1']^{-1}$. However, note that if the cost of $[2.1']^{-1}$ had been 2 or 3, then the critical point dept/emp-list would have been included with $[2.1']^{-1}$. Thus, the diagram shown in Figure 8.18 for the above calculation is the combined functional diagram for this example.

8.8 SUMMARY

The functional requirements of a knowledge system have been discussed, these contain query and update requirements for knowledge as well as for information and data. The knowledge base engineering problem is the problem of deriving a selection of least complexity. We have shown that this problem is NP-complete. Some very coarse complexity measures have been introduced which have enabled us to measure the complexity of groups. Two Algorithms have been quoted which should derive a "reasonable" solution to the knowledge base engineering problem in polynomial time.

⑨ Knowledge base implementation

9.1 INTRODUCTION

In this chapter we address the final problem in the design of a knowledge system; this concerns the implementation of the system. As our treatment is primarily concerned with modeling, and is intended to be independent of any particular language for implementing knowledge systems, the final problem that we address is that of deciding which populations and relations will actually be stored and which will be deduced. Thus, this Chapter finishes with the derivation of the three system models for the knowledge system. These models, together with the supporting documentation, comprise a complete system specification which may be passed to programming staff for implementation in any chosen language. As with the problem considered in the previous Chapter, the problem considered here is surprisingly complex. The complexity of the knowledge base implementation problem is established in Section 9.5, and that Section will appeal only to the mathematically-minded reader. In practice, the work described in this Chapter is mechanized so if the reader's interests are primarily with modeling knowledge, then the reader may choose not to study this Chapter in great detail. In any case, the reader is advised to study Section 9.3 carefully.

Knowledge base implementation is the fourth and last phase in the design of a knowledge system. In simple terms, knowledge base implementation is concerned with taking the product of the previous phase, namely knowledge base engineering, adding the operational constraints and deriving a model of an implemented system which will perform the required tasks, which satisfies the operational constraints, and is, in some sense, optimal. The input to the knowledge base implementation phase is the data, information and knowledge, selected by knowledge base engineering, as summarized on the combined functional diagram. The output of this phase is an implementation model for the system; this model will be represented as the three system models in their final form. The product of this phase may also be thought of as annotations to the combined functional diagram.

In this Chapter we first discuss the specification of the operational constraints of a knowledge system. The "knowledge base implementation problem" is then introduced as the problem of deciding which of the relations shown on the combined functional diagram should be stored and which should be deduced; the complexity of this problem is investigated. The knowledge base implementation problem might thus be described as the "storage allocation problem". To enable us to state that one solution to the knowledge base implementation problem is "better than" another, we introduce cost measures for particular storage allocations. An Algorithm which finds reasonable solutions to the

216

knowledge base implementation problem fairly quickly is then discussed. Finally, the worked example discussed in the previous Chapter is extended into this knowledge base implementation phase.

This Chapter contains Algorithms and techniques which give rise to fairly extensive calculations. These calculations are illustrated in worked examples. We wish to stress that in practice these calculations are not performed by hand.

9.2 OPERATIONAL CONSTRAINTS

The operational constraints for a knowledge system are usually expressed in terms of the query types and update types identified during knowledge base engineering, and in terms of the integrity checks identified during knowledge acquisition, knowledge analysis and knowledge base maintenance. The *operational constraints* could include:

1. the maximum permissible response time for each query type. This gives a limit to the amount of computation and the amount of reference to storage for each query type;
2. the maximum permissible service time for each update type. This gives a limit to the amount of computation and the amount of reference to storage for each update type. In particular, this gives a limit to the amount of stored information that can be updated by each update type;
3. the maximum permissible run time for each knowledge system integrity check. This gives a limit to the amount of computation and the amount of reference to storage for each integrity check type;
4. an estimation of the expected frequency of presentation of each query type, update type and integrity check. This provides a foundation for the notion of an "optimal" solution to the knowledge base implementation problem;
5. the amount of available storage. This gives a limit to the total amount of stored information;
6. some measure of the "flexibility" of the storage allocation. Informally, the notion *flexibility* is a measure of the likelihood of the storage allocation to be able to cope with additional query functions without modification. For example, for it to be able to support a new query type; in this case, if the query relations were precisely the stored relations, then the system would be as inflexible as it could be, but if the update relations were the stored relations, then the system would be as flexible as it could be expected to be. It is easy to see that placing a value on increased flexibility of query types will establish a preference for the real relations to be "close" to the update relations;
7. some measure of the cost of maintaining the internal consistency of the real relations. Placing a value on keeping this cost low will establish a preference for low redundancy in the storage allocation.

An *admissible solution* to the knowledge base implementation problem is a storage allocation which satisfies the operational constraints. It is clear that a particular set of operational constraints may mean that there can be no admissible solution. For example, there will be no admissible solution if the maximum allowed response times for all query and update types permitted one relation reference only. (Except in the trivial case when all query relations are update relations, and all query types use the key of the corresponding query relation.) The knowledge base implementation problem is to determine which admissible solution is the "optimal" solution.

9.3 THE KNOWLEDGE BASE IMPLEMENTATION PROBLEM

The product of the previous phase, namely knowledge base engineering, will be a selection of the data, information and knowledge gathered during knowledge analysis. This selection is chosen so that the query types may be satisfied on the basis of the update types. A useful presentation of this selection is provided by the combined functional diagram. The *knowledge base implementation problem* is:

- to decide which of the populations and relations shown on the combined functional diagram should actually be stored; and, having decided that
- to design suitable system integrity checks to preserve the validity of the stored information; so that
- the overall system performance is "optimal".

When a knowledge system is implemented, some populations and relations will actually be stored and their values *retrieved* when required: these populations and relations will be referred to collectively as a *storage allocation*, or as the *real populations* and the *real relations*. On the other hand, some populations and relations, which have been defined in terms of other populations and relations, will not be stored and their values will be *calculated* when required: these populations and relations will be referred to collectively as the *virtual populations* and the *virtual relations*. Satisfaction of the operational constraints of the system will determine in part which populations and relations are real and which are virtual. In fact, the first step in the knowledge base implementation problem is to decide whether each population and relation on the combined functional diagram should be real or virtual.

It is important to appreciate that the update populations and relations will not necessarily be real. In practice, however, a history of the update transactions will normally be retained on auxiliary storage media for reference during update transactions and to enable the system to be restarted in event of catastrophic failure. Data and information retained in auxiliary storage for archival, or system back-up purposes is *not* referred to as "real".

The definition of the knowledge base implementation problem given above refers to "optimal" system performance. We define the *system performance* of a storage allocation to be:

$$\sum_{q \in Q} \tau(q) \times f(q) \quad + \quad \sum_{u \in U} \tau(u) \times f(u) \quad + \quad \sum_{i \in I} \tau(i) \times f(i)$$

where Q is the set of query types, U is the set of update types and I is the set of integrity checks. τ is a "cost function"; for example, $\tau(q)$ is the "cost to service the query q"; and f is the "expected frequency function"; for example, $f(q)$ is the "expected frequency of presentation of the query q".

For each query type q, update type u and integrity check i, let T(q), T(u) and T(i) respectively denote the maximum permissible cost of response. For each relation r, let $\gamma(r)$ denote the cost of storing r, and let C denote the total cost of the available storage. We are now in a position to give a formal statement of the knowledge base implementation problem.

The knowledge base implementation problem

Given a combined functional diagram, given T(q), T(u) and T(i) for each $q \in Q$, $u \in U$ and $i \in I$, and given C, to choose a set of populations and relations R to be the real such that:

$$(\forall q \in Q) \; \tau(q) \leq T(q)$$
$$(\forall u \in U) \; \tau(u) \leq T(u)$$
$$(\forall i \in I) \; \tau(i) \leq T(i)$$

$$\sum_{r \in R} \gamma(r) \leq C$$

are satisfied and:

$$\sum_{q \in Q} \tau(q) \times f(q) \;\; + \sum_{u \in U} \tau(u) \times f(u) \;\; + \sum_{i \in I} \tau(i) \times f(i)$$

is minimized.

A group in the combined functional diagram *either* is used when servicing a query to retrieve values of a virtual population or relation by reference to other populations and relations, *or* is used when servicing an update to calculate values for one population or relation in terms of values in other populations and relations. The groups that have been gathered during knowledge analysis but are not shown on the combined functional diagram either become integrity checks or reside in the dormant model which is a reservoir of spare knowledge. We will refer to groups as being *query groups, update groups, integrity check groups* or *dormant groups* respectively; these sets of groups are disjoint. Thus, part of the knowledge base engineering problem can be expressed as the problem of determining which of the groups gathered during knowledge analysis should be either query groups, update groups, integrity check groups or dormant groups. An alternative, complete statement of the knowledge base implementation problem is to decide, for those groups chosen during knowledge base engineering, which should be query groups and which should be update groups, and then to decide which of the other groups identified by knowledge analysis should be employed as integrity check groups, so that the overall system performance is optimal.

In this discussion, it is necessary for us to restrict the form of recursion used in the logic. As in the previous Chapter, we will restrict ourselves here to primary recursion only. (Note that the notion of "primary recursion" was introduced in the previous Chapter.) In our experience, this does not impose a significant restriction in practical applications.

A knowledge base implementation technique must incorporate the following:

- a method for deciding which relations are to be actually stored so that the performance of the system satisfies the operational constraints, and;
- a method for designing an effective integrity checking strategy, so that;
- the overall system performance is optimal.

In addition, the following is a desirable feature of a knowledge base implementation technique:

- a method for automatically rearranging the implementation in response to changing demands.

9.4 THE CALCULATION OF MINIMAL STORAGE

Recall the notation for the set of groups selected by knowledge base engineering; this is the combined functional diagram for that set of groups. For example, given the three groups:

$$
\begin{aligned}
&A \leftarrow A, B, C \qquad A \leftarrow B, D \\
&B \leftarrow C, E \qquad\quad B \leftarrow E \\
&D \leftarrow D, E
\end{aligned}
$$

the combined functional diagram is as shown in Figure 9.1. By convention, combined functional diagrams are drawn with arrows going from right to left.

In a connected, combined functional diagram:

- The nodes which represent populations and relations which are associated in a natural way with the major query types are called *query nodes*, we presume that the set of query nodes will include all nodes which have no out-going arcs.

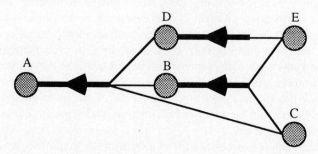

Figure 9.1 Combined functional diagram

- The nodes which represent populations and relations which are associated in a natural way with the major update types are called *update nodes*, we presume that the set of update nodes will be all nodes which have no in-coming arcs.

Thus, recalling the definition of "support", the groups summarized by the combined functional diagram support the query nodes on the update nodes. For example, in the above combined functional diagram, A is a query node, and E and C are the only update nodes. In a combined functional diagram, a node X is said to *depend* on node Y if there is a path *from* Y *to* X in that diagram. In the above example, D depends on E, B depends on E and C, and A depends on all the other nodes in the diagram.

Consider a set of groups, derived by knowledge base engineering, and summarized on a combined functional diagram. There are a number of ways in which this set of groups could be implemented. Three possible alternatives are:

- All the populations and relations could be stored, in which case the storage costs and update costs would be high.
- Just the query populations and relations could be stored, in which case the update costs would be high.
- Just the update populations and relations could be stored, in which case the query costs would be high.

It is important to appreciate that the update populations and relations need not necessarily be stored in the high speed memory. The values of updates may be retained in some sort of archive; these values may be required during subsequent update operations and may be required to regenerate the system in the event of a disaster. All that matters is:

- that all the values in all the real populations and relations can be deduced from the values in the update populations and relations; and
- that all the values in all the query populations and relations can be deduced from the values in the real populations and relations.

Thus, we see that the set of stored populations and relations will, in a sense, divide the combined functional diagram into two portions. Thus, informally, we may think of a *storage allocation* as a subset of the set of nodes such that if the storage allocation were removed from the diagram, then the resulting diagram would consist of two connected, possibly empty, components with one component containing no query nodes and the other component containing no update nodes. In a combined functional diagram, a storage allocation will support the set of query nodes, and the set of update nodes will support the storage allocation. The idea is that the storage allocation represents those populations and relations which are actually stored; in other words, those nodes which are *not* in the storage allocation represent populations and relations which will be calculated when required. In the previous example, four different storage allocations show that A is supported by the sets {B, C, D}, {D, E, C}, {E, B, C} and {C, E}. These four sets are identified by the four different lines shown on the diagram in Figure 9.2.

An *irredundant storage allocation* is a storage allocation with the property that if a node is removed from the storage allocation, then the resulting set ceases to be a storage

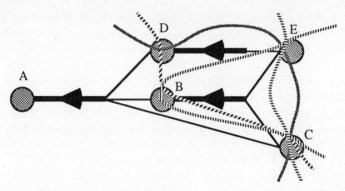

Figure 9.2 Four different storage allocations

allocation. An irredundant storage allocation can be visualized as a minimal set of nodes which divides the graph into two portions. In a combined group diagram, as an "irredundant storage allocation" is a "storage allocation", an irredundant storage allocation clearly supports the set of query nodes, and the set of update nodes clearly supports the irredundant storage allocation. If a storage allocation is not irredundant, it is called a *redundant storage allocation*. In the previous example, two of the storage allocations quoted are irredundant storage allocations; they are {B, C, D} and {C, E}. Note that for the storage allocation {B, C, D} the values of the update relation E cannot be recovered from {B, C, D} unless suitable, additional (clause) groups are available. In this case, if the values of E might be subsequently required, then they would have to be stored in some sort of archive.

A storage allocation, selected from a combined functional diagram, is a *division* if it contains no two nodes which depend on each other. As there are no superfluous groups in a combined functional diagram, if a selection is a "division", then that selection will cease to be a storage allocation if any node is removed from the storage allocation; in other words, all divisions are irredundant storage allocations. It is important to understand the difference between an irredundant storage allocation and a division. In the combined functional diagram shown in Figure 9.3 the storage allocation { C, D, F } is an irredundant storage allocation because if any one of these three nodes were removed it would cease to be a storage allocation; but, { C, D, F } is *not* a division because D depends on C. On the other hand, the storage allocation { B, D, F } *is* a division.

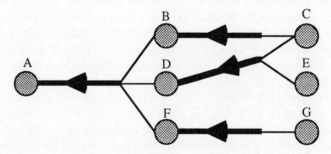

Figure 9.3 Combined functional diagram

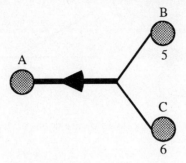

Figure 9.4 Dependency diagram with costs

A division may be visualized as a storage allocation chosen by cutting the graph in half where the cut goes "from top to bottom without straying unduly to left or right". At first glance there would seem to be little value in storage allocations which are not divisions; however, a single node can be used in different ways by different queries (or updates). We will see that non-division storage allocations are often desirable. Divisions are of great practical significance because if a storage allocation contains one node that depends on another, then the updates to the second node will also have to be reflected in the first. In other words, when updates are being performed on-line, divisions should require less elaborate file locking than storage allocations which are not divisions.

We now mark costs on the combined functional diagram. These costs are intended to represent the cost of storing each population or relation, and are written beside the node which represents the population or relation to which the costs apply. For example, if the cost of storing relation B was 5 and the cost of storing relation C was 6, and B and C were in a dependency diagram with head predicate A, then this would be denoted as shown on the diagram in Figure 9.4.

A storage allocation is called a *minimal storage allocation* if the storage allocation is the least cost set which supports the query nodes in the combined functional diagram. It is easy to show that minimal storage allocations are irredundant storage allocations but are not necessarily divisions. For example, consider the combined functional diagram as shown in Figure 9.5, the minimal storage allocation is the set { C, D, F } which is irredundant but is not a division. We will now consider the calculation of both the division with least cost and the minimal storage allocation.

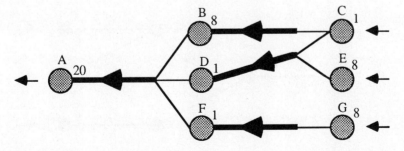

Figure 9.5 Combined functional diagram

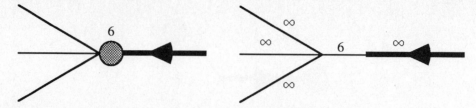

Figure 9.6 The node on the left is replaced by the figure on the right

Problem 1
To calculate the division with least cost.

This problem can be solved by applying the (polynomial time) minimum-cut Algorithm to a modified version of the combined functional diagram. This modification is performed in two steps. First, we mark all arcs on the diagram with "infinite" cost, and replace each node with a "pseudo-arc" marked with the node cost. For example, the node shown on the left of Figure 9.6 will be replaced by the node shown on the right. In the second step, all arcs marked with infinite cost are "collapsed" to a node. The resulting diagram is called the *division-dual diagram*. The solution to problem 1 may be found by applying the minimum-cut Algorithm to the division dual diagram. When the minimum-cut has been calculated, the pseudo-arcs which lie on the minimum-cut will correspond to the nodes in the division with least cost. (*See* Even, 1979 or any good book on Algorithmic graph theory, for a description of the minimum-cut Algorithm.)

For example, consider the combined functional diagram shown in Figure 9.5; its division-dual diagram is as shown in Figure 9.7 from which we readily see that the division of least cost is { C, E, F } or { B, D, F } with a total cost of 10. Note that an arc in the division-dual diagram corresponds to a node in the original diagram, and vice versa.

We now consider the calculation of the minimal storage allocation.

Problem 2
To calculate the irredundant storage allocation with least cost; this is the minimal storage allocation.

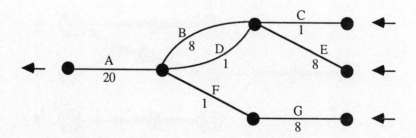

Figure 9.7 Division-dual diagram

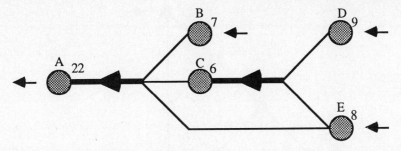

Figure 9.8 Combined functional diagram

This problem can be solved by applying the (polynomial time) minimum-cut Algorithm to a modified version of the combined functional diagram which is similar to that considered in the solution to problem 1. This modification is performed in three steps. First, all of the "thick" arcs in the combined functional diagram are "collapsed" to a point and then the remaining "thin" arcs are marked with "infinite cost". Second, replace each node with a "pseudo-polygon" as follows:

• A node which is directly connected to one or two other nodes is represented by a pseudo-arc as in the solution to problem 1. This pseudo-arc is marked with the node cost.
• A node which is directly connected to n other nodes, where $n > 2$, is represented by an n-sided pseudo-polygon with one corner of the polygon connected to the arc which is connected to each of the n nodes; the sides of the polygon are marked with the original node cost divided by two.

In the third step, all arcs marked with infinite cost are "collapsed" to a node. The resulting diagram is called the *dual diagram*. The solution to problem 2 may be found by applying the minimum-cut Algorithm to this dual diagram. When the minimum-cut has

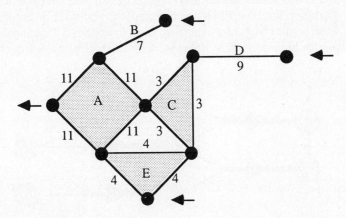

Figure 9.9 Dual diagram

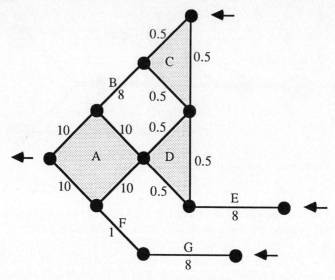

Figure 9.10 Dual diagram

been calculated, the pseudo-polygons which lie on the cut will correspond to the nodes in the minimal storage allocation.

For example, the combined functional diagram shown in Figure 9.8 will generate the dual diagram shown in Figure 9.9 from which we see that the minimal storage allocation is { B, C, E } with a cost of 21.

Also, for example, consider the combined functional diagram shown in Figure 9.5; its dual diagram is as shown in Figure 9.10 from which we readily see that the minimum-cut is { C, D, F } with a total cost of 3.

In practice we are not always interested in divisions; in fact, the operational constraints may even require that the storage allocation be non-minimal.

We conclude this Section with a notation that can be used to design interesting, redundant storage allocations; this notation is essentially a "tree" version of the combined functional diagram. We now formalize this idea. Given a set of groups, derived by knowledge base engineering, and summarized on a combined functional diagram, the *separated-diagram* is constructed by drawing a tree which supports each query node on the

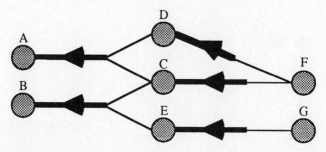

Figure 9.11 Combined functional diagram

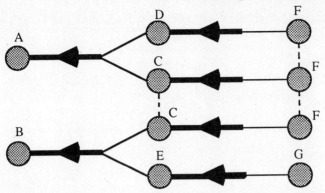

Figure 9.12 Separated diagram

update nodes. By convention, occurrences of the same node label on different branches of the trees are drawn one above each other (this is always possible); these different occurrences of the same label are joined by undirected dotted arcs. For example, if the given combined functional diagram had been as shown in Figure 9.11, then the separated diagram would be as shown in Figure 9.12. It is easy to see that the arcs in the combined functional diagram will correspond to equivalence classes of arcs in the separated-diagram defined by the dotted lines. The costs can now be marked on the separated diagram. The minimal storage allocation for each query node can then be considered separately, and a strategy devised for deducing an overall, possibly redundant, storage allocation.

9.5 COMPLEXITY OF THE KNOWLEDGE BASE IMPLEMENTATION PROBLEM

The operational constraints and optimality criteria noted above together comprise a complex set of conflicting constraints. We now show that the problem of determining an optimal, minimal storage allocation is difficult even when gross simplifications are made to the constraints. In fact, we will show that the problem of determining an admissible solution, never mind an optimal solution, to the knowledge base implementation problem is very hard.

RESULT
The knowledge base implementation problem is NP-complete.

Proof
We will restrict the knowledge base implementation problem, and will show that this restriction is equivalent to the "Minimum-Cut Into Bounded Sets" problem which is known to be NP-complete (Garey, Johnson and Stockmeyer, 1979).

First, assume that there is only one query type, q, one update type, u, and no integrity checks. Then the knowledge base implementation problem now reads: Given a combined functional diagram, given constants T(q), T(u) and C, to choose a set of relations R to be the real relations such that:

$$\tau(q) \leq T(q)$$
$$\tau(u) \leq T(u)$$

$$\sum_{r \in R} \gamma(r) \leq C$$

are satisfied, and:

$$(\tau(q) \times f(q)) \;+\; (\tau(u) \times f(u))$$

is minimized.

Second, adopt the following trivial measure for τ, this measure defines $\tau(q)$ to be the number of groups involved in servicing the query type q, and $\tau(u)$ is just the number of groups involved in servicing the update type u. In other words, $\tau(q)$ is the number of groups required to support q on R, $\tau(u)$ is the number of groups required to support R on u. In addition we further restrict the problem to the special case when $T(q) = T(u) = T$. Then the knowledge base implementation problem may be stated as:- Given a combined functional diagram, given constants T and C, to choose a set of relations R to be the real relations such that:

The number of groups needed to support q on R is less than or equal to T.
The number of groups needed to support R on u is less than or equal to T.

$$\sum_{r \in R} \gamma(r) \leq C$$

are satisfied, and:

$$(\tau(q) \times f(q)) \;+\; (\tau(u) \times f(u))$$

is minimized.

We now interpret this restriction of the knowledge base implementation problem in terms of the division dual diagram representation discussed in the previous Section. We will ignore the expression to be minimized, that is, we will just state the constraints. Recall that on the division dual diagram, populations and relations are denoted by arcs and groups are denoted by nodes. The knowledge base implementation problem as restricted so far now reads:- Given a division dual diagram, constants T and C, to choose a partition of the nodes of the diagram into two disjoint sets V_1 and V_2 such that the single query node q is directly connected to a node in V_1 and the single update node u is directly connected to a node in V_2 such that:

$$|V_1| \leq T$$
$$|V_2| \leq T$$

$$\sum_{r \in R} \gamma(r) \leq C$$

where |V| means "the number of elements in the set V", and R is the set of arcs with one node in V_1 and the other in V_2.

This final restriction of the knowledge base implementation problem is precisely the "Minimum-Cut into Bounded Sets" problem. This completes the proof.

We note from the proof of the theorem that what has actually been demonstrated is that the problem of finding an *admissible* solution to the knowledge base implementation problem is NP-complete, never mind the problem of finding an *optimal* admissible solution. Thus we have:

Corollary
Given a combined functional diagram, the problem of finding an admissible solution, which is not necessarily optimal, to the knowledge base implementation problem is NP-complete.

The "Minimum-Cut into Bounded Sets" problem remains NP-complete even if $\gamma(r) = 1$ ($\forall r \in R$), and if $T = |V| \div 2$. Thus, we note that the following restriction of the knowledge base implementation problem is also NP-complete. Given a dual diagram and constant C, to choose a partition of the nodes of the diagram into two disjoint sets V_1 and V_2 such that the single query node q is connected to a node in V_1 and the single update node u is connected to a node in V_2 such that:

$$|V_1| = |V| \div 2$$
$$|V_2| = |V| \div 2$$
$$|R| \leq C$$

In the special case when $T = |V|$ it is clear that the problem of finding an admissible, but not necessarily optimal, solution to the knowledge base implementation problem reduces to satisfying the single constraint:

$$\sum_{r \in R} \gamma(r) \leq C$$

which can be solved in polynomial time by the minimum-cut Algorithm.

The proof of the above result employs the restriction that there be only one query node and only one update node; and, as this restriction is NP-complete, the general case, with any number of query and update nodes, is also NP-complete. This restriction also leads to another interesting form of the knowledge base implementation problem. The knowledge base implementation problem refers to a "given combined functional diagram", on this diagram connect all query nodes to a single "dummy query node" q'; likewise, connect all update nodes to another, single "dummy update node" u'. In this version of the problem, suppose that the cost function, $\kappa(q)$, is the number of groups involved in servicing q in the *separated diagram*; likewise, $\kappa(u)$ is the number of groups involved in servicing u in the *separated diagram*. Then the constraints for this problem read:

$$\kappa(q') = \sum_{q \in Q} \kappa(q) \leq T(q')$$

$$\kappa(u') = \sum_{u \in U} \kappa(u) \leq T(u')$$

$$\sum_{r \in R} \gamma(r) \leq C$$

Dividing by suitable constants, and introducing T' and T":

$$\frac{1}{|Q|} \times \kappa(q') = \frac{1}{|Q|} \times \sum_{q \in Q} \kappa(q) \leq T' = \frac{1}{|Q|} \times T(q')$$

$$\frac{1}{|U|} \times \kappa(u') = \frac{1}{|U|} \times \sum_{u \in U} \kappa(u) \leq T'' = \frac{1}{|U|} \times T(u')$$

$$\sum_{r \in R} \gamma(r) \leq C$$

from which we see that the following variation of the knowledge base implementation problem is also NP-complete: "Given a combined functional diagram, constants T', T" and C, to choose a set of relations R to be the real relations such that:

The mean cost of servicing the query types is less than or equal to T'.
The mean cost of servicing the update types is less than or equal to T".

$$\sum_{r \in R} \gamma(r) \leq C$$

are satisfied and:

$$\sum_{q \in Q} \kappa(q) \times f(q) \quad + \sum_{u \in U} \kappa(u) \times f(u)$$

is minimal. As before, the problem of finding an admissible, but not necessarily optimal, solution to this problem is also NP-complete.

9.6 SUB-OPTIMAL STORAGE ALLOCATION

In the previous Section we have seen that the knowledge base implementation problem is NP-complete. However, this does not imply that identifiable classes of sub-problems encountered in practice need necessarily be NP-complete. For example, the costs on the arcs in either the separated diagram or the combined functional diagram are often related to each other. Perhaps investigation of this observation, and others like it, might lead to some simplification.

Whether, in practical terms, it is NP-complete or not, the knowledge base implementation problem still has to be solved. So we have the choice of either defining a (polynomial time) soluble sub-problem or looking for a sub-optimal (polynomial time) solution. We conclude our discussion with a sub-optimal Algorithm for calculating the (hopefully) minimal storage allocation which satisfies query and update response constraints. This Algorithm yields acceptable results in practice when the application is not heavily constrained. If the application has heavy query and update constraints, then the Algorithm may not find a solution. In the statement of our Algorithm, integrity checks are ignored.

The Algorithm begins with the unconstrained minimal storage allocation as calculated in Section 9.4. This minimal storage allocation is then "modified" to form other storage allocations which are all irredundant; thus, it is reasonable to "hope" that these modifications will remain within the available storage constraint. In fact, the Algorithm makes no reference to the satisfaction of the total storage constraint for which there are three reasons. First, the availability of storage does not tend to be a problem in practice. Second, the update constraints impose an implicit constraint on the amount of storage used; for example, if a large number of populations and relations are stored, then the update operations will necessarily be slow. Third, the Algorithm produces an irredundant storage allocation and this should ensure that storage costs are "low". (Recall, however, that there is often value in having storage allocations which are not divisions, and occasionally value in having storage allocations which are non-irredundant.)

In the statement of the following Algorithm, we will use the following notation. If, in a combined functional diagram, S is an irredundant storage allocation and n is a node not in S, then $S \uparrow \{n\}$ denotes the set of nodes obtained by adding n to S and removing from S any nodes which, as a result of n being added, prevent $S \cup \{n\}$ from being irredundant.

Algorithm
Find the minimal storage allocation. This may be done by employing our method given in Section 9.4 on the dual diagram. If there is more than one such storage allocation, then choose the storage allocation which violates fewest operational (i.e. query or update) constraints. (Recall that a storage allocation consists of a set of relations; on the dual diagram this set will be represented by a set of arcs.) Represent this minimal storage allocation as a "cut" on the combined functional diagram. Then:

begin(constraints)
> **let** the storage allocation S **be** the minimal storage allocation as described above
> **while** there are query nodes with unsatisfied operational constraints
> **do**   **let** P^Q **be** the nodes in S on which query nodes with unsatisfied operational constraints depend
>   **let** P^{GB} **be** the set of groups with at least one body node in P^Q

> **let** P^H **be** { n : n $\not\subseteq$ S and n is the head node of a group in P^{GB} }
> **if** there is a node n in P^H such that S $\uparrow$ {n} satisfies a presently unsatisfied query constraint **then let** N **be** n **else let** N **be** the node with the property that the storage allocation S $\uparrow$ {N} has the lowest query cost of all the storage allocations { S $\uparrow$ {n} : n $\in$ P^H }
> **let** S **be**   S $\uparrow$ {N}
>
endwhile

(By this stage S will be an irredundant storage allocation which satisfies all the query operational constraints.)

> **while**   there are update nodes with unsatisfied operational constraints
> **do**   **let** P^U **be** the nodes in S which depend on one or more update nodes with unsatisfied operational constraints
> **let** P^{GH} **be** the set of groups with head node in P^U
> **let** P^B **be** { n : n $\not\subseteq$ S, n is a body node of a group in P^{GH} and S $\uparrow$ {n} violates no query constraints}
> **if** P^B = $\emptyset$ **then halt**("unsuccessful") **else**
> **if** there is a node n in P^B such that S $\uparrow$ {n} satisfies a presently unsatisfied update constraint **then let** N **be** n **else let** N **be** the node with the property that the storage allocation S $\uparrow$ {N} has the lowest update cost of all the storage allocations { S $\uparrow$ {n} : n $\in$ P^B }
> **let** S **be** S $\uparrow$ {N}
>
endwhile
end

(By this stage S will be an irredundant storage allocation which satisfies all the query and update operational constraints but may not give rise to optimal system performance.)

begin(optimize)
> **let** P^{GH} **be** the set of groups with head node in S
> **let** P^B **be** { n : n $\not\subseteq$ S, n is a body node of a group in P^{GH} and S $\uparrow$ {n} violates no query and update constraints }
> **let** P^{GB} **be** the set of groups with at least one body node in S
> **let** P^H **be** { n : n $\not\subseteq$ S, n is the head node of a group in P^{GB} and S $\uparrow$ {n} violates no query or update constraints }
> **if** P^B $\cup$ P^H = $\emptyset$ **then halt**("successful") **else**
> **let** P^O **be** { n : n $\in$ P^B $\cup$ P^H such that the system performance of S $\uparrow$ {n} is lower than the system performance of S }
> **if** P^O = $\emptyset$ **then halt**("successful") **else**
> **let** N **be** the node in P^O with the property that the storage allocation S $\uparrow$ {N}   has the lowest system performance of all the storage allocations { S $\uparrow$ {n} : n $\in$ P^O }
> **let** S **be** S $\uparrow$ {N}
> **go to** optimize
end

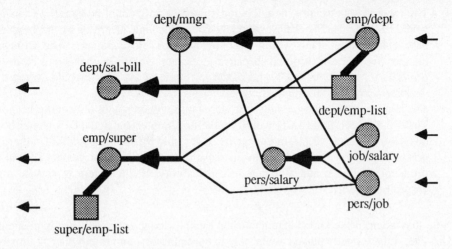

Figure 9.13 Combined functional diagram for worked example

It can be shown that if the Algorithm halts signalling "successful", then it will halt in polynomial time.

9.7 WORKED EXAMPLE

The final step in our discussion is, given the combined functional diagram, to design an implementation of the knowledge base. The single, key problem is to decide which populations and relations will actually be stored and which will be calculated in terms of the stored populations and relations. This is the knowledge base implementation problem, and solutions to it will be substantially determined by the operational constraints.

In our worked example the combined functional diagram is shown in Figure 9.13.

Before solving the knowledge base implementation problem for our worked example analytically, we will consider the relative merits of the following five different solutions:

1. All relations could be stored, in which case servicing queries should be inexpensive and fast, updates would be slow and storage requirements expensive. All the logic identified by the knowledge base engineering stage would become the update mechanism.
2. The update relations only could be stored, in which case the servicing of queries could be slow and expensive, storage requirements inexpensive (but not, in general, minimal) and updates fast and inexpensive. All the logic identified by the knowledge base engineering stage would become the query mechanism.
3. The query relations only could be stored, in which case the updates would be slow and expensive, storage requirements probably not minimal, and the amount of deduction involved in servicing queries minimal. All the logic identified by the knowledge base engineering stage would become the update mechanism.

4. The relations pers/salary, pers/job and emp/dept only could be stored. Then [3.1] would be the update mechanism; and the rest of the logic identified by the knowledge base engineering stage would become the query mechanism. The storage is inexpensive but not minimal, because job/salary would be cheaper to store than pers/salary. However, storing pers/salary in place of job/salary would decrease the response time of the fourth query type.
5. The relations pers/salary, emp/super, dept/mngr and emp/dept only could be stored. Then [2.1'], [2.4"] and [3.1] would be the update mechanism; [4.1'] would be the query mechanism. It might appear more sensible to store dept/sal-bill rather than pers/salary. However, this would increase the processing time for the second and third update types, and would reduce the ability of the system to service other, unspecified queries.

Note that much of the knowledge identified by knowledge analysis is not implemented. However, it has already played a vital role in normalization, and it will play an important role in designing integrity checks, providing a framework for knowledge base maintenance, and possibly for supporting future query types.

We now solve the knowledge base implementation problem for our worked example. We stress that this calculation is not normally attempted by hand for realistic problems. Using the Algorithm presented in Section 9.6, we first calculate the minimal storage allocation. Suppose that the costs associated with each relation are as shown in Figure 9.14. (Note: These costs are rather unrealistic and have been chosen to ensure that the following calculation is interesting.)

We then calculate the dual diagram which is as shown in Figure 9.15 where we have labeled the diagram as follows: A = dept/sal-bill, B = pers/salary, C = job/salary, D = pers/job,   E = emp/super,   F = super/emp-list,   G = dept/mngr, H = dept/emp-list, I = emp/dept.

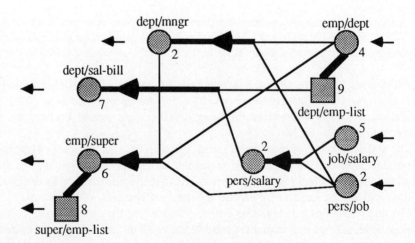

Figure 9.14 Combined functional diagram with costs

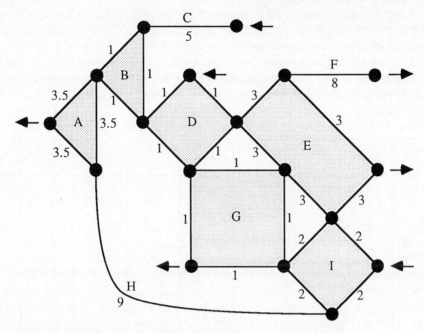

Figure 9.15 Dual diagram for worked example

We then apply the minimum-cut Algorithm and find that the minimal storage allocation is { B, D, I }.

Suppose that the operational constraints are as follows:

1. Maximum permissible response times for query types:
   - dept/mngr permitted to employ 1 group;
   - dept/sal-bill permitted to employ 2 groups;
   - emp/super permitted to employ 1 group;
   - super/emp-list permitted to employ 1 group.
2. Maximum permissible service time for update types:
   - emp/dept permitted to employ 1 group;
   - job/salary permitted to employ 1 group;
   - pers/job permitted to employ 1 group.
3. The storage allocation should be irredundant.

The only violation of the operational constraints is the query type super/emp-list. Thus, in the procedure "constraints" S is initially set to { B, D, I }. $P^Q = \{ D, I \}$. $P^H = \{ E, H \}$. $N = E$, and the new value of S is $S = \{ B, E, D, I \}$ which actually satisfies all query and update operational constraints. Note that this storage allocation is precisely the storage allocation discussed in (e) above.

As the "optimize" procedure given above is structurally very similar to the "constraints" procedure, there is little to be gained in completing this example by hand calculation. The reader may wish to specify values for the frequency of presentation of each query and update type and to calculate the optimal storage allocation for those frequencies. For the sake of argument, let us suppose that the optimal storage allocation is the storage allocation found above, namely { B, E, D, I }. In that case the final version of the three systems models will be as shown in Figures 9.16, 9.17 and 9.18. These three models, and the attendant documentation provide a complete specification of the implementation model for the system, no matter what language is to be employed for implementation.

Thing-population	Bundle	Sub-type of	Name-population	Labels	Population constraints	Label constraints	Fixed labels	Class
bus	1		business-name	Egs P/L	one label only			dormant
pers	2		person-name	(see 2.3)	each label unique			live
super	13	pers			= job GM and DM			live
emp	8	pers			= job DM and Workr			live
mngr	12	emp, super			= job DM			live
dept	9		dept-name	(see 9.3)	4 unique labels		all	live
job	6		job-name	(see 6.3)	3 unique labels	= GM,DM Workr	all	live
salary	16		salary-rate	(see 16.3)	3 labels or less	positive integer		live
gen-man	20	super		Mr Boss	one label only			real
sal-bill	21		sal-bill-amount	(see 21.3)		positive integer		live

Figure 9.16 The data model

9.8 SUMMARY

We have discussed several factors which will influence the choice of storage allocation for a knowledge system. Two solutions have been proposed for un-constrained applications. It has been argued that when realistic constraints are present, the determination of the optimal storage allocation is NP-complete. A sub-optimal Algorithm has been given which operates in polynomial time when the application is not heavily constrained. The final product of the work in this Chapter is a complete specification of the knowledge system which may be passed to a programmer for implementation in any chosen language.

Relation	Bundle	Key domain	Other domains	Tuples	Relation constraints	Tuple constraints	Associated with	Class
bus/pers	3		business-name person-name	(see 3.2)	IC1.1			dormant
pers/job	7	person-name	job-name	(see 7.3)	IC2.1		U2	real
emp/dept	10	emp-name	dept-name	(see 10.3)	IC3.1	IC3.2	U1	real
dept/mngr	11	dept-name	mngr-name	(see 11.3)	IC4.1	IC4.2	Q3	virtual query
emp/super	14	emp-name	super-name	(see 14.3)	IC5.1	IC5.2	Q1, Q2	real
pers/salary	17	person-name	salary-rate	(see 17.3)	IC6.1	IC6.2		real
job/salary	19	job-name	salary-rate	(see 19.3)	IC7.1	IC7.2	U3	virtual update
dept/sal-bill	22	dept-name	sal-bill-amount		IC8.1		Q4	virtual query

Figure 9.17 The information model

Cluster	Bundle	Group	Head	Body	Cluster constraints	Group constraints	Associated with	Class
[2]	15				complete			
	15.1	[2.1']	emp/super	pers/job emp/dept dpt/mngr		categ. & unique	Q5, Q6	update
	15.4.1	[2.2']	pers/job	emp/super		categ. & unique		dormant
	15.5.1	[2.3]	emp/dept	emp/super dept/mngr		categ. & unique		dormant
	15.6.1	[2.4"]	dept/mngr	pers/job emp/dept		categ. & unique	Q5, Q6	query
[3]	18				pers/salary only			
	18.1	[3.1]	pers/salary	job/salary pers/job		categ. & unique		update
[4]	23				dept/sal-bill only			
	23.1	[4.1']	dept/sal-bill	pers/salary emp/dept		categ. & unique	Q5, Q6	query

Figure 9.18 The knowledge model

10 Management and maintenance

10.1 INTRODUCTION

In this chapter we consider some managerial issues in the design, implementation and maintenance of knowledge systems. The material presented in Sections 10.1 to 10.6 inclusive is non-technical and should interest all readers. In Section 10.7 some maintenance operations on our worked example are discussed; these are a little tedious to work through but they do illustrate the way in which the whole method hangs together.

We have claimed that the design technique presented here is suitable for team work. However, if it is to be used by a team, then there are a number of aspects of the management of the application of the technique to which the project manager should pay close attention. In this chapter we address those essentially managerial issues.

First, we consider managerial issues involved in handling knowledge as such and then the issues involved in managing the whole design process. Issues involved in managing a team of maintenance staff for a knowledge system are discussed. Next, we introduce constraints and integrity checks as powerful devices for managing the preservation of consistency and correctness of a knowledge system. And last, we consider the problem of managing large knowledge systems.

10.2 MANAGEMENT OF KNOWLEDGE

We now discuss the key features of knowledge that the project manager should note when directing any aspect of a knowledge system development. Knowledge is explicit functional associations between items of information and/or data. The project manager will be concerned with represented knowledge. Thus, the key issues in the management of knowledge are related both to the management of the representation of explicit functional associations themselves and to the management of the representation of the information and/or data in terms of which the knowledge is expressed.

We first discuss the issues in the management of the representation of explicit functional associations. These issues are principally concerned with ensuring that the correct explicit functional associations have, in fact, been identified within the "real" knowledge. We have seen that raw facts are often presented in a form that does not imply any particular knowledge dependency. For example, the fact "the selling price for an item is the purchase price multiplied by the mark-up rate" contains no particular implied knowledge dependency. An analyst might thus be excused for interpreting this fact as:

if an item's buying price is known **and** an item's mark-up rate is known, **then** the
item's selling price is the buying price multiplied by the mark-up rate.

However, it is possible that:

if an item's selling price is known **and** an item's mark-up rate is known, **then** the item's buying price is the selling price divided by the mark-up rate.

and that:

if an item's selling price is known **and** an item's buying price is known, **then** the mark-up rate is the quotient of the selling price and the buying price.

are also valid consequences of the stated fact. The important point to realize is that these three forms are logically independent. In other words, if they are all valid, then they should all be stated. Thus, it is important for the analyst to be sure to determine which of these three functional associations are intended by the domain expert. In short, when representing a fact, which contains a particular knowledge dependency, in a notation which is knowledge goal-dependent, the analyst must take great care to determine which of the possible knowledge-dependent interpretations are valid and which are not.

Another problem in representing knowledge occurs when the analyst incorrectly concludes that the presented fact only contains one particular knowledge dependency. This can often occur if the analyst interprets a causal connection as a logical implication. For example, the fact "worn piston rings will produce blue smoke in the exhaust" might appear to be in the functional form:

if the piston rings are worn, **then** the exhaust will contain blue smoke.

However, if the analyst only records this form, then the valuable diagnostic rule which enables a mechanic to deduce the probability of a car's piston rings being worn, given that the exhaust contains blue smoke, will have been lost. Such a rule might have the form:

if the exhaust contains blue smoke, **then with probability 0.6**[the piston rings are worn]

The truth of both of these statements can clearly be related to each other using Bayes' theorem, but the important point is that, in the absence of other information, these two forms are logically independent. Another situation in which the analyst can incorrectly assume that a presented fact contains one particular knowledge dependency is when the fact seems to establish an "answer", that is, the fact seems to establish an answer to a question which the analyst feels is "bound to reflect the deductive flow of the system". For example, when presented with the fact "the selling price for an item is the purchase price multiplied by the mark-up rate" the analyst may come to the conclusion that although this fact may imply that the form:

if an item's selling price is known **and** an item's mark-up rate is known, **then** the item's buying price is the selling price divided by the mark-up rate.

is valid, this form "could never be of any use".

We have just noted two scenarios in which the analyst might not gather all the knowledge dependencies in a fact. It is important to realize that the business of constructing all valid knowledge-dependent forms does not necessarily amount to "permuting" the wording as in the simple "buying price versus selling price" example considered above. For example, re-examine the "worn piston rings" example above or the knowledge represented in bundle 15 in the worked example developed in Chapter 7. Thus, we conclude that the construction of each valid knowledge-dependent representation must be done in careful consultation with the domain expert.

We have also seen in our worked example that the process of gathering all knowledge-dependent forms of a given fact can, via the normalization process, lead to an improved representation of those knowledge dependent forms. For example, recall that in Chapter 7 [2.2'] was used to normalize [2.4'] (*see* Section 7.6.1). In that example, when the breach of normal form K.1.1 caused by the presence of the label "Mr Boss" has been rectified, cluster [2] is as shown in Figure 10.1. Then note that [2.2'] was used to normalize [2.4'] to produce [2.4"]. Then note that as a result of this normalization, an attempt was made to use [2.4"] to normalize [2.1']; this attempt was not in fact successful. Thus, it is incorrect to view the different knowledge-dependent forms of a fact as being independent of each other. In the example of cluster [2] just referred to, one of these forms is employed to normalize another, then this normalized form becomes a candidate for normalizing yet another. In other words, it is incorrect to view the business of completing a cluster as an apparently futile exercise which gathers largely unusable knowledge; it is an integral part of the model building process and a vital part of the normalization process. It is also incorrect to view the groups of an unnormalized cluster as being "orthogonal" to each other, where by *orthogonal* we mean that each group is independent of the remainder.

As we have noted, knowledge is explicit functional associations between items of information and/or data. Thus, we now discuss the problems in the management of the

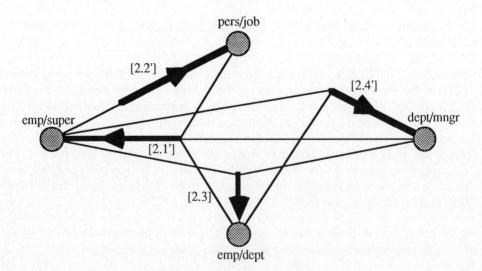

Figure 10.1 The combined group diagram for cluster [2]

representation of the information and/or data in terms of which the knowledge will be expressed. We have already made the case that, in a real sense, information is "simpler stuff" than knowledge. In particular, the problem of ensuring that the correct implicit functional associations have been identified is not as complex an issue as it is for the explicit functional associations. The technology for gathering and maintaining both data and information is well known. However it is important to clearly understand the way in which the established technology, which is used to manage data and information, interfaces with our new technology which is used to manage the knowledge. For example, if the B-R modelling approach is used for information, then the knowledge will be principally expressed in terms of binary relations; this may, or may not, be appropriate.

A simple, but vital, problem with the management of information and/or data in terms of which the knowledge will be expressed is the problem of preserving the correctness of the information and data models. In Section 5.1 we noted the potential added cost caused by duplicate names being recorded for the same "real" population. We also noted that this potential added cost is far more significant in the knowledge than it is in the information. Thus, the project manager will be concerned with ensuring that at all times the populations identified are genuinely independent of one another. Furthermore, it is important to ensure that the information model remains both accurate and normal. Note that any changes to the data model will usually cause changes to both the information and the knowledge model, and changes to the information model will usually cause changes to the knowledge model.

10.3 MANAGING THE DESIGN PROCESS

A central feature of our approach to knowledge systems design is the construction of the application model and the three system models. The application model is constructed first and contains a representation of the application in quasi-natural language. The three system models are constructed during data analysis, information analysis and knowledge analysis. We have seen that the data model determines the vocabulary in terms of which the information model is expressed, and that the data and information models together determine the vocabulary in terms of which the knowledge model is expressed. Furthermore, we have seen that the three system models interact with, and cause modification to each other as they, and the system are developed. Once they have been normalized, the four models taken together are referred to as the *normalized model*. The normalized model should be seen as an integrated and interrelated structure which provides the interface between the domain expert and the programmer as depicted in Figure 10.2. The normalized model will be constructed and maintained by the knowledge analysts. Additional facts, pronounced by the domain expert, will be analysed and normalized by the knowledge analysts, and will finally be represented in the normalized model. In its final form, the normalized model provides the programming staff with a formal specification of the knowledge system. Thus, the normalized model plays a key role in the management of the design process. It is a complete, structural and precise representation of the facts that have been presented to the knowledge analyst. Furthermore, the normalized model is the formal specification from which the knowledge system itself is constructed. Thus, the

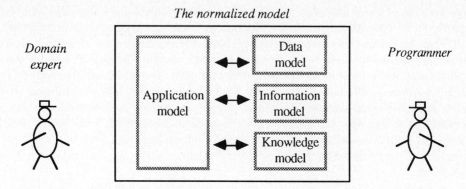

Figure 10.2 Interface between domain expert and programmer

derivation and preservation of this model should be seen as the most vital function of the whole design and maintenance process. It is not possible to overemphasize the importance of ensuring that the normalized model is correct, and that it is, in fact, normal.

Having noted the central role of the normalized model, it is useful to regard this model as dividing the design process into two distinct parts. The first part is concerned with the construction of the normalized model itself, and the second part is concerned with using the normalized model to construct an operational system. We now consider the management issues associated with these two parts. The first part consists of knowledge acquisition and knowledge analysis. The second part consists of knowledge base engineering and knowledge base implementation. The business of knowledge base maintenance is considered separately in the next section.

One of the key problems in managing the knowledge acquisition phase is ensuring that gathered facts, which may have been gleaned from different sources by different analysts, are phrased consistently with each other. This problem is addressed by the "uniqueness requirement" and the "type identification requirement". These requirements insists that a data dictionary should be carefully maintained, especially when members of a team of analysts are working together. In other words, we claim that it is essential that the members of a team of analysts operate with a common set of primitive concepts in terms of which their analysis will be expressed. As this may require regular, detailed communication between analysts, it is not easy to achieve in practice. It is probably the most complex issue confronting the project manager during knowledge acquisition.

The key problems in managing the knowledge analysis phase are ensuring uniformity in information analysis, ensuring uniformity in object classification, and normalization. Despite the fact that information is, in a sense, "built out of data", there is great flexibility in deriving the information model even when the data model has been determined. It is important to ensure that the information model derived is sufficient for the needs of the whole system and that all analysts are fully acquainted with it. Likewise, it is vital that object classification is determined in a uniform way. For example, it is essential that if one analyst represents a fact as information then all other analysts will be aware of this and will not represent the same fact, or similar facts, as data or knowledge later on. A key step in the construction of the normalized model is the normalization of knowledge, as well as the normalization of the information and data. An important feature of knowledge is that the business of normalization is highly technical. By contrast, the normalization of information can often be achieved on the basis of an intuitive understanding of the problem. The potential cost of maintaining unnormalized knowledge can be very high. Thus, in applications which are being designed for maintenance, there appears to be no alternative to the often laborious business of re-interviewing the domain expert while the normalized form of the knowledge is being constructed. An important conclusion drawn from this is that when a human expert is not available for questioning, such as when the expertise has been gleaned from a printed source or some inductive inference system, it may just not be possible to normalize the knowledge and, as a result, may not be possible to construct a knowledge system which can be maintained simply.

Once the normalized model has been constructed, the two phases of design that remain are knowledge base engineering and knowledge base implementation. These two phases are highly technical in nature but should be carried out automatically by the knowledge base management system. Thus, the management of these two phases is considerably simpler than the earlier phases. There is, however, one issue that deserves special mention. On completion of the knowledge base implementation phase, the system integrity checks should be designed. The business of designing system integrity checks is considered below.

10.4 STRATEGY FOR MAINTENANCE

We will relate the business of knowledge systems maintenance to our approach to knowledge systems design. The first two stages in the design process are "knowledge acquisition" and "knowledge analysis". These two stages can be represented as shown in Figure 10.3.

Thus the first two stages of the design process can be summarized as a process which has as input the raw application and as output the normalized model. Then, following our design methodology, we add the functional requirements to the normalized

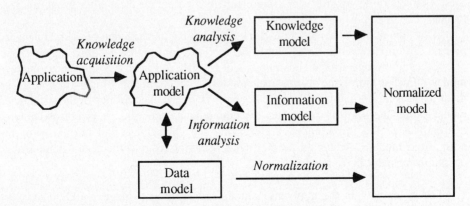

Figure 10.3 Knowledge acquisition and knowledge analysis

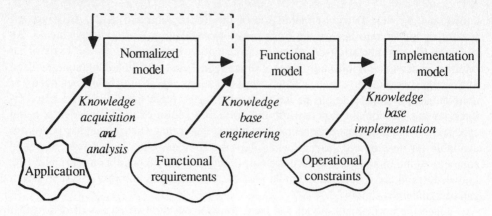

Figure 10.4 The whole design process

model and, using knowledge base engineering, derive the functional model. Then, we add the operational constraints to the functional model and, using knowledge base implementation, derive the implementation model. The whole design process can be represented as shown in Figure 10.4.

Recall that when the functional requirements are added in during knowledge base engineering this often leads to a "partial revisit" to the knowledge acquisition stage; this has been denoted on the diagram in Figure 10.4 by a dotted line. By a "partial revisit", we mean that such subsequent knowledge acquisition will usually be quite consistent with the normalized model derived to that point. With the proviso that developing or modifying the functional requirements *may* entail additional knowledge acquisition, we now observe a simple hierarchy for knowledge base maintenance operations. Changes to the operational constraints may be accommodated by revisiting the knowledge base implementation stage only. Changes to the functional requirements may be accommodated by revisiting the knowledge base engineering stage only. Other changes to the application will require that the knowledge acquisition phase be revisited and that the changes will then be passed through the whole design process. We will show shortly that these changes often require very little effort to incorporate them into the normalized model.

Thus, the normalized model plays a key role in the management of the maintenance process. All modifications, except for trivial modifications to the functional requirements or changes in the operational constraints, will be reflected in changes to the normalized model. Furthermore, the normalized model is the point at which all non-trivial modifications are formally fed into the system. Thus, the maintenance of the normalized model should be seen as crucial to the maintenance process. It is not possible to overemphasize the importance of preserving the correctness and normality of the normalized model. As far as the normalized model is concerned, any maintenance operation consists of five steps:

1. The statements in the application model which are no longer valid, if any, are identified.

2. Those statements which are no longer valid are removed from the application model and representations of these statements are removed from the system models.
3. Any new bundles of statements are added to the application model.
4. The analysis and normalization is performed to generate a new normalized model.
5. The resulting modifications to the three system models are presented to the programming staff for implementation.

In a typical application, changes to the operational constraints are often the most common class of alterations to the application. Common changes to the operational requirements include changes to the frequency of presentation of the query or update types, and changes to the maximum permissible response time for a query type. In a substantial application which is in heavy use, small changes to the operational constraints may occur daily. Thus, it is important to define criteria which identify when sufficient changes to the operational constraints have been observed to justify revisiting the knowledge base implementation phase. Once it has been acknowledged that substantial changes to the operational constraints have been observed, then the knowledge base implementation phase should be revisited. The important thing to appreciate is that the knowledge base implementation Algorithms should be embedded in the system so this should result in in the knowledge base "automatically reorganizing" itself so that its response is more satisfactory.

Changes to the functional requirements are often the second most common class of alterations to the application. Common changes to the functional requirements include the identification of new system query types or modifications to existing system update types. Once a change in the functional requirements has occurred, the key question is to decide whether or not it will be necessary to revisit the knowledge analysis phase. This question can be decided using the following criteria. If the new functional requirements can be expressed in terms of the populations, relations and groups identified in the normalized model, then it is not necessary to revisit the knowledge analysis phase; otherwise it will be necessary.

Changes to the application are essentially of two types; first, those that require modification to existing statements in the application model and, second, those that do not in which case such a change can be effected by an addition to the application model. An important class of changes to the application are changes to labels which are not designated as being "fixed" in the data model; these changes can be effected by simply changing the appropriate label in the data model. Another important class of changes to the application are changes to the information and knowledge that the system has been designed to accommodate; it should be possible to permit programming staff to effect changes in this class. Important changes outside this class include changes to "fixed" labels and changes to items of knowledge which have not been constrained and designed for modification; for changes of this form an analyst should be made responsible for ensuring that the change is processed correctly.

10.5 CONSTRAINTS AND INTEGRITY CHECKS

The practical importance of system constraints and integrity checks to the maintenance of information systems is well understood. As far as system maintenance is concerned, the difference between information systems and knowledge systems is that, in general, a knowledge system is designed to receive modifications and updates to the knowledge component on a day-to-day basis. Thus, in addition to the conventional constraints and integrity checks for the data and information, constraints and integrity checks for knowledge will be required. Constraints for knowledge have been discussed in Chapter 7; they are vital to the survival of a knowledge system. The project manager should ensure that knowledge constraints are carefully built into the system and are themselves kept up to date. Then, if a knowledge constraint is violated, the matter should be referred to the system architect for resolution. Constraints for knowledge play two important roles. First, constraints may be seen as a safety alarm which sounds when errors are made. Second, constraints may be seen as a specification of the bounds within which modifications may be made without de-stabilizing the system. It is important to remember both of these roles when designing constraints for knowledge.

Once the knowledge base implementation phase has been performed and the whole design process is complete, there should be an abundant supply of knowledge which has not been selected for the implemented system. This spare knowledge is a source of material for the system integrity checks. A classic example of an integrity check is when sufficient knowledge is used to calculate values for an update relation in terms of the values in the real stored relations. It is important to appreciate that these calculations can be carried out automatically in much the same way that information model consistency is established. Thus, if the processing of integrity checks is scheduled during periods of low system usage, a powerful array of checks can be applied for a very low additional cost. The project manager should take full advantage of this inexpensive means of checking the correctness of the knowledge, information and data.

10.6 PARTITIONING LARGE SYSTEMS

The design technique that we have proposed is sufficiently methodical to support development by a design team. In Sections 10.2 and 10.3 we have emphasized the management aspects of the design process that require supervision if the technique is to be used by a team successfully. Thus, in principle, the technique can be employed to build "large" systems. A crude, but useful measure of the size of a system is the number of groups in the combined functional diagram for that system. As a rough rule, we might say that a system was large if it contained more than two or three hundred groups. In simple terms, a system can be "large" in two different ways. First, a system can contain substantial "depth" of knowledge, and second, a system can contain substantial "breadth" of knowledge. Three important measures of the *depth* of a knowledge system are the "maximum", "minimum" and "mean" depth. The *depth* of a relation is the length of the longest path from that relation to the update relations in the combined functional diagram. For example, in the diagram shown in Figure 10.5, relation A has depth 3. The *maximum depth*, *minimum depth* and *mean depth* of a knowledge system are defined respectively to be the maximum, minimum and mean, over all query relations, of the depth of the query relations. For example, the maximum depth in the example shown in Figure 10.5 is 3, the minimum depth is 2 and the mean depth is 2.6.

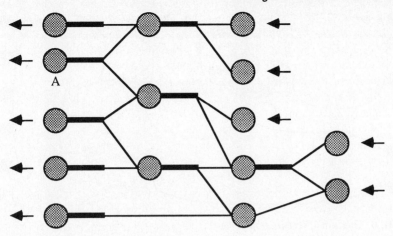

Figure 10.5 Combined functional diagram

Three important measures of the *breadth* of a knowledge system are the "maximum", "minimum" and "mean" breadth. The *maximum breadth*, *minimum breadth* and *mean breadth* of a knowledge system are defined respectively to be the maximum, minimum and mean, over all divisions on the combined functional diagram, of the number of relations in those divisions. For example, the maximum breadth in the example shown above is 5, the minimum breadth is 4, and the mean breadth is 4.8.

The problem with systems of substantial size, be it substantial breadth or substantial depth, is that the normalized model becomes too large for an analyst to comprehend effectively. That is, a maintenance analyst would find it difficult to relate modifications in the application to the normalized model accurately. In other words, when the system becomes large the practical value of the design and maintenance process, as we have described it, breaks down. A natural way of dealing with a system that is too large is to break it up into a number of smaller sub-systems. We refer to this process as *partitioning* a system.

There are two ways of approaching partitioning. First, all the knowledge can be gathered, analysed and normalized then, using some Algorithm, the combined functional diagram can be broken up into workable chunks in such a way as to minimize the number of links between its chunks. We do not advocate this method as it will probably lead to a partitioning that does not reflect the way in which the problem might be divided naturally. The second approach to partitioning is to design the partitions deliberately to reflect a natural partition of the knowledge. One such natural partition is determined by the source of the knowledge. For example, if knowledge is being drawn from four experts who interact in the natural course of their business then the knowledge system can be partitioned into four components which interact in the same way as the experts. No matter how the system has been partitioned, note that when this has been done the query relations in one partition may be the update relations in another partition. For example, consider the diagram shown in Figure 10.6. Note also that modifications performed on a partition will only be local to that partition if they do not affect the meaning of the query and update relations in that partition.

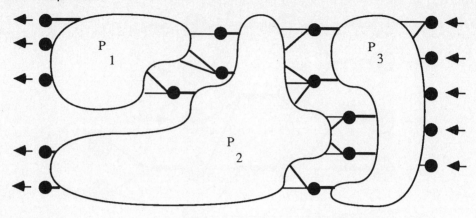

Figure 10.6 System in three partitions

There is more to partitioning than simply "splitting up" the knowledge. For example, we should consider how to manage the information and data, much of which may be shared by a number of partitions of the knowledge. We advocate that each partition should be completely modeled separately; that is, each partition will have its own data, information and knowledge models. At first glance, this may seem like lunacy as it appears to be advocating the replication of much of the data and information within the different partitions. Note, however, that we are advocating the construction of independent normalized models for each partition; we have yet to address the design of the implemented system. Having analysed the application into separate partitions, we now consider the problem of, at least partially, synthesizing a good implementation from the separate partitions. The key to achieving this synthesis is the construction of a "system data model". The system data model contains entries for every data item in each partition and maintains links to those data items as shown in the diagram in Figure 10.7.

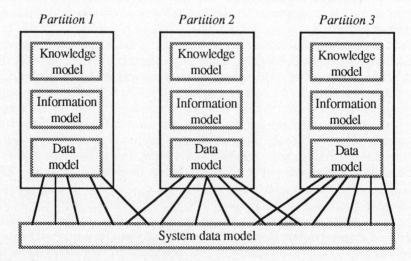

Figure 10.7 The system data model

Having related the data models in each partition to the system data model, the business of identifying relations which are common to more than one partition is comparatively simple. Thus, once again, we note the fundamental structural importance of a correct data model.

10.7 WORKED EXAMPLE

Before we consider some maintenance operations on the worked example developed through Chapters 7, 8 and 9, we quote the normalized model as it is at this point in our discussion. Note that the application model now contains the query and update types, and the three system models now contain a column headed "associated with" which contains the query or update types associated with each data, information and knowledge item. In fact, in this example, only the information and knowledge model have an "associated with" column as the "associated with" column for the data model would have contained no entries. The three system models also contain a "class" column which contains the result of the knowledge base implementation phase. The application model is:

1.1   There are businesses.
1.2   Businesses are identified by a business-name.
1.3   "Egs P/L" is the name of a business.
1.4   Egs P/L is the only business name.
2.1   There are persons.
2.2   Each person is identified by a unique person-name.
2.3   The "personnel file" contains all person-names.
3.1   Persons work at businesses.
3.2   All persons work at the business named Egs P/L.
6.1   There are jobs.
6.2   Jobs are identified by a job-name.
6.3   "General-Manager", "Department-Manager" and "Worker" are the only job names.
7.1   Persons have jobs.
7.2   Each person has exactly one job.
7.3   The personnel file contains the job-name for each person.
8.1   There are employees.
8.2   The employees are the persons listed in the personnel file excluding the particular person whose job is General-Manager.
8.3   All employees are persons.
9.1   There are departments.
9.2   Each department is identified by a unique department-name.
9.3   The organization chart contains all the department names.
9.4   There are four department-names.
10.1   Employees are assigned to departments.
10.2   Each employee is assigned to one particular department.
10.3   The organization chart shows a department for each employee.
11.1   Departments have department-managers.

11.2   Each department has a unique department-manager.

11.3   The organization chart contains the name of the department-manager for each department.

12.1   There are department-managers.

12.2   Department-managers are employees.

12.3   The department-managers are listed in the personnel file.

13.1   The are supervisors.

13.2   Supervisors are persons.

13.3   The supervisors are listed in the personnel file.

13.4   Department managers are supervisors.

14.1   Employees are supervised by supervisors.

14.2   Each employee has a unique supervisor.

14.3   The organization chart contains the name of the supervisor for each employee.

15.1   The supervisor of an employee may be deduced from that employee's job and that employee's department.

15.2   **if** an employee's job is a worker **and** if that employee works in a certain department, **then** that employee is supervised by the Department Manager of that department.

15.3   **if** an employee's job is a Department Manager, **then** that employee is supervised by the General Manager.

15.4.1 The job of an employee may be deduced from knowing that employee's supervisor.

15.4.2 **if** an employee is supervised by the General Manager, **then** that employee's job is Department Manager.

15.4.3 **if** an employee's supervisor is in turn supervised by the General Manager, **then** that employee's job is Worker.

15.5.1 The department in which an employee works may be deduced from knowing that employee's supervisor and the managers of each department.

15.5.2 **if** a person is manager of a department, **then** that person is said to work in that department.

15.5.3 **if** a person has a supervisor who is manager of a department, **then** that person works in that same department.

15.6.1 The manager of a department may be deduced from knowing the employees in that department and the jobs of the employees in that department.

15.6.2 **if** an employee has the job of department manager **and** that employee works in some particular department, **then** that employee is manager of that department.

16.1   There are salaries.

16.2   Salaries are identified by a salary-rate expressed in dollars per annum.

16.3 $50,000, $40,000 and $30,000 are the only salary rates.

16.4   There are at most three different salary-rates.

17.1   Persons receive salaries.

17.2   Each person receives a single salary.

17.3   The personnel file contains the salary for each person.

18.1   A person's salary may be deduced from that person's job.

18.2   **if** a person has job "General Manager", **then** that person receives a salary of $50,000, **and if** a person has job "Department Manager", **then** that person receives a salary of $40,000, **and if** a person has job "Worker", **then** that person receives a salary of $30,000.

19.1   Job is associated with salary.

19.2   Each job-name is associated with a unique salary-rate.

19.3   Managing-Director is associated with $50,000, Department-Manager is associated with $40,000 and Worker is associated with $30,000.

20.1   There are general managers.

20.2   General managers are supervisors.

20.3   There is only one general manager.

20.4   "Mr Boss" is a general manager.

21.1   There are total-salary-bills.

21.2   total-salary-bills are identified by a salary-bill-amount expressed in dollars per annum.

21.3   salary-bill-amounts must be positive integers.

22.1   Each department is associated with a total salary bill.

22.2   Each department is associated with a unique total salary bill.

23.1   The total salary bill for a department may be deduced from the salaries of the employees who work in that department.

23.2   **if** a department has a collection of employees working in that department **and** the salary of each employee is known, **then** the total salary bill for that department is the sum of the salaries of the employees working in that department.

Q1   To find the supervisor of any given employee.

Q2   To find the list of employees supervised by a given person.

Q3   To find the manager of any given department.

Q4   To calculate the total salary for any given department.

Q5   To explain how the above four query types may be satisfied in general.

Q6   To explain how any particular answer to one of the above four query types was derived.

U1   For any employee, the department, if any, in which that employee works.

U2   For any employee, the title of the job which that employee holds.

U3   For any job description, the salary rate for that job.

The three system models for the worked example are shown in Figures 10.8, 10.9 and 10.10; Figure 10.8 shows the data model where:

- business-name(x) means "x is the name of a business, at present Egs P/L is the only business name";
- person-name(x) means " x is the name of a person";
- dept-name(x) means "x is the name of a department";
- job-name(x) means "x is the name of a job";
- salary-rate(x) means "x is a salary expressed in dollars per annum";
- sal-bill-amount(x) means "x is a salary bill expressed in dollars per annum".

Thing-population	Bundle	Sub-type of	Name-population	Labels	Population constraints	Label constraints	Fixed labels	Class
bus	1		business-name	Egs P/L	one label only			dormant
pers	2		person-name	(see 2.3)	each label unique			live
super	13	pers			= job GM and DM			live
emp	8	pers			= job DM and Workr			live
mngr	12	emp, super			= job DM			live
dept	9		dept-name	(see 9.3)	4 unique labels		all	live
job	6		job-name	(see 6.3)	3 unique labels	= GM,DM Workr	all	live
salary	16		salary-rate	(see 16.3)	3 labels or less	positive integer		live
gen-man	20	super		Mr Boss	one label only			real
sal-bill	21		sal-bill-amount	(see 21.3)		positive integer		live

Figure 10.8 The data model

Figure 10.9 shows the information model where the constraints are as listed in Section 7.5.1 and, in addition:

- IC8.1 is "domain-1 is total"

and where:

- bus/pers(x, y) means "x is the name of a business and y is the name of a person who works at that business";
- pers/job(x, y) means "x is the name of a person and y is the name of the unique job that that person has";
- emp/dept(x, y) means "x is the name of an employee and y is the name of the unique department in which that employee works";
- dept/mngr(x, y) means "x is the name of a department and y is the name of the unique manager of that department";
- emp/super(x, y) means "x is the name of an employee and y is the name of the unique supervisor of that employee";
- pers/salary(x, y) means "x is the name of a person and y is the unique salary in dollars per annum of that person";

Relation	Bundle	Key domain	Other domains	Tuples	Relation constraints	Tuple constraints	Associated with	Class
bus/pers	3		business-name person-name	(see 3.2)	IC1.1			dormant
pers/job	7	person-name	job-name	(see 7.3)	IC2.1		U2	real
emp/dept	10	emp-name	dept-name	(see 10.3)	IC3.1	IC3.2	U1	real
dept/mngr	11	dept-name	mngr-name	(see 11.3)	IC4.1	IC4.2	Q3	virtual query
emp/super	14	emp-name	super-name	(see 14.3)	IC5.1	IC5.2	Q1, Q2	real
pers/salary	17	person-name	salary-rate	(see 17.3)	IC6.1	IC6.2		real
job/salary	19	job-name	salary-rate	(see 19.3)	IC7.1	IC7.2	U3	virtual update
dept/sal-bill	22	dept-name	sal-bill-amount		IC8.1		Q4	virtual query

Figure 10.9 The information model

- job/salary(x, y) means "x is the name of a job and y is the unique salary in dollars per annum associated with that job";
- dept/sal-bill(x, y) means "x is the name of a department and y is the total salary bill in dollars per annum associated with that department".

The knowledge model is as shown in Figure 10.10.

We now consider some sample maintenance operations. For each problem we will assume that the starting point is the normalized model quoted above, and will follow through the five steps described in Section 10.4. To avoid using an inordinate amount of space, we have presented the working that follows in a summary form only. In particular, the knowledge analysis and normalization steps are not mentioned explicitly as such. The reader may wish to work through the examples in a complete and systematic way. In any case, note carefully how the procedure operates; in particular, note how the links between the four models assist the maintenance process. For example, in the first example considered below, note how the observation that 9.3 is now invalid automatically leads to the population "dept" in the data model through the reference to bundle 9 in that model. Then, once the population "dept" has been earmarked for modification, it is referenced by the relations "emp/dept", "dept/mngr" and "dept/sal-bill" in the information model. In turn, these three relations are linked to bundles 10, U1, 11, Q3, 22 and Q4 in the information model so even if our domain expert had failed to identify 10.3, 11.3 and 22.1 as invalid, the structure of the information model itself would have ensured that the analyst confirm the validity of these bundles. Furthermore, these three relations identified are linked to bundles 15, Q5 and Q6 (groups [2.1'], [2.3] and [2.4"]) and to bundles 23.1,

Cluster	Bundle	Group	Head	Body	Cluster constraints	Group constraints	Associated with	Class
[2]	15				complete			
	15.1	[2.1']	emp/super	pers/job emp/dept dpt/mngr		categ. & unique	Q5, Q6	update
	15.4.1	[2.2']	pers/job	emp/super		categ. & unique		dormant
	15.5.1	[2.3]	emp/dept	emp/super dept/mngr		categ. & unique		dormant
	15.6.1	[2.4"]	dept/mngr	pers/job emp/dept		categ. & unique	Q5, Q6	query
[3]	18				pers/salary only			
	18.1	[3.1]	pers/salary	job/salary pers/job		categ. & unique		update
[4]	23				dept/sal-bill only			
	23.1	[4.1']	dept/sal-bill	pers/salary emp/dept		categ. & unique	Q5, Q6	query

Figure 10.10 The knowledge model

Q5 and Q6 (group [4.1']) in the knowledge model so even if our domain expert had failed to identify 23.1 as invalid, the structure of the knowledge model itself would have ensured that the analyst confirmed the validity of bundles 15 and 23. Thus, the normalized model should be seen as a fairly robust and stable structure which should help to prevent the introduction of inconsistencies.

Maintenance Problem 1
"The Hardware Department is to be re-named the Home Supplies Department."

1. **9.3, 10.3, 11.3, 22.1** and **23.1** are invalid.
2. **9.3** the new organization chart dated "today" contains all the department names.
   10.3 the new organization chart dated "today" shows a department for each employee.
   11.3 the new organization chart dated "today" contains the name of the department-manager for each department.
   22.1 each department listed in the new organization chart dated "today" is associated with a total salary bill.
   23.1 the total salary bill for each department list in the new organization chart dated "today" may be deduced from the salaries of the employees who work in that department.

3. None.
4. "Home Supplies" replaces "Hardware" under the thing-population "dept" in the data model, as the labels for the thing-population "dept" are fixed, it is necessary to check all relations and clauses which refer to the thing-population "dept".

   The domain dept-name in the relation emp/dept in the information model now refers to the new department names.

   The domain dept-name in the relation dept/mngr in the information model now refers to the new department names.

   The domain dept-name in the relation dept/sal-bill in the information model now refers to the new department names.

   Group [4.1'] is checked to see if it refers to the "Hardware" Department explicitly; in fact it does not therefore no change to this group is required.
5. The programmer has to make the appropriate changes from "Hardware" to "Home Supplies" under the population name "dept" in the data base.

   The programmer has to adjust any of the relations emp/dept, dept/mngr and dept/sal-bill which are real relations in the information base.

Maintenance Problem 2
"Mr Boss, the General Manager, has retired. The new General Manager is Mr Head."

1. **20.4** is invalid.
2. **20.4** "Mr Head" is a general manager.
3. None.
4. "Mr Head" replaces "Mr Boss" under the thing-population gen-man in the data model, as the labels for the thing-population gen-man are not fixed, this change is all that has to be done.
5. All the programmer has to do is to make the appropriate change from Mr Boss to Mr Head in the data base.

Maintenance Problem 3
"The title of Department Manager is to be changed to Assistant Manager."

1. **6.3, 7.3, 15.2, 15.3, 15.4.2, 15.6.2, 18.2** and **19.3** are invalid.
2. **6.3** "General-Manager", "Assistant-Manager" and "Worker" are the only job names.

   7.3 the new personnel file dated "today" contains the job-name for each person.

   15.2 **if** an employee's job is a worker **and** if that employee works in a certain department, **then** that employee is supervised by the Assistant Manager of that department.

   15.3 **if** an employee's job is an Assistant Manager, **then** that employee is supervised by the General Manager.

   15.4.2 **if** an employee is supervised by the General Manager, **then** that employee's job is Assistant Manager.

   15.6.2 **if** an employee has the job of Assistant Manager **and** that employee works in some particular department, **then** that employee is manager of that department.

18.2 **if** a person has job "General Manager", **then** that person receives a salary of $50,000, **and if** a person has job "Assistant Manager", **then** that person receives a salary of $40,000, **and if** a person has job "Worker", **then** that person receives a salary of $30,000.

19.3 Managing-Director is associated with $50,000, Assistant-Manager is associated with $40,000 and Worker is associated with $30,000.

3.   None.

4.   Population constraints for super, emp and mngr are adjusted, and the label constraints for job are adjusted.

The domain "job-name" in the relations pers/job and job/salary now refers to the new job names.

Groups [2.1'], [2.2'] and [2.4"] are adjusted.

5.   The programmer has to make the appropriate changes from "Department Manager" to "Assistant Manager" under the population name "job" in the data base.

The programmer has to adjust either of the relations pers/job and job/salary if they are real relations in the information base.

The implementations of groups [2.1'], [2.2'] and [2.4"] are adjusted in the knowledge base.

Maintenance Problem 4

"Persons are now to be paid a wage which consists of a pay which is determined by their job (as previously for salary) plus a loading which is calculated at $100 per annum for every year the person has worked for Egs P/L. The query type 'To calculate the total salary for any given department' becomes 'To calculate the total wage for any given department' and the update type 'For any job description, the salary rate for that job' becomes 'For any job description, the pay rate for that job'."

1.   **16.1, 16.2, 16.3, 17.1, 17.2, 17.3, 19.1, 19.2, 19.3, 21.1, 21.2, 21.3, 22.1, 23.1, 23.2, Q4** and **U3** are invalid.

2.   **16.1** there are pays.

16.2 pays are identified by a pay-rate expressed in dollars per annum.

16.3 $50,000, $40,000 and $30,000 are the only pay rates.

17.1 persons have pay.

17.2 each person has a single pay.

17.3 the new personnel file dated "today" contains the pay for each person.

19.1 job is associated with pay.

19.2 each job-name is associated with a unique pay-rate.

19.3 Managing Director is associated with $50,000, Department-Manager is associated with $40,000 and Worker is associated with $30,000.

21.1 there are total-wage-bills.

21.2 total-wage-bills are identified by a wage-bill-amount expressed in dollars per annum.

21.3 wage-bill-amounts must be positive integers.

22.1 each department is associated with a total wage bill.

23.1 the total wage bill for a department may be deduced from the wages of the employees who work in that department.

23.2 **if** a department has a collection of employees working in that department **and** the wage of each employee is known, **then** the total wage bill for that department is the sum of the wages of the employees working in that department.

Q4 to calculate the total wage for any given department.

U3 for any job description, the pay rate for that job.

3.   **24.1** there are wages.

24.2 wages are identified by a wage-rate expressed in dollars per annum.

25.1 there are loadings.

25.2 loadings are identified by a loading-rate expressed in dollars per annum.

26.1 there are services.

26.2 each service is identified by years-of-service in years.

27.1 each person has a service (as in years of service).

27.2 each person has just one service.

27.3 the personnel file contains the service for each person.

28.1 each person has a loading.

28.2 each person has just one loading.

28.3 the personnel file contains the loading for each person.

29.1 a person's loading may be deduced from that person's service.

29.2 **if** a person has n years of service, **then** that person's loading is $n \times 100$ dollars per annum,

30.1 persons receive wages.

30.2 each person receives a single wage.

30.3 the personnel file contains the wage for each person.

31.1 a person's wage may be deduced from that person's salary and that person's loading.

31.2 **if** a person's salary is x **and** that persons loading is y, **then** that person's wage is $x + y$.

4.   "salary" is changed to "pay" in the data model.

"sal-bill" is changed to "wage-bill" in the data model.

"wages", "loadings" and "services" are introduced into the data model with name-populations wage-rate, loading-rate and years-of-service respectively, and are associated with bundles 24, 25 and 26 respectively.

The relation pers/salary is changed to pers/pay in the information model.

The relation job/salary is changed to job/pay in the information model.

The relation dept/sal-bill is changed to dept/wage-bill in the information model.

The relations pers/service, pers/loading and pers/wage are introduced into the information model and are identified with bundles 27, 28 and 30 respectively.

"dept/sal-bill" is changed to "dept/wage-bill" in the information model.

The knowledge represented in [4.1'] is changed, in line with bundle 23.1, in the application model.

The clause:

$$\text{pers/load(} x, y \text{)} \leftarrow \text{pers/serv(} x, z \text{)}, y = z \times 100 \qquad [5.1]$$

is established as the first clause in cluster [5] in the knowledge model and is associated with bundle 29.

The clause:

$$\text{pers/wage}(\ x, y\ ) \leftarrow \text{pers/salary}(\ x, z\ ),\ \text{pers/load}(\ x, w\ ),\ y = z + w \qquad [6.1]$$

is established as the first clause in cluster [6] in the knowledge model and is associated with bundle 31.

5.   "salary" and "sal-bill" are deleted from the data base.
"pay", "wage-bill", "wages", "loadings" and "services" are added to the data base.
"pers/salary", "job/salary" and "dept/sal-bill" are deleted from the information base.
"dept/wage-bill", "pers/pay", "job/pay", "pers/serv", "pers/load" and "pers/wage" are added to the information base and those that are real relations are populated accordingly.
Implementations of [5.1] and [6.1] are added to the knowledge base in line with bundles 29 and 31 respectively.
The implementation of [4.1'] is adjusted in line with bundle 23.

10.8 SOFTWARE

"The Knowledge Analyst's Assistant"
A software package which implements the design technique described in this text is scheduled to be ready for distribution late in 1989. The software is being prepared by the Australian Commonwealth Scientific and Industrial Research Organization within their Division of Information Technology's laboratory at North Ryde, Sydney, Australia. The software package will be distributed world wide, mainly through local agents. Enquiries for wholesale or retail sales should be directed to:

Knowledge Systems Design Project,
C.S.I.R.O.,
Division of Information Technology,
PO Box 1599,
North Ryde, NSW 2113,
Australia.

This software functions as a complete "knowledge base design and maintenance assistant". It is designed to run on a workstation which is either "stand alone" or is linked to a mainframe which supports some form of knowledge processing software. The Knowledge Analyst's Assistant provides the following the functions:

•   complete support for the knowledge acquisition process, including the construction of the application model and the supporting data model;
•   a means of entering the derived information model. In line with the method presented in this text, the software does not attempt to interfere with the information analysis process which is assumed to be conducted in keeping with local, established practice;
•   complete support for the normalization process by the provision of prompts which identify candidates for normalization; the presentation of these prompts may be

controlled either to occur as the knowledge is entered or after it has all been entered;

- complete support for the development of the knowledge model; by this stage the system contains a representation of a robust "normalized model" in which the application model, the data model, the information model and the knowledge model are all interlinked;
- complete support for the knowledge base engineering phase, including the development of the update types and the query types, as well as the automatic derivation of the combined functional diagram;
- complete support for the knowledge base implementation phase, including the specification of the operational constraints, query, update and integrity check presentation frequencies, and the automatic derivation of the "hopefully optimal" storage allocation;
- a prototyping facility in which either sample information can be entered directly and the knowledge base trialed without the need for an external information base, or the information can be accessed from a host via simple user-provided procedures;
- the output from the package is in a system independent form which has been chosen for ease of translation to the target formalism; the idea being that the knowledge module designed by the package may be uploaded into a mainframe knowledge processing environment;
- complete support for the knowledge base maintenance process, including assistance with the classification of maintenance operations and automatic constraint checking for all maintenance tasks for which constraints have been provided;
- a facility for the design and implementation of system integrity checks, both within the prototyping module and as part of the final system as designed using the package.

As is noted above, the "Knowledge Analyst's Assistant" generates a simple text file representation of the designed knowledge. Simple procedures will have to be written by the user to translate the contents of these text files into the expert system shell being used for mainline implementation. In addition, the specification is given for simple user-provided procedures which enable the information base on the mainline host to be accessed for prototyping the gathered knowledge. In this way the software is completely integrated with existing investments in both information processing and knowledge processing and generality of application is assured. However it is important to stress that the links between the workstation and the host will operate slowly and are only intended to support file transfer and prototyping.

10.9 SUMMARY

We have noted the problems in dealing with knowledge, in particular the problem of identifying the "right" functional associations within real knowledge. We have also noted that the business of completing clusters is, in fact, an integral part of the normalization process. We have stressed the importance of a well designed data model to the design of the whole system. We have seen that the normalized model plays a key role in the design and maintenance process, and have discussed key managerial issues in the knowledge acquisition, knowledge analysis, knowledge base engineering and knowledge base implementation phases. A strategy for maintaining knowledge systems has been presented, and we have given criteria for determining the amount of the design process that has to be executed for any given modification. The value of constraints and integrity checks has been explored and a technique for dealing with large knowledge systems based on "partitioning" has been presented. Finally, our worked example is presented in its final form and various modifications are performed on it. We have noted the useful assistance that the normalized model gives to the maintenance process in helping to preserve consistency and correctness.

Appendix: Case study

A.1 INTRODUCTION

The object of this appendix is to establish a framework in which the reader can practice the techniques presented in this text. The appendix will thus be of considerable assistance in the development of assignment work if the text is used for instruction. The appendix contains the description of a case study which has been designed specifically to enable the reader to use the *new* techniques presented in the earlier chapters. The working given for the case study deals in detail with the application of established work, that is, data analysis and information analysis, placing the reader in a position to continue to develop the case study and to practice the new skills of knowledge analysis, knowledge base engineering, knowledge base implementation and knowledge base maintenance. This case study has been specifically designed to be suitable for the addition of substantial quantities of further knowledge and so it should be useful as the basis for exercises when the text is being used for instruction.

A.2 THE PROBLEM

In the case study an analyst has been asked to construct a knowledge system which implements some particular expertise. The expertise in question is held by a senior salesman, called the "domain expert" of an insurance company called "Giraffe Insurance". The expertise relates in particular to the sale of illness insurance. To acquaint the analyst

Figure A.1 The client file

Policy holder	Client name	Client address	Client type	Occupat group	Age in years	Gross earns	Expense
six digit number							

Figure A.2 The policy file

Policy number	Policy holder	Policy type	Policy details	Policy status	Benefit rate	Waiting period	Benefit period	Paid to date
seven digit number	six digit number							

with the problem, the domain expert has given the analyst a copy of the company's client file, a copy of the company's policy file, a copy of the company's claims file, and a copy of the company's handbook on illness insurance. The client file contains records of the form shown in Figure A.1; the policy file contains records of the form shown in Figure A.2; the claims file contains records of the form shown in Figure A.3 and the company's handbook on illness insurance is reproduced below.

Giraffe Insurance Co

Illness Insurance

These policies are available for individuals only and provide an income benefit during periods of total disablement resulting from illness, which continues beyond a selected "waiting period". The client can select a waiting period which may be 1, 2, 4 or 6 weeks. The client may also select the maximum benefit period, that is, the maximum time for which the client may receive a benefit; the (maximum) benefit period may be 1, 2 or 5 years, or "up to age 60" or "up to age 65". Premiums will be waived while the benefit is payable; this is achieved by refunding the premium pro rata as the benefit is paid. Thus, the client is always responsible for paying the annual premium on a policy. Each policy automatically terminates when the client reaches the "policy expiry age". To determine terms and conditions of a policy, and the premium payable on a policy, Giraffe Insurance

Figure A.3 The claims file

Disable number	Policy number	Disable cause	Start date	Finish date	Status
nine digit positive integer					

Figure A.4 Policy expiry age and waiting period

Occupation group	Benefit period (years)	Policy expiry age	Waiting period (weeks)
All	1	60	6
All	2	60	4,6
All	5	60	2,4,6
A,B,C,D	to age 60	60	1,2,4,6
A,B,C,D	to age 65	65	1,2,4,6

classify people by their occupation into "occupation groups" A, B, C, D, E or "other". Clients in the "other" occupation group are not eligible for this form of insurance. The table shown in Figure A.4 gives the policy expiry age and the possible waiting periods for the different occupation groups and chosen benefit periods.

Notes:

1. The **one week waiting period** is only available to the "A" occupation group.
2. The "E" occupation group is only eligible for 1,2 and 5 year benefit periods.

AVAILABLITY
Policies are available to people who are actively engaged, on a full time basis, in jobs which are in one of the identified occupation groups, and whose ages are:

- 18 to 50 next birthday for policies expiring at age 60;
- 18 to 55 next birthday for policies expiring at age 65.

INSURABLE BENEFIT
The **minimum** insurable benefit is $12,000 per annum.
The **maximum** annual insurable benefit is calculated as follows:

- 75% of the first $72,000 per annum of "net earnings before tax";
- plus 50% of the balance between $72,000 and $132,000;
- plus 25% of the balance over $132,000,

and is also subject to the maximum benefit available for each occupation group which is:

- $20,000 per annum for occupation group "E";
- $40,000 per annum for occupation group "D";

- $60,000 per annum for occupation group "C";
- $80,000 per annum for occupation group "B";
- $100,000 per annum for occupation group "A".

Notes:

1. "Net earnings before tax" means income earned in the client's nominated profession after deduction of expenses incurred in earning that income but before the deduction of income tax.
   INVESTMENT INCOME CANNOT BE INCLUDED.
2. The earnings used for calculation will generally be that earned in the latest tax year or latest 12 months if appropriate.

MEDICAL
A medical report stating total disability to work for the whole period for which a claim is made is required before benefits will be paid.

OCCUPATION GROUPS

Class A.
Includes occupations for which either membership of a professional body, or membership of a Government body, or post-graduate qualifications are necessary.
(e.g. doctor, university-professor.)
This classification is only used to allow a different definition of the maximum benefit. The premium rate is the same as for Class B.

Class B.
Includes occupations which are primarily desk-based, which do not involve manual labour, which do not require a substantial amount of traveling and which are not included in Class A.
(e.g. most "white-collar" workers.)

Class C.
Includes occupations which do not involve manual labour, and which are not included in Classes A and B.
(e.g. traveling salesman or factory supervisor.)

Class D.
Includes occupations which involve light manual work, which do require technical qualifications, and which are not included in Classes A, B or C.
(e.g. electrician.)

Class E.
Includes occupations which require some degree of skill, and which are not included in Classes A, B, C or D.
(e.g. handyman.)

PREMIUM DESCRIPTION

OCCUPATION GROUP FACTORS

The Basic Premium Rates shown in the standard tables, see Figure A.5 for a sample, are those applying to the "A" and "B" groups.

For other groups, the premium rates are calculated using the "occupation group factors" as follows:

- Group C = 1.5 times the A rate;
- Group D = 2.0 times the A rate;
- Group E = 2.5 times the A rate.

PREMIUM CALCULATION

There are tables which show the Basic Premium Rate per annual benefit of $12,000 for various ages, waiting periods and benefit periods; a sample table is shown in Figure A.5. To calculate the Annual Premium Payable:

1. Note the age, the required benefit period and the required waiting period.
2. Read off the Basic Premium Rate from the appropriate table.
3. Multiply the Basic Premium Rate by the Occupation Group Factor.
4. Multiply by a factor for the required annual benefit; (e.g. if an annual benefit of $30,000 is required then multiply by 2.5).
5. Add on stamp duty at 7 percent, and this is the annual premium payable.

Figure A.5 Sample table for basic premium rate

SAMPLE TABLE
BENEFIT PERIOD: 5 YEARS

Age	Waiting period (weeks)			
	1	2	4	6
	$	$	$	$
< 26	281	214	163	147
26	287	219	167	151
27	295	227	173	156
28	304	233	178	160
29	315	243	186	166

Having studied the Company's handbook on illness insurance, the analyst decides to conduct the initial knowledge acquisition in two stages. During the first stage an application model and associated data model will be built which represents only the facts directly implied by the handbook, the client file, the policy file and the claims file. During the second stage, the analyst will develop and extend these two models in consultation with the domain expert.

A.3 KNOWLEDGE ACQUISITION: 1

On the basis of the facts contained in the handbook, the client file, the policy file, and the claims file, the analyst constructs the following application model:

1.1	There are insurance companies.
1.2	Insurance companies are identified by a business-name.
1.3	"Giraffe Insurance Co" is a business-name.
1.4	"Giraffe Insurance Co" is the only business-name.
2.1	There are clients.
2.2	Clients are identified by a client-number.
2.3	The "client file" contains a list of all client-numbers.
2.4	Client-numbers are six digit positive integers.
3.1	There are client types.
3.2	Client types are identified by a client-type-description.
3.3	"individual" is a client-type-description.
4.1	Clients have client types.
4.2	Each client has a unique client type.
4.3	The client type for each client is shown in the "client file".
5.1	There are individual clients.
5.2	All individual clients are clients.
5.3	All individual clients have client type "individual".
6.1	There are policies.
6.2	Policies are identified by a policy-number.
6.3	The "policy file" contains a list of all policy-numbers.
6.4	Policy-numbers are seven digit positive integers.
7.1	There are policy types.
7.2	Policy types are identified by a policy-type-description.
7.3	"illness insurance" is a policy-type-description.
8.1	Policies have a policy type.
8.2	Each policy has a unique policy type.
8.3	The policy type for each policy is shown in the "policy file".
9.1	Policies are written by insurance companies.
9.2	Each policy is written by a unique insurance company.
9.3	All policies are written by "Giraffe Insurance Co".
10.1	Policies have clients.
10.2	Each policy has exactly one client.
10.3	The "policy file" contains the client for each policy.

10.4 <u>if</u> a policy has type "illness", **then** the client has type "individual".

11.1 There are waiting periods.

11.2 Waiting periods are identified by a waiting-period-in-weeks.

11.3 1, 2, 4 and 6 weeks are waiting-periods-in-weeks.

11.4 1, 2, 4 and 6 weeks are the only waiting-periods-in-weeks.

12.1 There are maximum benefit periods.

12.2 Maximum benefit periods are identified by a maximum-benefit-period-description which may either be a number of years or an age in years.

12.3 1, 2, 5, "up to age 60" and "up to age 65" are maximum-benefit-period-descriptions.

12.4 1, 2, 5, "up to age 60" and "up to age 65" are the only maximum-benefit-period-descriptions.

13.1 There are policy expiry ages.

13.2 Policy expiry ages are identified by a policy-expiry-age-in-years.

13.3 60 years and 65 years are policy-expiry-ages-in-years.

13.4 60 years and 65 years are the only policy-expiry-ages-in-years.

14.1 There are policy statuses.

14.2 Policy statuses are identified by a policy-status-description.

14.3 "terminated" is a policy-status-description.

15.1 Policies have policy status.

15.2 Each policy has a unique policy status.

15.3 The "policy file" shows the policy-status-description of each policy-number.

16.1 There are income benefits.

16.2 Income benefits are identified by an income-benefit-$-per-month.

17.1 There are premiums.

17.2 Premiums are identified by a premium-$-per-annum.

18.1 There are premium statuses.

18.2 Premium statuses are identified by a premium-status-description.

18.3 "waived" is a premium-status-description.

19.1 There are disablements.

19.2 Disablements are identified by a disablement-number.

19.3 The "claims file" contains all disablement-numbers.

19.4 Disablement numbers are nine digit integers.

20.1 There are disablement causes.

20.2 Disablement causes are identified by a disablement-cause-description.

20.3 "illness" is a disablement-cause-description.

21.1 Disablements have disablement causes.

21.2 Each disablement has a unique disablement cause.

21.3 The "claims file" contains the disablement cause for each disablement.

22.1 There are disablement starting dates.

22.2 Each disablement starting date is identified by a standard-disablement-starting-date which is an integer representing days since 1/1/80.

23.1 Disablements have disablement starting dates.

23.2 Each disablement has a unique disablement starting date.

23.3 The "claims file" contains the disablement starting date for each disablement.

24.1 There are disablement statuses.

24.2   Disablement statuses are identified by a disablement-status-description.

24.3   "terminated" and "on-going" are disablement-status-descriptions.

24.4   "terminated" and "on-going" are the only disablement-status-descriptions.

25.1   Disablements have disablement statuses.

25.2   Each disablement has a unique disablement status.

25.3   The "claims file" contains the disablement status for each disablement.

26.1   There are disablement finishing dates.

26.2   Each disablement finishing date is identified by a disablement-finishing-date-description which is either "unknown" or a positive integer representing the date of the finish of the disablement measured in days since 1/1/80.

27.1   Disablements have disablement finishing dates.

27.2   Each disablement has a unique disablement finishing date.

27.3   The "claims file" contains the disablement finishing date for each disablement.

28.1   The disablement finishing date may sometimes be deduced from the disablement status.

28.2   **if** a disablement has status "terminated", **then** the disablement finishing date is not "unknown".

28.3   **if** a disablement has status "on-going", **then** the disablement finishing date is "unknown".

29.1   There are benefit rates.

29.2   Benefit rates are identified by a benefit-rate-description in $s per annum.

30.1   Policies have benefit rates.

30.2   Each policy has a unique benefit rate.

30.3   The benefit rate for each policy is shown in the "policy file".

31.1   Policies have waiting periods.

31.2   Each policy has a unique waiting period.

31.3   The waiting period for each policy is shown in the "policy file".

32.1   Policies have (maximum) benefit periods.

32.2   Each policy has a unique (maximum) benefit period.

32.3   The (maximum) benefit period for each policy is shown in the "policy file".

Figure A.6 Policy expiry age

Benefit period (years)	Policy expiry age
1	60
2	60
5	60
≤60	60
≤65	65

33.1 There are occupation groups.

33.2 Occupation groups are identified by an occupation-group-description.

33.3 A, B, C, D, E and "other" are occupation-group-descriptions.

33.4 A, B, C, D, E and "other" are the only occupation-group-descriptions.

34.1 Individual clients have occupation groups.

34.2 Each individual client has a unique occupation group.

34.3 The "client file" contains the occupation group for each individual client.

35.1 Policies have policy expiry ages.

35.2 Each policy has a unique policy expiry age.

36.1 Benefit periods have policy expiry ages.

36.2 Each benefit period has a unique policy expiry age.

36.3 The table shown in Figure A.6 gives the policy expiry age for each benefit period.

37.1 There are allowable waiting periods.

37.2 Allowable waiting periods are identified by a four-tuple of waiting periods.

37.3 The allowable four-tuples of waiting periods are shown in the table in Figure A.7.

37.4 The only allowable four-tuples of waiting periods are shown in the table in Figure A.7.

38.1 Benefit periods have allowable waiting periods.

38.2 Each benefit period has a unique four-tuple of waiting periods.

38.3 The table shown in Figure A.7 gives the four-tuple of waiting periods for each benefit period.

39.1 There are allowable benefit periods.

39.2 Allowable benefit periods are identified by a five-tuple of benefit periods.

39.3 The allowable five-tuples of benefit periods are shown in the table in Figure A.8.

39.4 The only allowable five-tuples of benefit periods are shown in the table in Figure A.8.

40.1 Occupation groups have allowable benefit periods.

Figure A.7 Allowable waiting periods

Benefit period (years)	Allowable waiting period (weeks)			
	1	2	4	6
1	No	No	No	Yes
2	No	No	Yes	Yes
5	No	Yes	Yes	Yes
≤60	Yes	Yes	Yes	Yes
≤65	Yes	Yes	Yes	Yes

Figure A.8 Allowable benefit periods

Occupation group	Allowable benefit periods (years)				
	1	2	5	≤60	≤65
A	Yes	Yes	Yes	Yes	Yes
B	Yes	Yes	Yes	Yes	Yes
C	Yes	Yes	Yes	Yes	Yes
D	Yes	Yes	Yes	Yes	Yes
E	Yes	Yes	Yes	No	No

40.2	Each occupation group has a unique five-tuple of benefit periods.
40.3	The table shown in Figure A.8 gives the five-tuples of benefit periods for each occupation group.
41.1	There are eligible age brackets.
41.2	Eligible age brackets are identified by a two-tuple-age-next birthday.
41.3	(18, 50) and (18, 55) are two-tuple-age-next-birthday values.
41.4	(18, 50) and (18, 55) are the only two-tuple-age-next-birthday values.
42.1	Policies have eligible age brackets.
42.2	Each policy has a unique eligible age bracket.
43.1	The eligible age bracket for a policy may be deduced from the expiry age of the policy.
43.2	**if** the policy has an expiry age of 60, **then** the eligible age bracket of the policy is (18, 50).
43.3	**if** the policy has an expiry age of 65, **then** the eligible age bracket of the policy is (18, 55).
44.1	There are minimum insurable benefits.
44.2	Minimum insurable benefits are identified by minimum-benefit-$s.
44.3	12,000 is a minimum-benefit-$s.
44.4	12,000 is the only minimum-benefit-$s.
45.1	Individual clients have minimum insurable benefits.
45.2	Each individual client has a unique minimum insurable benefit.
45.3	Each individual client has a $12,000 minimum insurable benefit.
46.1	There are maximum insurable benefits.
46.2	Maximum insurable benefits are identified by maximum-benefit-$s.
47.1	Individual clients have maximum insurable benefits.
47.2	Each individual client has a unique maximum insurable benefit.
48.1	There are net earnings before tax.
48.2	Net earnings before tax are identified by earnings-before-tax-$s.
49.1	Individual clients have net earnings before tax.
49.2	Each individual client has a unique net earnings before tax.
50.1	There are gross earnings.

50.2 Gross earnings are identified by gross-earnings-$s.

51.1 Individual clients have gross earnings.

51.2 Each individual client has a unique gross earnings.

51.3 The gross earnings for each client are shown in the "client file".

52.1 There are expenses.

52.2 Expenses are identified by expenses-$s.

53.1 Individual clients have expenses.

53.2 Each individual client has a unique expenses.

53.3 The expenses for each client are shown in the "client file".

54.1 An individual client's net earnings before tax may be deduced from that individual client's gross earnings and that individual client's expenses.

54.2 **if** a individual client has $x gross earnings **and** that individual client has $y expenses, **then** that individual client has ($x - $y) net earnings

55.1 There are maximum benefits available.

55.2 Maximum benefits available are identified by maximum-available-benefits-$s.

55.3 Maximum-available-benefits-$s are shown in the table in Figure A.9.

55.4 The only maximum-available-benefits-$s are shown in the table in Figure A.9.

56.1 Occupation groups have maximum benefits available.

56.2 Each occupation group has a unique maximum benefits available.

56.3 The maximum benefits available for each occupation group are shown in the table in Figure A.9.

57.1 An individual client's maximum insurable benefit may be deduced from that individual client's net earnings before tax and that individual client's occupation group.

57.2 **if** an individual client's income, when split into a three-tuple in the three ranges "less than $72,000", "between $72,000 and $132,000" and "over 132,000" is ($x, $y, $z) **and** let $w = 0.75 \times $x + 0.5 \times $y +0.25 \times $z **and** that individual client has a job which is in a certain occupation group **and** the maximum benefit available for that occupation group is $v, **then** that individual client's maximum insurable benefit is the least of $w and $v reduced by the amount of any other benefit income.

Figure A.9 Maximum benefit available

Occupation group	Maximum benefit available
A	100,000
B	80,000
C	60,000
D	40,000
E	20,000

Figure A.10 Occupational group factors

Occupational group	Occupational group factor
A	1.0
B	1.0
C	1.5
D	2.0
E	2.5

58.1	There are occupation group factors.
58.2	Occupation group factors are identified by occ-gp-factor-value.
58.3	Occ-gp-factor-values are shown in the table in Figure A.10.
58.4	The only occ-gp-factor-values are shown in the table in Figure A.10.
59.1	Occupation groups have occupation group factors.
59.2	Each occupation group has a unique occupation group factor.
59.3	The occupation group factors for each occupation group are shown in the table in Figure A.10.
60.1	There are ages.
60.2	Ages are identified by an age-in-years.
61.1	There are individual client-policy types. (Note: "individual client-policy types" are a fictitious population introduced to ensure that all relations are binary. In fact, "individual client-policy type" is a compound population comprising the age of the policy holder, the maximum benefit period and the waiting period.)
61.2	Individual client-policy types are identified by a cl-pol-type-description.
62.1	Individual client-policy types have ages.
62.2	Each individual client-policy type has a unique age.
63.1	Individual client-policy types have maximum benefit periods.
63.2	Each individual client-policy type has a unique maximum benefit period.
64.1	Individual client-policy types has waiting periods.
64.2	Each individual client-policy type has a unique waiting period.
65.1	There are basic premium rates.
65.2	Basic premium rates are identified by basic-premium-rate-value.
65.3	Basic-premium-rate-values are shown in the tables in Figure A.11.
65.4	The only basic-premium-rate-values are shown in the tables in Figure A.11.
66.1	Individual client-policy types have basic premium rates.
66.2	Each individual client-policy type has a unique basic premium rate.
66.3	The basic premium rate for each individual client-policy type is shown in the set of tables one of which is reproduced in Figure A.11.
67.1	There are occupations.
67.2	Occupations are identified by an occupation-description.
68.1	Individuals have occupations.

Figure A.11 Sample table for basic premium rate

SAMPLE TABLE
BENEFIT PERIOD: 5 YEARS

Age	Waiting period (weeks)			
	1	2	4	6
	$	$	$	$
< 26	281	214	163	147
26	287	219	167	151
27	295	227	173	156
28	304	233	178	160
29	315	243	186	166

68.2	Each individual has a unique occupation.
69.1	There are required skills.
69.2	Required skills are identified by a skill-description.
69.3	The only skill-descriptions are "post-graduate", "technical", "basic skills" and "none".
70.1	Occupations have required skills.
70.2	Each occupation has a unique required skill.
71.1	There are required memberships.
71.2	Required memberships are identified by a membership-description
71.3	The only membership descriptions are "professional", "government-body" and "none".
72.1	Occupations have required memberships.
72.2	Each occupation has a unique required membership.
73.1	There are occupation styles.
73.2	Occupation styles are identified by an occupation-style-description.
73.3	The only occupation-style-descriptions are "desk-based" and "non-desk-based".
74.1	Occupations have occupation styles.
74.2	Each occupation has a unique occupation style.
75.1	There are occupation types.
75.2	Occupation types are identified by an occupation-type-description.
75.3	The only occupation type descriptions are "heavy-manual", "light-manual" and "non-manual".
76.1	Occupations have occupation types.
76.2	Each occupation has a unique occupation type.
77.1	There are occupation mobilities.

77.2   Occupation mobilities are identified by an occupation-mobility-description.

77.3   The only occupation-mobility-descriptions are "traveling" and "non-traveling".

78.1   Occupations have occupation mobilities.

78.2   Each occupation has a unique occupation mobility.

79.1   Occupations have occupation groups.

79.2   Each occupation has a unique occupation group.

80.1   The occupation group for an occupation may be deduced from: the required skills for that occupation, the required membership for that occupation, the occupation style for that occupation, the occupation type for that occupation and the occupation mobility for that occupation.

80.2   **if** the required skills for an occupation are "post-graduate", **then** that occupation has occupation group "A".

80.3   **if** the required memberships for an occupation are "professional", **then** that occupation has occupation group "A".

80.4   **if** the required memberships for an occupation are "government-body", **then** that occupation has occupation group "A".

80.5   **if** the occupation style for an occupation is "desk-bound" **and** the occupation type for that occupation is "non-manual" **and** the occupation mobility for that occupation is "non-traveling" **and** it is **not** the case that the occupation group for that occupation is "A", **then** the occupation group for that occupation is "B".

80.6   **if** the occupation type for an occupation is "non-manual" **and** it is **not** the case that the occupation group for that occupation is "A" **and** it is **not** the case that the occupation group for that occupation is "B", **then** the occupation group for that occupation is "C".

80.7   **if** an occupation type for an occupation is "light-manual" **and** the required skills for that occupation are "technical" **and** it is **not** the case that the occupation group for that occupation is "A" **and** it is **not** the case that the occupation group for that occupation is "B" **and** it is **not** the case that the occupation group for that occupation is "C", **then** the occupation group for that occupation is "D".

80.8   **if** the required skills for an occupation are "basic-skills" **and** it is **not** the case that the occupation group for that occupation is "A" **and** it is **not** the case that the occupation group for that occupation is "B" **and** it is **not** the case that the occupation group for that occupation is "C" **and** it is **not** the case that the occupation group for that occupation is "D", **then** the occupation group for that occupation is "E".

80.9   **if** it is **not** the case that the occupation group for an occupation is "A" **and** it is **not** the case that the occupation group for that occupation is "B" **and** it is **not** the case that the occupation group for that occupation is "C" **and** it is **not** the case that the occupation group for that occupation is "D" **and** it is **not** the case that the occupation group for that occupation is "E", **then** the occupation group for that occupation is "other".

81.1   There are required benefits.

81.2   Required benefits are identified by a required-benefit-description-$s-per-annum.

82.1   Policies have required benefits.

82.2   Each policy has a unique required benefit.
83.1   Policies have client-policy types.
83.2   Each policy has a unique client-policy type.
83.3   The "policy file" and the "client file" together give the client-policy type for each policy number.
84.1   Policies have premiums.
84.2   Each policy has a unique premium.
85.1   There are stamp duties.
85.2   Stamp duties are identified by stamp-duty-%.
85.3   There is only one stamp-duty-%.
86.1   The premium payable on a policy for an individual may be deduced from the client-policy type for that policy, the occupation group factor for the individual's occupation, the required benefit for the policy and the stamp duty rate.
86.2   **if** a policy has type "illness" **and** that policy is held by an individual client **and** that policy has a certain client-policy type **and** that client-policy type has a certain basic premium rate **and** that client has a certain occupational group **and** that occupational group has a certain occupational group factor, **then** the premium on that policy is:

((basic premium rate) $\times$ (occupational group factor) $\times$ (required benefit) $\div$ 12000) $\times$ (1 + stamp-duty-% $\div$ 100)

The data model, which has been constructed along with the application model, is shown in Figures A.12a, A.12b and A.12c.

A.4 KNOWLEDGE ACQUISITION: 2

Having constructed the application model and the data model as shown in the previous section, the analyst now interviews the domain expert. The first step is for the analyst to ask the domain expert to check that the application model constructed so far is correct. Let us suppose that the domain expert agrees that it is correct. The analyst then identifies GEFs which may not be complete and asks the domain expert to complete them.

The analyst notes that "individual" is a client-type-description. [Q] "Is 'individual' the only client-type-description?", [A] "No, the only other one is 'corporate'." Thus:

3.3   "individual" and "corporate" are client-type descriptions.
3.4   "individual" and "corporate" are the only client-type descriptions.

[Q] "Is 'illness insurance' the only policy-type-description?", [A] "As far as this investigation is concerned, Yes.". Thus:

7.4   "illness insurance" is the only policy-type-description.

[Q] "Is 'terminated' the only policy-status-description?", [A] "No, there is also 'active'.". Thus:

14.3   "terminated" and "active" are policy-status-descriptions.
14.4   "terminated" and "active" are the only policy-status-descriptions.

The data model, which has been constructed along with the application model, is shown in Figures A.12a, A.12b and A.12c.

Thing-population	Bundle	Sub-type of	Name-population	Labels	Population constraints	Label constraints	Fixed labels
insurance companies	1		business-name	Giraffe Insurance	one label only		
clients	2		client-number	(see 2.3)	each label unique	six digit positive int	
client types	3		client-type-description	individual			all
individual clients	5	clients			=client type "individual"		
policies	6		policy-number	(see 6.3)	each label unique	seven digit positive int	
policy types	7		policy-type-description	illness			all
waiting periods	11		wait-period-in-weeks	1, 2, 4, 6 weeks	four labels only	= 1, 2, 4 or 6	all
max benefit periods	12		max-ben-period-desc	(see 12.3)	five labels only	= 1, 2, 3, ≤60, ≤65	all
policy expiry age	13		pol-expiry-age-in-yrs	60 years, 65 years	two labels only	= 60 or 65	all
policy status	14		pol-status-description	terminated			all
income benefits	16		inc-benef-$s/month				
premiums	17		premium-$s/annum				
premium status	18		prem-status-description	waived			all
dis-ablements	19		disable-number	(see 19.3)	each label unique	nine digit positive int	
disable causes	20		dis-cause-description	illness			all

Figure A.12a The initial data model: Part "a"

Thing-population	*Bundle*	*Sub-type of*	*Name-population*	*Labels*	*Population constraints*	*Label constraints*	*Fixed labels*
disable-start-date	22		std-disable-start-date			positive integer	
disable status	24		disab-stat-description	terminated, on-going	two labels only	= term, on-going	all
disable-finish-date	26		disab-finish-date-desc			pos int, or "unknown"	
benefit rates	29		benef-rate-description			positive integer	
occupation groups	33		occup-grp-description	A, B, C, D, E, other	six labels only	= A, B, C, D, E, other	all
allowable waiting pds	37		4-tuple-waiting-pds	(see 37.3)	five labels only		
allowable benefit pds	39		5-tuple-benefit-pds	(see 39.3)	five labels only		
eligible age brackets	41		2-tuple-age-next-bday	(see 41.3)	two labels only		all
min-ins-benefit	44		minimum-benefit-$s	12,000	one label only	= 12,000	
max-ins-benefit	46		maximum-benefit-$s			positive integer	
net earnings	48		earn-before-tax-$s			positive integer	
gross earnings	50		gross-earns-$s			positive integer	
expenses	52		expenses-$s			positive integer	
maximum benefit av	55		max-avail-benefit-$s	(see 55.3)	five labels only	positive integer	
occupation group facs	58		occ-gp-factor-value	(see 58.3)	five labels only	real ≥ 1	
ages	60		age-in-years			positive integer	

Figure A.12b The initial data model: Part "b"

Thing-population	*Bundle*	*Sub-type of*	*Name-population*	*Labels*	*Population constraints*	*Label constraints*	*Fixed labels*
client-policy types	61		cl-pol-type-description				
basic premium rt	65		bas-prem-rate-value			positive integer	
occupation	67		occupation-description				
required skills	69		skill-description	(see 69.3)	four labels only		all
occupation styles	73		occup-style-description	desk-based non-desk-b	two labels only		all
occupation types	75		occup-type-description	(see 75.3)	three labels only		all
mobilities	77		oc-mobil-description	travel, non-travel	two labels only		all
required benefits	81		req-benef-desc-$'s				
stamp duty	85		stamp-duty-%	7%	one label only		

Figure A.12c The initial data model: Part "c"

[Q] "Is 'waived' the only premium status?", [A] "No, 'payable' and 'non-payable' are also premium statuses.". Then:

18.3   "waived", "payable" and "non-payable" are premium statuses.
18.4   "waived", "payable" and "non-payable" are the only premium statuses.

[Q] "Is 'illness' the only disablement-cause-description?", [A] "No, but as far as this investigation goes the only other one is 'non-illness'.". Then:

20.3   "illness" and "non-illness" are disablement-cause-descriptions.
20.4   "illness" and "non-illness" are the only disablement-cause-descriptions.

[Q] "Can the disablement finishing date always be deduced from the disablement status?", [A] "No, only when the finishing date is 'unknown'.".

Next, the analyst attempts to discover whether the PAFs in any of the GEFs can be deduced from knowledge other GEFs.

The domain expert advises that the PAFs in the GEFs in bundles 4, 8, 9 and 10 cannot be deduced from knowledge involving other GEFs. However, for bundle 15, the domain expert advises that "the status of a policy may be deduced from the age of the policy holder, the policy expiry age for the policy and whether or not the policy is paid up". Thus, the analyst notes that:

87.1 There are payments.

87.2 Payments are identified by a payment-description.

87.3 "paid-up" and "not-paid-up" are payment descriptions.

87.4 "paid-up" and "not-paid-up" are the only payment descriptions.

88.1 Policies have payments.

88.2 Each policy has a unique payment.

89.1 The status of a policy may be deduced from the age of the policy holder, the policy expiry age for the policy and whether or not the policy is paid up.

89.2 **if** a policy holder has a certain age **and** the policy has a certain policy expiry age **and** the policy holder's age is greater than the policy's expiry age **then** the policy status is "terminated".

89.3 **if** a policy holder has a certain age **and** the policy has a certain policy expiry age **and** the policy holder's age is less than or equal to the policy's expiry age **and** the payment on the policy is "not-paid-up", **then** the policy status is "terminated".

89.4 **if** a policy holder has a certain age **and** the policy has a certain policy expiry age **and** the policy holder's age is less than or equal to the policy's expiry age **and** the payment on the policy is "paid-up", **then** the policy status is "active".

The domain expert advises that the PAFs in the GEFs in bundles 21, 23, 25, and 27 cannot be deduced from knowledge involving other GEFs. However, for bundle 30 the domain expert advises that:

90.1 The benefit rate for an illness insurance policy can be deduced from the required benefit for that policy, the annual premium for that policy, the minimum insurable benefit for the policy holder, the maximum insurable benefit for the policy holder and the status of the policy.

90.2 **if** the required benefit for a policy is less than the minimum insurable benefit for the holder of that policy **then** the benefit rate for that policy is zero.

90.3 **if** the required benefit for a policy is greater than the maximum insurable benefit for the holder of that policy, **then** the benefit rate for that policy is zero.

90.4 **if** the status of a policy is "terminated", **then** the benefit rate for that policy is zero.

90.5 **if** the required benefit for a policy is less than the maximum insurable benefit for the holder of that policy **and** the required benefit for that policy is greater than the minimum insurable benefit for the holder of that policy **and** the status of the policy is "active", **then** the benefit rate for that policy is the required benefit for that policy plus a pro rata refund of the premium on that policy.

The domain expert advises that the PAFs in the GEFs in bundles 31 and 32 cannot be deduced from knowledge involving other GEFs. However, for bundle 34, the domain expert advises that:

91.1 The occupation group for an individual may be deduced from the occupation of that individual and the occupation group for that individual's occupation.

91.2 **if** an individual has a certain occupation **and** the occupation group for that occupation is known, **then** the individual has that occupation group.

The domain expert advises that the PAFs in the GEFs in bundles 35, 36, 38 and 40 cannot be deduced from knowledge involving other GEFs. Bundle 43 states how the PAFs in the GEF introduced in bundle 42 may be deduced. Bundle 45 is trivial. Bundle 57 states how the PAFs in the GEF introduced in bundle 47 may be deduced. The domain expert advises that the PAFs in the GEFs introduced in bundles 56, 59, 62, 63, 64, 66, 68, 70, 72, 74, 76 and 78 cannot be deduced from knowledge involving other GEFs. Bundle 80 states how the PAFs in the GEF introduced by bundle 79 may be deduced. The domain expert advises that the PAFs in the GEFs introduced in bundles 82 and 83 cannot be deduced from knowledge involving other GEFs. Bundle 86 states how the PAFs in the GEF introduced in bundle 84 may be deduced. For bundle 88 the domain expert advises that:

92.1 There are paid-to dates.

92.2 Paid-to dates are identified by standard-paid-to-dates measured in days since 1–1–80.

93.1 Policies have paid-to dates.

93.2 Each policy has a unique paid-to date.

93.3 The paid-to date for each policy is shown in the "policy file".

94.1 The payment on a policy may be deduced from the paid-to date and today's date.

94.2 **if** the paid to date on a policy is before today's date, **then** the payment on that policy is "not-paid-up".

94.3 **if** the paid-to date on a policy is not before today's date, **then** the payment on that policy in "paid-up".

When the additions and modifications noted above have been included in the application model, the final data model should read as shown in Figures A.13a, A.13b and A.13c.

In figures A.13a, A.13b and A.13c the meaning of the name-populations is as follows:

- business-name(x) means "x is the name of an insurance company".
- client-number(x) means "x is the number of a client".
- client-type-description(x) means "x is a client-type-description, at present these are 'individual' or 'corporate' ".
- policy-number(x) means "x is the number of an insurance policy".
- policy-type-description(x) means "x is the description of an insurance policy, for the present 'illness' is the only policy-type-description".
- wait-period-in-weeks(x) means "x is a waiting period in weeks, for example, the waiting period during which a policy holder will receive no benefits even if disabled due to illness".
- max-ben-period-desc(x) means "x is a maximum benefit period, for example the period during which the policy holder will receive benefits when disabled due to illness".

Figure A.13a The final data model: Part "a"

Thing-population	Bundle	Sub-type of	Name-population	Labels	Population constraints	Label constraints	Fixed labels
insurance companies	1		business-name	Giraffe Insurance	one label only		
clients	2		client-number	(see 2.3)	each label unique	six digit positive int	
client types	3		client-type-description	individual, corporate	two labels only		all
individual clients	5	clients			=client type "individual"		
policies	6		policy-number	(see 6.3)	each label unique	seven digit positive int	
policy types	7		policy-type-description	illness	one label only		all
waiting periods	11		wait-period-in-weeks	1, 2, 4, 6 weeks	four labels only	= 1, 2, 4 or 6	all
max benefit periods	12		max-ben-period-desc	(see 12.3)	five labels only	= 1, 2, 3, ≤60, ≤65	all
policy expiry age	13		pol-expiry-age-in-yrs	60 years, 65 years	two labels only	= 60 or 65	all
policy status	14		pol-status-description	terminated, active	two labels only		all
income benefits	16		inc-benef-$s/month				
premiums	17		premium-$s/annum				
premium status	18		prem-status-description	waived pay non-pay	three labels only		all
dis-ablements	19		disable-number	(see 19.3)	each label unique	nine digit positive int	
disable causes	20		dis-cause-description	illness, non-illness	two labels only		all

Figure A.13b The final data model: Part "b"

Thing-population	*Bundle*	*Sub-type of*	*Name-population*	*Labels*	*Population constraints*	*Label constraints*	*Fixed labels*
disable-start-date	22		std-disable-start-date			positive integer	
disable status	24		disab-stat-description	terminated, on-going	two labels only	= term, on-going	all
disable-finish-date	26		disab-finish-date-desc			pos int, or "unknown"	
benefit rates	29		benef-rate-description			positive integer	
occupation groups	33		occup-grp-description	A, B, C, D, E, other	six labels only	= A, B, C, D, E, other	all
allowable waiting pds	37		4-tuple-waiting-pds	(see 37.3)	five labels only		
allowable benefit pds	39		5-tuple-benefit-pds	(see 39.3)	five labels only		
eligible age brackets	41		2-tuple-age-next-bday	(see 41.3)	two labels only		all
min-ins-benefit	44		minimum-benefit-$s	12,000	one label only	= 12,000	
max-ins-benefit	46		maximum-benefit-$s			positive integer	
net earnings	48		earn-before-tax-$s			positive integer	
gross earnings	50		gross-earns-$s			positive integer	
expenses	52		expenses-$s			positive integer	
maximum benefit av	55		max-avail-benefit-$s	(see 55.3)	five labels only	positive integer	
occupation group facs	58		occ-gp-factor-value	(see 58.3)	five labels only	real ≥ 1	
ages	60		age-in-years			positive integer	

Figure A.13c The final data model: Part "c"

Thing-population	Bundle	Sub-type of	Name-population	Labels	Population constraints	Label constraints	Fixed labels
client-pol types	61		cl-pol-type-description				
basic premium rt	65		bas-prem-rate-value			positive integer	
occupation	67		occupation-description				
required skills	69		skill-description	(see 69.3)	four labels only		all
occupation styles	73		occup-style-description	desk-based non-desk-b	two labels only		all
occupation types	75		occup-type-description	(see 75.3)	three labels only		all
mobilities	77		oc-mobil-description	travel, non-travel	two labels only		all
required benefits	81		req-benef-desc-$s				
stamp duty	85		stamp-duty-%	7%	one label only		
payments	87		payment-description	paid-up, not-paid-up	two labels only		all
paid-to-date	92		std-paid-to-date				

- pol-expiry-age-in-yrs(x) means "x is a policy expiry age; for example, the age beyond which the policy holder will not receive benefits, at present the only values for pol-expiry-age-in-yrs are 60 and 65".
- pol-status-description(x) means "x is the status of a policy, at present the only values for pol-status-description are 'terminated' and 'active' ".
- inc-benef-$s/month(x) means "x is an income benefit in dollars per month".
- premium-$s/annum(x) means "x is a premium in $s per annum".
- prem-status-description(x) means "x is a status of a premium, at present these indicate whether or not it is payable".
- disable-number(x) means "x is the number of a registered disablement, for example, as part of a claim".
- dis-cause-description(x) means "x is the description of the cause of a disability".
- std-disable-srt-date(x) means "x is the starting date of a registered disability, at present this is measured in days since 1-1-80".
- disab-stat-description(x) means "x is the description of a disability status. At present this is either terminated or on-going".
- disab-finish-date-desc(x) means "x is the finishing date of a registered disability, at present this will either be "unknown" for a continuing disability, or the date of the finish of the disability measured in days since 1-1-80".
- benef-rate-description(x) means "x is a benefit rate measured in dollars per annum".
- occup-grp-description(x) means "x is the name of an occupation group, at present these are A, B, C, D, E and other".
- 4-tuple-waiting-pds(x) means "x is a binary four-tuple, each member of which denotes whether 1, 2, 4 or 6 week waiting periods respectively are available".
- 5-tuple-benefit-pds(x) means "x is a binary five-tuple, each member of which denotes whether the allowable benefit periods 1 year, 2 years, 5 years, up to 60 years, or up to 65 years are available".
- 2-tuple-age-next-bday(x) means "x is a two-tuple of ages, for example denoting the allowable age bracket in which a policy holder must be"
- minimum-benefit-$s(x) means "x is a least annual benefit, for example, the least annual benefit which a policy may provide".
- maximum-benefit-$s(x) means "x is a greatest annual benefit, for example, the greatest annual benefit which a policy may provide".
- earn-before-tax-$s(x) means "x is an income, after the deduction of expenses but before the deduction of tax, expressed in dollars per annum".
- gross-earns-$s(x) means "x is a gross income, before the deduction of expenses and before the deduction of tax, expressed in dollars per annum".
- expenses-$s(x) means "x is the gross expenses expressed in dollars per annum".
- max-avail-benefit-$s(x) means "x is the maximum benefit available, for example the maximum benefit available to an individual".
- occ-gp-factor-value(x) means "x is the value, as a real number, of an occupation group factor".
- age-in-years(x) means "x is an age in years".
- cl-pol-type-description(x) means "x is a client-policy type description"
- bas-prem-rate-value(x) means "x is a basic premium rate in dollars per annum".
- occupation-description(x) means "x is the name of an occupation".

- skill-description(x) means "x is a description of a skill, at present these are 'post-graduate', 'technical', 'basic skills' and 'none' ".
- occup-style-description(x) means "x is a description of an occupation style, at present these are 'desk-based' and 'not desk-based' ".
- occup-type-description(x) means "x is a description of the type of an occupation, at present these are 'heavy manual', 'light manual' and 'non-manual' ".
- oc-mobil-description(x) means "x is a description of the mobility of an occupation, at present these are 'travel' and 'non-travel' ".
- req-benef-desc-$s(x) means "x is a value, in dollars per annum, of a required benefit".
- stamp-duty-%(x) means "x is a value percent of the stamp duty".
- payment-description(x) means "x is a description of a payment, at present these are 'paid-up' and 'not paid-up' ".
- std-paid-to-date(x) means "x is a date, in days since 1-1-80, of a date to which payment has been made".

A.5 INFORMATION ANALYSIS

We now presume that using some technique for information analysis, an information model is derived. The information in this information model could well be as represented in Figures A.14a, A.14b and A.14c.

The meanings of the relations introduced in Figures A.14a, A.14b and A.14c are:

- client/cl-tp(x, y) means "x is the number of a client whose client type description is y".
- pol/pl-type(x, y) means "x is the number of a policy whose type is y".
- pol/ins-co(x, y) means "x is the number of a policy which has been written by company name y".
- pol/client(x, y) means "x is the number of a policy which has been written for client number y".
- pol/status(x, y) means "x is the number of a policy whose policy status description is y".
- disab/cause(x, y) means "x is the number of a disability whose cause is y".
- disab/start(x, y) means "x is the number of a disability whose starting date is y".
- disab/status(x, y) means "x is the number of a disability whose status is y".
- disab/finish(x, y) means "x is the number of a disability whose finishing date is y, where y can be 'unknown' ".
- pol/ben-rate(x, y) means "x is the number of a policy whose benefit rate is y dollars per annum".
- pol/wait-pd(x, y) means "x is the number of a policy whose waiting period is y weeks".
- pol/ben-pd(x, y) means "x is the number of a policy whose maximum benefit period is y".
- indiv/oc-gp(x, y) means "x is the number of an individual whose occupation group is y".

Figure A.14a The information model: Part "a"

Relation	Bundle	Key domain	Other domains	Tuples	Relation constraints	Tuple constraints	Associated with
client/cl-tp	4	client-number	client-type-description	(see 4.3)			
pol/pol-typ	8	policy-number	policy-typ-description	(see 8.3)			
pol/ins-co	9	policy-number	business-name	(see 9.3)		2nd dom = Giraffe	
pol/client	10	policy-number	client-number	(see 10.3)			
pol/status	15	policy-number	pol-status -description	(see 15.3)			
disab/cause	21	disable-number	dis-cause-description	(see 21.3)			
disab/start	23	disable-number	std-disab-start-date	(see 23.3)			
disab/status	25	disable-number	disab-status -decription	(see 25.3)			
disab/finish	27	disable-number	disab-finish -date-desc	(see 27.3)			
pol/ben-rate	30	policy-number	benef-rate-description	(see 30.3)			
pol/wait-pd	31	policy-number	wait-period -in-weeks	(see 31.3)			
pol/ben-pd	32	policy-number	max-ben-period-desc	(see 32.3)			
indiv/oc-gp	34	client-number	occup-gp-description	(see 34.3)			
pol/exp-age	35	policy-number	pol-expiry -age-in-yrs				
ben-pd/ exp-age	36	max-ben-period-desc	pol-expiry -age-in-yrs	(see 36.3)			
ben-pd/ al-wait-pd	38	max-ben-period-desc	4-tuple-waiting-pd	(see 38.3)			
oc-gp/ al-benef-pd	40	occup-gp-description	5-tuple-benef-pf	(see 40.3)			

Figure A.14b The information model: Part "b"

Relation	Bundle	Key domain	Other domains	Tuples	Relation constraints	Tuple constraints	Associated with
pol/el-age	42	policy-number	2-tuple-age-next-b				
indiv/min-ins-benefit	45	client-number	minimum-benefit-$s	(see 45.3)		2nd dom = 12,000	
indiv/max-ins-benefit	47	client-number	maximum-benefit-$s				
indiv/net-earn	49	client-number	earn-bef-tax-$s				
indiv/gross-earn	51	client-number	gross-earnings-$s	(see 51.3)			
indiv/expenses	53	client-number	expenses-$s	(see 53.3)			
oc-gp/max-ben-av	56	occup-gp-description	maximum-benefit-$s	(see 56.3)			
oc-gp/oc-gp-fac	59	occup-gp-description	oc-gp-factor-value	(see 59.3)			
cl-pol-type/age	62	cl-pol-type-description	age-in-years				
cl-pol-type/max-ben-pd	63	cl-pol-type-description	max-ben-period-desc				
cl-pol-type/wait-period	64	cl-pol-type-description	wait-period-in-weeks				
cl-pol-type/bas-prem-rt	66	cl-pol-type-description	basic-prem-rate-value	(see 66.3)			
indiv/occupation	68	client-number	occupation-description				
occupation/requ-skills	70	occupation-description	skill-description				
occupation/requ-memb	72	occupation-description	membership-description				
occupation/occup-style	74	occupation-description	occupation-style-desc				
occupation/occup-type	76	occupation-description	occupation-type-desc				

Figure A.14c The information model: Part "c"

Relation	Bundle	Key domain	Other domains	Tuples	Relation constraints	Tuple constraints	Associated with
occupation/ mobility	78	occupation-description	occupation-mobil-desc				
occupation/ occ-group	79	occupation-description	occup-gp-description				
policy/ req-benef	82	policy-number	req-benef-desc-$s				
policy/ cl-pol-type	83	policy-number	cl-pol-type -description	(see 83.3)			
policy/ premium	84	policy-number	premium-$s/annum				
policy/ payment	88	policy-number	payment-description				
policy/ paid-to-date	93	policy-number	std-paid-to-date	(see 93.3)			

- pol/exp-age(x, y) means "x is the number of a policy which expires when the policy holder reaches the age of y years".
- ben-pd/exp-age(x, y) means "x is the benefit period of a policy and y is the corresponding expiry age, i.e. when the age of the policy holder exceeds the expiry age the policy terminates".
- ben-pd/al-wait-pd(x, y) means "x is the benefit period of a policy and y is a binary four-tuple indicating which of four allowable waiting periods are available for that policy".
- oc-gp/al-benef-pd(x, y) means "x is an occupation group of a person and y is a binary five-tuple indicating which of five allowable benefit periods are are available to that person".
- pol/el-age(x, y) means "x is a policy number and y is a two-tuple indicating the range of ages within which a prospective policy holder's age must lie".
- indiv/min-ins-benefit(x, y) means "x is a number of a client and y is the minimum insurable benefit in dollars pr annum for that client".
- indiv/max-ins-benefit(x, y) means "x is a number of a client and y is the maximum insurable benefit in dollars per annum for that client".
- indiv/net-earn(x, y) means "x is the number of a client and y is the net earnings before tax of that client in dollars per annum".
- indiv/gross-earn(x, y) means "x is the number of a client and y is the gross earnings, before the deduction of any expenses of that client in dollars per annum.
- indiv/expenses(x, y) means "x is the number of a client and y is the expenses in dollars per annum of that client".

- oc-gp/max-ben-av(x, y) means "x is an occupation group and y is the maximum benefit available for that group in dollars per annum".
- oc-gp/oc-gp-fac(x, y) means "x is an occupation group and y is the occupation group factor that applies for that occupation group".
- cl-pol-type/age(x, y) means "x is a client-policy type and y is the age of that client-policy type".
- cl-pol-type/max-ben-pd(x, y) means "x is a client policy type and y is the maximum benefit period of that client-policy type".
- cl-pol-type/wait-period(x, y) means "x is a client-policy type and y is the waiting period of that client-policy type".
- cl-pol-type/bas-prem-rt(x, y) means "x is a client-policy type and y is the basic premium rate for that client-policy type".
- indiv/occupation(x, y) means "x is the number of a client and y is the occupation of that client".
- occupation/requ-skills(x, y) means "x is an occupation and y is the required skill for practicing that occupation".
- occupation/requ-memb(x, y)   means "x is an occupation and y is the required memberships for practising that occupation".
- occupation/occup-style(x, y) means "x is an occupation and y is style of that occupation (i.e. 'desk based' or 'not desk based')".
- occupation/occup-type(x, y) means "x is an occupation and y is the type of that occupation (i.e. 'heavy manual', 'light manual' or 'non-manual')".
- occupation/mobility(x, y) means "x is an occupation and y is the degree of mobility associated with that occupation".
- occupation/occ-group(x, y) means "x is an occupation and y is the occupation group in which that occupation lies".
- policy/req-benef(x, y) means "x is the number of a policy and y is the benefits required from that policy".
- policy/cl-pol-type(x, y) means "x is the number of a policy and y is the client-policy type of that policy and its associated client".
- policy/premium(x, y) means "x is the number of a policy and y is the annual premium payable on that policy in dollars".
- policy/payment(x, y) means "x is the number of a policy and y is the payment description (i.e. "paid-up" or "non paid-up") for that policy".
- policy/paid-to-date(x, y) means "x is the number of a policy and y is the date to which that policy is paid".

Note that the relation constraints and the tuple constraints in the information model as shown in Figure A.14a, A.14b and A.14c are largely unspecified. We suggest that, before considering knowledge analysis, the reader should address the important matter of designing suitable constraints for the information and data models quoted above.

A.6 KNOWLEDGE ANALYSIS

The intention of this case study is to provide a framework within which the reader can develop the new skills presented herein. The next stage in the development of our model of the application is knowledge analysis. We will leave this stage largely to the reader as an exercise.

The first step in knowledge analysis is to represent the rules identified so far. One of these is in bundle 86. This rule could be represented as:

policy/premium(x, y) ← pol/pol-type(x, 'illness'),
               pol/client(x, z), client/cl-tp(z, 'individual'),
               policy/cl-pol-type(x, w), cl-pol-type/bas-prem-rt(w, u),
               policy/req-benef(x, s), indiv/oc-gp(z, v), oc-gp/oc-gp-fac(v, t),
               is-the[stamp-duty-%](p),
               $y = (u \times t \times s \div 12000) \times (1 + p \div 100)$ [1.1]

The reader is encouraged to represent all the rules in bundles 28, 43, 54, 57, 80, 86, 89, 90, 91 and 94 in logic. Then the dependency diagrams for each rule should be constructed. Using simulated interviews with an imaginary domain expert, these ten clusters should be completed and normalized. And last, the knowledge model should be constructed. The reader may then wish to introduce some query and update types and proceed with the knowledge base engineering and knowledge base implementation stages before considering the execution of maintenance operations on the whole design.

Further, the rich data and information models developed above have been designed to form a basis for the statement of substantial quantities of additional knowledge. This should prove useful if this text is being used for instruction.

Bibliography

ADDIS, T.R. (1985), *Designing Knowledge-Based Systems*, Kogan-Page.

AMAMIYA, M., HAKOZAKI, K., YOKOI, T., FUSAOKA, A. and TANAKA, Y. (1982), "New architecture for knowledge base mechanisms", in *Proceedings of the International Conference on Fifth Generation Computer Systems*, North-Holland (T. Moto-Oka, ed.), pp. 179-88.

BOWEN, K.A. and KOWALSKI, R. (1982), "Amalgamating language and metalanguage in logic programming", in *Logic Programming* (K.L. Clark and S.A. Tarnlund, eds), Academic Press, pp. 153-72.

BUCHANAN, B.G. and FEIGENBAUM, E.A. (1978), "DENDRAL and meta-DENDRAL: Their application dimension", *Artificial Intelligence*, Vol. 11.

BUNDY, A. (1983), *The Computer Modelling of Mathematical Reasoning*, Academic Press.

CHAKRAVARTHY, U.S., MINKER, J. and TRAN, D. (1982), "Interfacing predicate-logic languages and relational data bases", in *Proceedings of the First International Logic Programming Conference*, Faculte des Sciences de Luminy, Marseille, France, 14-17 September 1982, pp. 91-8.

CHANG, C-L. and LEE, R.C-T. (1973), *Symbolic Logic and Mechanical Theorem Proving*, Academic Press.

CLARK, K.L. (1978), "Negation as Failure", in *Logic and Data Bases* (H. Gallaire and J. Minker, eds), pp. 293-322.

CLARK, K.L. and McCABE, F.G. (1982), "PROLOG: A language for implementing expert systems", in *Machine Intelligence 10*, (Hayes, J. and Michie, D. eds) Ellis and Horwood, pp. 455-76.

CLARK, K.L., McCABE, F.G. and GREGORY, S. (1982), "IC-PROLOG language features", in *Logic Programming* (K.L. Clark and S.A. Tarnlund, eds), Academic Press, pp. 253-66.

CLOCKSIN, W.F. and MELLISH, C.S. (1981), *Programming in PROLOG*, Springer-Verlag.

CODD, E.F. (1971), "Normalized database structure: A brief tutorial", *ACM SIGFIDET Workshop on Data Description*, Access and Control, November 1971, pp. 1-17.

COHEN, J. (1988), "A view of the origins and development of prolog", C. ACM, Vol. 31, No. 1, pp. 26-37.

DAHL, V. (1982), "On database systems development through logic", *ACM Transactions on Database Systems*, Vol. 7, No. 1, pp. 102-23.

DATE, C.J. (1986), *An Introduction to Database Systems* (4th ed), Addison-Wesley.

DEBENHAM, J.K. (1984), "The atorage allocation problem for logic systems", in *Proceedings Seventh Australian Computer Science Conference*, Adelaide, 1984, pp. 25.1-25.10.

DEBENHAM, J.K. (1985a), "Knowledge base design", *Australian Computer Journal*, 1985, Vol. 17, No. 1, pp. 187-96.

DEBENHAM, J.K. (1985b), "Knowledge base engineering", in *Proceedings of the Eighth Australian Computer Science Conference*, Melbourne, 1985.

DEBENHAM, J.K. (1986), "Style in logic programs", in *Proceedings Australian Computer Conference*, Gold Coast, Queensland, 1986.

DEBENHAM, J.K. (1987a), "Expert systems: An information processing perspective", in *Applications of Expert Systems* (J.R. Quinlan, ed), Addison-Wesley, 1987, pp. 200-16.

DEBENHAM, J.K. (1987b), "The integration of expert systems and information systems", in *Proceedings Australian Computer Conference*, Melbourne, 1987, pp. 702-21.

DEBENHAM, J.K. (1988), "Knowledge acquisition: A systematic approach", in *Proceedings Fourth Australian Conference on Applications of Expert Systems*, 1988.

DEBENHAM, J.K. and McGRATH, G.M. (1982), "The description in logic of large commercial data bases: A methodology put to the test", in *Proceedings of the Fifth Australian Computer Science Conference*, pp. 12-21.

DEBENHAM, J.K. and McGRATH, G.M. (1983), "LOFE: A language for virtual relational data base", *The Australian Computer Journal*, Vol. 15, No. 1, February 1983, pp. 2-8.

EVEN, S. (1979), *Graph Algorithms*, Computer Science Press.

FAGIN, B.S. and DESPAIN, A.M. (1984), "Performance studies of parallel prolog architecture", in *Proceedings 14th SIGARCH* , 1984, pp. 108-16

FEIGENBAUM, E.A. and McCORDUCK, P. (1983), *The Fifth Generation*, Addison Wesley.

FILMAN, R.E. (1988), "Reasoning with worlds and truth maintenance in a knowledge-based programming environment", in *C. A.C.M.*, Vol. 31, No. 4, pp. 382-401.

FUCHI, K. (1982), "Aiming for knowledge information processing systems", in *Proceedings of the International Conference on Fifth Generation Computer Systems*, North-Holland (T. Moto-Oka, ed.), pp. 107-20.

GAINES, B.R. (1987), "Foundations of knowledge engineering", in *Research and Development in Expert Systems III*, (M.A. Bramer, ed) Cambridge University Press.

GAREY, M.R. and JOHNSON, D.S. (1979), *Computers and Intractability*, Freeman.

GAREY, M.R., JOHNSON, D.S. and STOCKMEYER, L. (1976), "Some simplified NP-complete graph problems.", *Theoretical Computer Science*, Vol. 1, No. 3, pp. 237-67.

GASHNIG, J. (1981), "PROSPECTOR: An expert system for mineral exploration", in *Machine Intelligence*, Infotech State of the Art Report 9, No. 3.

GRAY, P. (1985), *Logic, Algebra and Databases*, Ellis Horwood.

GREEN, C.C. (1969), "Theorem-proving by resolution as a basis for question-answering systems", in *Machine Intelligence 4*, (B. Meltzer and D. Michie, eds), Edinburgh University Press, pp. 183-208.

GRIES, D. (1981), *The Science of Programming* Springer-Verlag.

HERTZBERGER, L.O. (1984), "The architecture of fifth generation inference computers", in *Future Generation Computer Systems*, Vol. 1, No. 1, July 1984, pp. 9-21.

HOGGER, C. (1984), *Introduction to Logic Programming*, Academic Press.

HORVITZ, E.J., BREESE, J.S. and HENRION, M. (1988), "Decision theory in expert systems and artificial intelligence", *International Journal of Approximate Reasoning*, Elsevier.

IOANNIDIS, Y.E. and WONG, E. (1988), "Transforming nonlinear recursion to linear recursion", in *Proceedings Second International Conference on Expert Database Systems*, George Mason University.

JANSEN, B. (1988), "Applying software engineering concepts to rule based expert systems", in *AI and Software Engineering* (D. Partridge, ed.), Ablex Publishing Company.

JANSEN, B. (1989), "A data dictionary approach to the software engineering of rule based expert systems", in *Artificial Intelligence Developments and Applications* (J.S. Gero and R. Stanton, eds), North Holland.

JANSEN, B. and COMPTON, P. (1988a), "The knowledge dictionary: An application of software engineering techniques to the design and maintenance of expert systems", in *Proceedings of the AAAI-88 Workshop on Integration of Knowledge Acquisition and Performance Systems*, August 1988, Minnesota, USA.

JANSEN, B. and COMPTON, P. (1988b), "The knowledge dictionary: A relational tool for the maintenance of expert systems", in *Proceedings of the International Conference on Fifth Generation Computing Systems*, Tokyo, November 1988.

KASHIWAGI, H. (1985), "The Japanese super speed computer project", in *Future Generation Computer Systems*, Vol. 1, No. 3, pp. 153-60.

KENT, W. (1983), "A simple guide to five normal forms in relational database theory", *C. ACM*, Vol. 26, No. 2, February 1983, pp. 120-25.

KERSCHBERG, L. (1986) (Ed.), *Expert Database Systems*, Proceedings from the First International Workshop, Benjamin Cummings.

KERSCHBERG, L. (1988) (Ed.), *Expert Database Systems*, Proceedings of the Second International Conference on Expert Database Systems, Virginia, United States.

KOWALSKI, R.A. (1975), "A proof procedure using connection graphs", *J. ACM* Vol. 22, No. 4 (October 1975).

KOWALSKI, R.A. (1979a), "Algorithm = Logic + Control", *C. ACM*, Vol. 22, No. 7, July 1979, pp. 424-36.

KOWALSKI, R.A. (1979b), *Logic for Problem Solving*, North-Holland.

KOWALSKI, R.A. (1982a), "Logic as a computer language", in *Logic Programming* (K.L. Clark and S.A. Tarnlund, eds), Academic Press, pp. 3-18.

KOWALSKI, R.A. (1982b), "Logic programming in the fifth generation", in *Proceedings of the Fifth Generation Conference*, SPL International, London, 7-9 July 1982.

KUROKAWA, T. (1982), "Logic programming - What does it bring to the software engineering", in *Proceedings of the First International Logic Programming Conference*, 14-17 September 1982, Faculte des Sciences de Luminy, Marseille, France, pp. 134-8.

LI, D. (1984), *A Prolog Database System*, Research Studies Press, UK.

LLOYD, J.W. (1983), "Introduction to deductive data base systems", *The Australian Computer Journal*, Vol. 15, No. 2, May 1983, pp. 52-7.

LLOYD, J.W. (1984), *Foundations of Logic Programming*, Springer Verlag.

LOVELAND, D.W. (1978), *Automated Theorem Proving: A Logical Basis*, North-Holland.

MALIK, R. (1983), "Behind the fifth generation", *Australasian Computer World*, 18 March, 1983.

MARTIN, N. (1988), *Software Engineering of Expert Systems*, Addison Wesley.

McDERMOTT, J. (1980), "R1: an expert in the computer systems domain", in *Proceedings of AAAI-80*.

MINKER, J. (1988), "Perspectives in deductive databases", in *Journal of Logic Programming*, Vol. 5, No. 1, pp. 33-60.

MIYACHI, T., KUNIFUJI, S., KITAKAMI, H., FURUKAWA, K., TAKEUCHI, A and YOKOTA, H. (1984), "A knowledge assimilation method for logic databases", in *Proceedings 1984 International Symposium on Logic Programming*, Atlantic City, New Jersey, United States.

MOTO-OKA, T., et al. (1982), "Challenge for knowledge information processing systems", in *Proceedings of the International Conference on Fifth Generation Computer Systems*, (T. Moto-Oka, ed.), North-Holland pp. 3-89.

NAKASHIMA, H., TOMURA, S. and UEDA, K. (1984), "What is a variable in PROLOG?", in *Proceedings of the International Conference on Fifth Generation Computer Systems*, 1984, (ICOT, ed.), pp. 327-32.

NAPHEYS, B. and HERKIMER, D. (1988), "A look at loosely-coupled prolog/database systems", in *Proceedings Second International Conference on Expert Database Systems*, George Mason University, pp. 107-16.

NEVES, J.C., ANDERSON, S.O. and WILLIAMS, M.H. (1983), "A prolog implementation of query-by-example", in *Proceedings of 7th International Computing Symposium*, 22-24 March, Nurnberg, Germany.

NIJSSEN, G.M. and HALPIN, T.A. (1989), *Conceptual Schema and Relational Data Base Design*, Prentice Hall.

PARTRIDGE, D. (1987), "The scope and limitations of first generation expert systems", *Future Generation Computer Systems*, Vol. 3, No. 1, February 1987.

POTTER, J.M. and VASAK, T. (1985), "Meta-logical control for logic programs", *Journal of Logic Programming*, Vol. 2, No. 5, October 1985.

POTTER, J.M. and VASAK, T. (1986), "Characterization of terminating logic programs", in *Proceedings of IEEE 3rd Symposium on Logic Programming*, Salt Lake City, September 1986.

QIAN, X. (1988), "Distribution design of integrity constraints", in *Proceedings of Second International Conference on Expert Database Systems*, George Mason University, pp. 75-84.

QUINLAN, J.R. (1986), "Induction of decision trees", in *Machine Learning 1*, Kluwer Academic Publications, Boston, pp. 81-106.

QUINLAN, J.R. (1987a), "Simplifying decision trees", in *International Journal for Man-Machine Studies*, Vol. 26.

QUINLAN, J.R. (1987b), "Decision trees as probabilistic classifiers", in *Proceedings Fourth International Machine Learning Conference*, Irvine, California.

QUINLAN, J.R. (1987c), "Generating production rules from decision trees", in *Proceedings International Joint Conference on Artificial Intelligence*, Milan, Italy.

RINGWOOD, G.A. (1988), "Parlog86 and the dining logicians", *C. ACM*, Vol. 31, No. 1, pp. 10-25.

ROBINSON, J.A. (1965), "A machine-oriented logic based on the resolution principle", *J. ACM*, Vol. 12, pp. 23-41.

SAHNI, S. (1974), "Computationally related problems", *SIAM Computing*, Vol. 3, No. 4, pp. 262-79.

SANTANE-TOTH, E. and SZEREDI, P. (1982), "PROLOG applications in Hungary", in *Logic Programming* (K.L. Clark and S.A. Tarnlund, eds), Academic Press, pp. 19-42.

SCHEFE, P. (1982), "Some fundamental issues in knowledge representation", in *Proceedings of the 6th German Workshop on Artificial Intelligence*, Bad Honnef, pp. 42-62.

SCHMIDT, J.W. and BRODIE, M.L. (1982), *Relational Data Base Systems: Analysis and Comparison*, Springer-Verlag.

SHEU, P.C. and LEE, W.S. (1987), "Efficient processing of integrity xonstraints in deductive databases", *Future Generation Computer Systems*, Vol. 3, No. 4, pp. 201-16.

SHORTLIFFE, E.H. (1976), *Computer-based medical consultation: MYCIN*, Elsevier.

SINCLAIR, C. (1984), "The Third Industrial Revolution", *Future Generation Computer Systems*, Vol. 1, No. 2, pp. 119-22.

STEELS, L.(1987), "Second generation expert systems", in *Research and Development in Expert Systems III*, (M.A. Bramer, ed.), Cambridge University Press.

STONIER, T. (1987), "What is information", in *Research and Development in Expert Systems III*, (M.A. Bramer, ed.), Cambridge University Press.

TSICHRITZIS, D.C. and LOCHOVSKY, F.H. (1982), *Data Models*, Prentice Hall.

TUCHERMAN, L. and FURTADO, A.L. (1988), "Update-oriented database structures", in *Proceedings Second International Conference on Expert Database Systems*, George Mason University.

UCHIDA, S. (1987), "Parallel inference machines at ICOT", *Future Generation Computer Systems*, Vol. 3, No. 4, pp. 245-52.

UEDA, K. (1988), *Guarded Horn Clauses*, MIT Press.

VAN EMDEN, M.H. (1977), "Programming with resolution logic", in *Machine Intelligence 8*, (E.W. Elcock and D. Michie, eds), Ellis Horwood, pp. 266-99.

VERHEIJEN, G.M.A and VAN BEKKUM, J. (1982), "NIAM: An information analysis method" in *Information Systems Design Methodologies: A Comparative Review*, (T.W. Olle and A.A. Verrijn-Stuart, eds), IFIP, North-Holland, 1982.

WALD, J.A. (1988), "Implementing constraints in a knowledge-base", in *Proceedings Second International Conference on Expert Database Systems*, George Mason University, pp. 53-62.

WALKER, A. (1987), *Knowledge Systems and Prolog*, Addison-Wesley, 1987.

WATERMAN, D.A. (1986), *A Guide to Expert Systems*, Addison Wesley.

ZLOOF, M.M. (1975), "Query by example", in *Proceedings of the National Computer Conference*, AFIPS Press, Vol. 44, pp 431-8.

Index